FOREIGN POLICIES OF INDIA
AND HER NEIGHBOURS

Also by Ashok Kapur

INDIA'S NUCLEAR OPTION
THE INDIAN OCEAN
INTERNATIONAL NUCLEAR PROLIFERATION
PAKISTAN'S NUCLEAR DEVELOPMENT

Also by A. Jeyaratnam Wilson

THE BREAK UP OF SRI LANKA

Foreign Policies of India and her Neighbours

Ashok Kapur
Professor of Political Science
University of Waterloo

with

A. Jeyaratnam Wilson
Professor of Political Science
University of New Brunswick

First published in Great Britain 1996 by
MACMILLAN PRESS LTD
Houndmills, Basingstoke, Hampshire RG21 6XS
and London
Companies and representatives
throughout the world

A catalogue record for this book is available
from the British Library.

ISBN 0-333-55829-4

 First published in the United States of America 1996 by
ST. MARTIN'S PRESS, INC.,
Scholarly and Reference Division,
175 Fifth Avenue,
New York, N.Y. 10010

ISBN 0-312-12380-9

Library of Congress Cataloging-in-Publication Data
Kapur, Ashok.
The foreign policy of India and her neighbours Ashok Kapur with
A. Jeyaratnam Wilson.
p. cm.
Includes bibliographical references and index.
ISBN 0-312-12380-9
1. India—Foreign relations—South Asia. 2. South Asia—Foreign
relations—India. 3. India—Foreign relations—1947-1984.
4. India—Foreign relations—1984- I. Wilson, A. Jeyaratnam.
II. Title.
DS450.S64K36 1996
327.54—dc20   95-18041
                                                                CIP

© Ashok Kapur and A. Jeyaratnam Wilson 1996

All rights reserved. No reproduction, copy or transmission of
this publication may be made without written permission.

No paragraph of this publication may be reproduced, copied or
transmitted save with written permission or in accordance with
the provisions of the Copyright, Designs and Patents Act 1988,
or under the terms of any licence permitting limited copying
issued by the Copyright Licensing Agency, 90 Tottenham Court
Road, London W1P 9HE.

Any person who does any unauthorised act in relation to this
publication may be liable to criminal prosecution and civil
claims for damages.

10 9   8   7   6   5   4   3   2   1
05 04 03 02 01 00 99 98 97 96

Printed in Great Britain by
Ipswich Book Co Ltd, Ipswich, Suffolk

Contents

List of Tables, Figures and Boxes	vii
Acknowledgements	ix

1 Introduction: Overview – the Historical Legacy and the Setting in 1947 — **1**
- Overview — 1
- The Historical Legacy — 5
- The Academic and Policy Setting in 1947 — 8
- Patterns and Trends — 15

2 The Structure of Power in South Asia: Literature Survey and Research Design — **21**
- Western Paradigms in the Study of South Asia — 22
- Research Questions — 23
- Stability via Regional Military and Diplomatic Conflict and Cooperation Formation — 30
- History of the Development of the Power Structure in South Asia: A General Overview — 42

3 Polarity and Alliances in South Asia, 1947 to the Mid-1950s — **51**
- The First Alignment — 56
- The Second Alignment — 56
- The Third Alignment — 60
- The Fourth Alignment — 66
- The Fifth Alignment — 72
- Summary — 75

4 Arms Race, War and Crisis in South Asia, 1955–71 — **77**
- The Themes — 79
- Variables in South Asian Wars, 1960s to 1971 — 87

5 The Foreign Policies of India's Immediate Neighbours — **111**
- Neighbours other than Pakistan — 114
- Pakistan's External Relations — 125

The South Asian Association for Regional Cooperation
     (SAARC) 130
  Conclusions 131

6 **India and Pakistan in the 1980s and Early 1990s: Crises and Nuclear Activities** **133**
  Overview 133
  The 1987 and 1989–90 Indo–Pakistani crises: The Pattern
     of Behaviour, the Players and their Calculations 138
  Summary 155

7 **Future Prospects** **156**

Notes and References 166

Index 178

List of Tables, Figures and Boxes

Tables

1.1	India and her neighbours – the orientation of the literature	10
1.2	Incidence of war, military crisis and terrorism	18
1.3	Alignment patterns in South Asia, 1947 to the mid-1990s	19
2.1	Competing paradigms of South Asian regional security	24
2.2	Interstate relations in South Asia	29
2.3	Walt's theory revised	34
2.4	Public enmities and friendships in South Asia	37
2.5	Dual elements of friendship and enmity in South Asian international relations	39
3.1	The first alignment: Pakistani government, 1947–51	57
3.2	The second alignment: shifts in Anglo–US ideology and policy, 1949–54	58
3.3	The third alignment: the cluster of ideas and forces, 1949–52	65
3.4	Pattern of treaty relations with the Himalayan kingdoms	68
6.1	Indo–Pakistani confidence-building measures	135
6.2	The escalatory potential of Indo–Pakistani nuclear activities, 1947–89	136
6.3	Processes in Indo–Pakistani affairs in the 1980s	138

Figures

2.1	Regional conflict and cooperation formation in South Asia	36
2.2	Simplified model of public enmities and friendships in South Asia	37
2.3	The complex model of enmities and friendships in each relationship in South Asia	39
6.1	Summary of the 1987 Indo–Pakistani crisis	145

Boxes

2.1	Walt's theory and South Asia	31
3.1	Elements and characteristics of cooperative and hostile relations between India and the Himalayan kingdoms	69

Acknowledgements

This study was made possible by the research and travel support provided to Professor Ashok Kapur by the Social Sciences and Humanities Research Council of Canada, and the Indo-Canadian Shastri Institute. This is greatly appreciated.

A. Jeyaratnam Wilson wishes to thank the Canadian Institute for International Peace and Security, the Military and Strategic Studies Fund, the University of New Brunswick and Professor S. Milner for financial support.

Both authors thank Carole Gray, Joanne Voisin and Mary-Lou Schagena for their skill and enthusiasm in preparing the manuscript for publication.

Finally the authors thank Mr T. M. Farmiloe of Macmillan for his encouragement in writing this book, and Mr Keith Povey for editing the work.

A. K.
A. J. W.

1 Introduction: Overview – the Historical Legacy and the Setting in 1947

OVERVIEW

This book is cast in a post-Nehruvian mould. In Nehru's world the emphasis was on Cold War rejection, the quest for world peace, nuclear disarmament, Asian unity, opposition to military pacts and opposition to balance of power policies and doctrines; there was a plea to advance the causes of non-alignment, Third-World development and international cooperation.[1] On the other hand the post-Nehruvian stress is on regional security and takes South Asia into serious consideration. South Asia is seen as a regional subsystem in international affairs. India has to shape its position and its ascendency in South Asia and to be mindful of developments in her neighbourhood, especially in Tibet, Burma (Myanmar), the Gulf and, with the break-up of the USSR, Central Asia.

In diplomatic and foreign affairs, India's policy makers must take into account continuous interactions between three kinds of elemental forces in domestic and international relations. First, there are enmities and socio-ideological differences (ethnic, racial, cultural) that divide peoples and define the 'us' versus 'them' differences. Second, there are risks of action or inaction in the policy sphere, and such risks include wrong timing. Here the matrix of calculation varies between doing something and losing, not doing something and losing, doing something and gaining, and not doing something and gaining. Finally, there are conceptions, usually competing ones, of good government and responsible behaviour at work in international relations. All three elements are usually present in diplomatic and military situations.[2] When the first element predominates, the result is social, political and military conflict. When the third predominates, the result is a process of confidence building and conflict resolution. The second element concerns tactics – leading to war or peace. In India the post-Nehruvian architects were Nehru's successors as prime minister: his daughter Indira Gandhi, Lal Bahadur Shastri, Morarji Desai, Rajiv Gandhi and Narasimha

Rao. They have tried to manage the interaction between the three elemental forces by intensifying the quest for Indian power as well as seeking regional and international consent. Their contributions no doubt vary in significance, yet all fall in the post-Nehru category.

This category reveals the ascendency of geopolitical thinking in the Indian government. It indicates a better fusion of India's political and military strategy for the development of a stable power structure in South Asia. Pakistan, and to a lesser extent the other South Asian states, continue to be concerned about the danger of Indian hegemony. Pakistan in particular, and to some extent Bangladesh (though not the other South Asian states), have given South Asian international relations an Islamic colouring. Pakistan sees itself as the guardian of Indian Muslims and Kashmiris and a defender against Indian expansionism. Most Indians reject both views. Nevertheless all South Asian states are preoccupied with the task of restructuring internal political, economic and social relationships and the development of bilateral relations with India, as well as relations between themselves and the international environment. So, despite policy and attitudinal differences among the elites of South Asian states, there is continuous interaction among these states. In this sense a pattern of relationships, of conflict and/or cooperation, has emerged in South Asia.

As Indian power in South Asian affairs progressed from the late 1940s, and as the major powers acknowledged India's role as a mature democracy and a non-expansionist power, the focus shifted to bilateral and intraregional agendas. The latter reveal three kinds of South Asian relations. Between India and Pakistan there is military and social conflict that is moderated by limited confidence-building measures. Between India and the Himalayan kingdoms and the Maldives there is a hegemonistic relationship. Between India and Sri Lanka and India and Bangladesh, the situation varies from occasional hostility to indifference over bilateral social, economic and military issues.

Our theme here is that relations between India and her neighbours after 1947 did not develop in a vacuum. At least *three formative experiences shaped post-1947 South Asian relations*. First, there was the presence of two competitive political traditions in Indian thinking and Indian history. Of these the former sought a peaceful synthesis of competing interests and cultures. The latter required a resort to intrigue, alliances and war in the quest for stabilising power. These traditions are to be found over an historical (from ancient India) time-span. Second, there was the Moghul impact on the subcontinent and on 'Indian' traditions. The Moghuls conquered important parts of India but they also adapted to it and contributed to its architecture, poetry and administration, and in the process they became indigenised. Finally, there was the British impact on the Indian subcontinent and Indian political traditions, and the consequent 'South Asian' reactions to its encounter with Imperial British power. These formative experiences led to an Indian subcontinental civilisational base among South Asian countries. On the other hand the political ethics of South Asian states have varied, often with competing interests, rivalries and outlooks and these have led to a variety of policies – diplomatic, economic, political and military – since the 1940s in internal and external affairs. As a result of a common civilisational–Indian pull, the basis of Indian subcontinental unity is cultural, not political or strategic. The common civilisational base is the result of history, which bilateral, interstate controversies since 1947 have not destroyed. In this sense it may be argued that subcontinentals in South Asia are really Indians at heart,[3] but the influence of this element varies according to the diplomatic, strategic and political imperatives of the prevailing political ethos.

The second theme is that the *relationships between India and its neighbours have passed through different phases* (involving wars, social and ethnic conflicts, diplomatic controversies, economic competition, arms races and propaganda wars) and a *structure of power relations has emerged*. Historically, two trends are highlighted. First, from the early 1600s until 1947, political and military relations in India were organised under British authority. London and its representative, the viceroy of India, proved a strong central authority from about the mid-1800s to the mid-1900s. With the withdrawal of Britain from India in 1947, a process of fragmentation of political power into several territorial units occurred. Second, under Nehru, and particularly Patel, India's first home minister (1947–50), and with Lord Mountbatten's endeavours as viceroy and later as India's first governor-general, the government of India sought to carve out a politically unified Indian union from more than 600 princely states and provinces. The groundwork and procedure for the development of a strong political centre in India was established in the Nehru days, but in the region itself, particularly in Indo–Pakistani affairs, the process of fragmentation set in from partition onwards. The communal Hindu–Muslim divisions of the 1920s led to partition in 1947. Partition led to fundamental divergences in the diplomatic, military, economic and political spheres, and Indo–Pakistani rivalry became institutionalised in internal affairs between the two countries. Moreover it became regionalised in South Asia and was internationalised in UN, East–West and Third World affairs.

The fragmentation of Indo–Pakistani relations however contrasted with the continuation of British–Indian treaty relations with the Himalayan kingdoms. In sum, the twin processes of consolidation (within India, and between India and the Himalayan kingdoms), and fragmentation (between India and Pakistan) were at work in the Nehru years. After Nehru's death, his successors proceeded to strengthen the unifying process in subcontinental strategic matters. After 1971 in particular, the trend was to consolidate Indian power in the subcontinent. As a result a unipolar regional security system emerged, with India as the regional power centre.

This view contradicts that of mainstream Western literature, which maintains that South Asia has two poles of power – India and Pakistan.[4] This study argues otherwise. We demonstrate that a unipolar system of power relations has emerged in South Asia in which India is the centre of regional power, but the government of India needs further to develop an openly consultative process and a mechanism to secure the consent of its South Asian neighbours vis-à-vis Indian policies for ensuring the interests of the region as a whole. This unipolar centre or system is likely to continue throughout the 1990s. To understand the emergence of this unipolar centre we need to review the developments and events in South Asia over that last forty years in historical perspective, and this we do in Chapters 3 and 4.

The third theme is that although India is the biggest country and the strongest power in the subcontinent, it is not an expansionist state. It has not seized opportunities to conquer its smaller neighbours or forcibly to intervene, except in the cases of Goa, Sikkim and Bangladesh. Its troops have intervened in Sri Lanka (1971, 1987–89), the Maldives (1989) and Bangladesh (1971), but they returned upon completion of their missions. These interventions were seen by the host countries at times as benign, and on other occasions as hostile. 'Hostile interventions' have raised the spectre of Indian hegemony, but 'benign interventions' have been welcomed as aiding the cause of regime security. King Tribhuvan of Nepal was restored to the throne in 1951 with Indian help, likewise the JVP insurgency in 1971 in Sri Lanka and the Maldives coup attempt was crushed in 1989 with India's military assistance.

In this introduction we will assess the South Asian historical legacy so as to be able to explain post-1947 patterns and trends in South Asian international affairs in subsequent chapters. We will also define policy making in 1947 as well as the Western academic orientation in South Asian studies since 1947. In the policy sphere, 1947 saw the departure from the Indian subcontinent of British power, which had held it together in military and political affairs for about three hundred years. It also marked the beginning of the East–West Cold War. The departure of the British heralded the break-up of the subcontinent into a number of states and the beginning of strategic disunity in the region. This was the beginning of a pattern of competition and mistrust among South Asian countries. This was nothing new among the peoples of the subcontinent, but what was new was that after 1947 the political and military organisation of the British raj was replaced by a number of new territorial units that saw themselves in competition with each other. Out of this competition came a pattern of relations between India and her neighbours. This book defines the main developments between India and her neighbours with a view to defining the relationships that emerged out of conflict, cooperation, indifference and competition.

THE HISTORICAL LEGACY

The historical legacy is revealed by the continuous existence of two 'Indian' traditions. These have dominated Indian thinking and Indian history for several thousand years. The first tradition may be called 'the pursuit of synthesis'.[5] Here one finds a continuous attempt by conflicting parties to integrate, merge and harmonise as far as possible a variety of ethnic and cultural streams, or group attitudes and policies. A continuous attempt to interrelate diverse nationalities or cultures and their interests may be studied in the context of Indian history. This pursuit can be seen in the relations between the Aryans and the non-Aryans in the subcontinent. It was also in play when the Aryans in India came into contact with Greek, Persian, Turkish and eventually Islamic forces. However the first encounter between native 'Indians' and the invading Moslem forces in the eleventh and the twelfth centuries was initially one of conqueror and conquered. Consequently a conflict between two different and major lines of thinking emerged. On the one hand was the theory (the ideals) of the state, which emphasised, along the lines of *Mahabharata*, that good polity required the development of state power along ethical lines. On the other hand lay the Islamic view, which holds that there is but one Book, and there can be no compromise between believer and non-believer. In Indian history there was the encounter between Indians and the Moghuls but, as the subsequent discussion shows, even this was accommodated by the Indian tradition of searching for synthesis. To this point we shall return later.

The second Indian tradition may be called *realpolitik* or the Kautilyan tradition.[6] It originated around 300 BC, and in this tradition the strategy was to promote rivalries between neighbours, to rely on intrigue, to fight, to develop alliances, to engage in territorial aggrandisement, to engage in subversion and intelligence activities, and generally to seek to maximise the king's and the state's power. But it also had a moral dimension, namely to engage in activities that advanced the wellbeing of the king's subjects. Despite this moral dimension, most experts judge it as an imperial tradition where the use of war, intrigue and territorial expansion became necessary. Indian political and military history from ancient times is replete with such examples, and furthermore British Indian history fits into this tradition. British Imperial attitudes and practices *vis-à-vis* the Indian princes and their policies and attitudes towards each other demonstrates the vitality of the Kautilyan approach.

In Indian history and thinking these traditions coexisted uneasily; and *realpolitik* never succeeded in replacing that which emphasised this synthesis. Because neither tradition dominated Indian thinking, there was an uneasy coexistence between the two; a balance of power and polarity was maintained between them. Indians therefore failed to develop a theory of power; on the other hand, due to frequent reliance on Kautilyan practices, the peaceful tradition failed to dominate.

The message of Islam baffled Indians because it was contrary to Indian practice, which stressed the value of synthesis. There were two reactions to the Muslim invasion of India. The first was that Indian Hindu society, when exposed to the Muslim encounter, closed itself against Islam. The caste system became rigid. The practise of *Sati* increased during this period because women were afraid that they would be taken and abused by the Moghul invaders: on hearing of the defeat of their men in battle they thought it was better to burn themselves in their husband's funeral pyre. This was a policy of non-cooperation with the invader. There was no attempt to seek a peaceful synthesis between Hindus and Muslims. But eventually this rigidity and non-cooperation was transformed into a situation of uneasy coexistence, because the longer the Moghul invaders stayed in India the more Indianised they became. For example Akbar became a vegetarian, wore caste marks on his head, married a Hindu princess, and his administration had elements of Moghul administration as well as practices developed from ancient Indian revenue administration. Akbar wanted to build a new religion that would bring together Hinduism, Islam and Christianity. Fatehpur Sikri was to be the new centre. His successors

– Jehangir, Shahjehan and Aurangzeb – were of a different political and religious temperament. They were less diligent, sectarian in their outlook (especially Aurangzeb) and had other interests. Consequently Akbar's dream had died by 1707.[7]

In the last days of the Moghul Empire, when the decay had already set in, British merchants in the form of the East India Company entered the Indian scene. This story has been told very well by Philip Mason and others.[8] The British started with a toehold in Madras and from thence the East India Company developed its commercial and political relations with Indians, including princes, and by the mid-1700s its presence in different parts of the subcontinent was established. After the Indian Mutiny of 1857 the affairs of the East India Company were taken over by Britain, and India became a part of the British Empire. The position and privileges of the East India Company and its relations and dealings with the Indian princes and people were taken over by the British Crown.

But the British presence in India under the East India Company and its successor, the Crown, had unique features. The British wanted to rule, not to synthesise. They relied on a different set of traditions; namely to divide and rule, and to engender rivalries among the neighbouring princes. The British experience was new to the Indians, even though their political and military behaviour was consistent with Kautilyan principles. The British wanted to exploit India and its fabulous riches. They wanted to subordinate Indians and to maintain British separateness and exclusivity. By the turn of the century the British had developed a sense of racial superiority in relation to the Indians. This experience completely disoriented the Indians because it ran counter to the historical idea that encounters between different peoples and different civilisations and cultures required conflict resolution by a process of synthesis, but there was no prospect of this happening between the British and the Indians. In this context, the real meaning of Indian independence lay not in the emergence of the Nehrus and the Indian National Congress nor in the adoption of Western-style parliamentary democracy and periodic elections in India, but in the rejection by Indians of the British theory of superiority and exclusivity, the separation of Indian communities according to religion, the British claim to racial superiority and Britain's subordination of Indians.

THE ACADEMIC AND POLICY SETTING IN 1947

South Asia makes up about one fifth of all humanity in a grouping of seven states: India, Pakistan, Nepal, Bangladesh, Bhutan, Sri Lanka and the Maldives. Throughout most of South Asian diplomatic and military history from 1947–95 the distribution of power has been quite uneven. It has favoured India in terms of area, population, economic strength, natural resources, military resources and the vitality of its political system. This unequal distribution has created a fear of Indian hegemony among other South Asian states, and is an important issue in the perceptions of most of these states and their elites. It has skewed South Asian diplomatic and military studies in a particular way. According to Leo Rose there is a great and permanent divide between India and her South Asian neighbours: 'All the other South Asian states have until recently considered India as the major threat to their security and national integrity.'[9]

This is a popular but superficial view of the relationships between India and her neighbours; it does not explain the complex factors at work in those relationships. Furthermore the literature stresses the internal problems in South Asia, but does not reveal the emergence of a dynamic system of states, where a set of players with diverse capacities have interests, values, perceptions and strategies, and their diplomatic–strategic behaviour has consequences. The literature fails to show how and when a regional order and a regional system of states emerged. Our concern is that, despite the size and complexity of South Asian states, there has been little systematic study of South Asian international relations. The history, patterns and trends in relations between India and her neighbours since 1947 have been neglected and generally speaking the region has been inadequately researched. In our view the quality of the literature, too, is inadequate. In comparison with international and regional studies of different parts of the world, South Asia is among the least studied. Table 1.1 shows the orientation of the academic literature.

In North America, South Asian studies are neglected and the teaching of South Asian diplomatic affairs in an integrated fashion is scattered among a few departments with few courses to offer. Likewise, in policy matters South Asia generally receives low priority in the United States and Canada, and Western policy concerns have marginalised academic work on South Asian diplomatic–military affairs. South Asia became peripheral to international affairs after 1947, and although the Canadian and British governments gave adequate consideration to Nehru in the first half of the 1950s,[10] the literature did not take Nehru, India or South Asia seriously. There are a number of reasons to explain this attitude. First, from 1947 the Truman administration was increasingly preoccupied with other issues: the Soviet threat in Western Europe and the Mediterranean area; Middle East oil security; European security problems; and North-East Asian affairs as a result of the US occupation of Japan and the Korean War.[11] Second, South Asian states were passive and of little value in world affairs.[12] Consequently Western thinkers generally neglected the South Asian region in their attempt to contain the USSR and develop a new US-power-driven world order. Pakistan, however, was judged important in Western thinking because of its utility as a base against Soviet expansion.[13]

Western policy attitudes have had a significant impact on Western academic work because scholarly concerns are driven by the policy agenda. As Gunnar Myrdal points out:

> The most perceptible political influence on the research approach in Western countries to the problems of South Asian countries is the pre-dominant role given to considerations of national power and international power relations. In a world full of perils to national security and survival, this tendency is understandable; it is often asserted to be a more realistic direction of social research. The implication is, however, that studies of the problems of underdeveloped countries are now undertaken, not with a view to the universal and timeless values that are our legacy from the Enlightenment, but with a view to the fortuitous and narrow political or, narrower still, military-strategic interests of one state or bloc of states. All sorts of studies are now justified by, or focused on, their contribution to the 'security' of Western countries. This officious accommodation by the scholarly profession to a new political 'realism' in research often borders on the ridiculous.[14]

To understand the academic and policy setting of South Asia in 1947 it is necessary to define the broad outline of the international setting and the structure of power in the Indian subcontinent before 1947. As noted earlier, until 1947 political authority concerning Indian subcontinental affairs was unified and in British hands. There were two decision-making centres from 1857 to 1947: in London there was the secretary of state of India; in Delhi the government was headed by the viceroy of India, who functioned as the eyes and ears of the British Indian Empire. The main mission of the Crown in India was to maintain British political authority in the subcontinent. This required

Table 1.1 India and her neighbours – the orientation of the literature

Author	Determinants of India/neighbour relations
1. Leo Rose and S. Kumar, 'South Asia', in W. J. Feld and G. Boyd (eds)., *Comparative Regional Systems*, (New York: Pergamon, 1980), pp. 268 and 264.	(a) India is hegemonic. (b) Smaller neighbours fear India: 'all the other South Asian states have until recently considered India as the major threat to their security and national integrity . . .' (c) There is a big divide between India and her neighbours. 'The perspective on security issues in Nepal, Bangladesh, Sri Lanka and Bhutan is similar to that of Pakistan in that the major problem for each is their relationship with India rather than with external powers.'
2. B. Buzan, in Buzan and Rizvi, *South Asian Insecurity and the Great Powers* (London: Macmillan, 1986), pp 9, 14, 1, 23 and 27.	(a) Indo–Pakistani relations rest on diplomatic, military and religious rivalry. (b) Indo–Pakistani rivalry defines the South Asian security complex. 'These two countries were both locked into a complicated rivalry that defined the central security problem for each of them. They easily overawed the smaller states which were geographically entangled within their sphere.' (c) 'The organising principle of Pakistan threatens India with secessionism, while that of India threatens Pakistan with either dismemberment or absorption.' (d) There is a bipolarity in the distribution of power between India and Pakistan. Despite Bangladesh, Pakistan has been 'strong enough and wilful enough to sustain bipolarity'. (e) In South Asia the 'status quo has been maintained'. South Asian wars 'have served more to reinforce existing hostility than either to eliminate it, or to break the bipolar power structure'.
3. G. Rivzi, in Buzan and Rizvi, op. cit., pp. 62 and 93.	(a) 'She [Pakistan] has fought three major wars with India and despite being truncated in 1971 has steadfastly refused a subordinate status in the subcontinent'.

(b) Leaders in India and Pakistan 'view Indo-Pakistan relations as a zero-sum game.... The rivalry is too deep-rooted either to disappear easily or to be capable of a rational solution'.

4. Mohammed Ayoob, 'India in South Asia: The Quest for Regional Predominance', *World Policy Journal*, 1990, pp. 108–9, 128, 119, and 124.

(a) India has regional pre-eminence (measured by objective criteria) but it lacks regional predominance 'measured by the other regional states' acceptance of such a role as legitimate'.
(b) 'The primary objective and overriding concern of Indian foreign policy since... 1947 has been the establishment of India's predominance in South Asia'.
(c) A bipolar configuration has enabled the smaller South Asian states to enlist external sources of support, especially the USA and China, and to neutralise India's inherent superiority in the subcontinent and India has failed to establish a strategic consensus in the subcontinent. A regional consensus on the role of India – the pivotal power – on security issues is lacking.
(d) Pakistan seeks an equal role with India in political and military affairs and it has been encouraged by outside powers. Pakistan's ability to 'borrow power from abroad' – mainly from the USA and China – has enabled it to maintain a position of 'near-parity' with India in military terms.
(e) India's regional policy is driven by the 'Indira Doctrine'. It maintains: 'India will neither intervene in the domestic affairs of any states in the region, unless requested to do so, nor tolerate such interference by an outside power; if external assistance is needed to meet an internal crisis, states should first look within the region for help'.

5. Sisir Gupta, in M. S. Rajan and S. Ganguly (eds), *Sisir Gupta: India and the International System* (New Delhi: Vikas, 1981), pp. 11, 12, 14, 1, 21, 144, 10, 11, 14, 1, and 17–8.

(a) Pakistan's identity crisis (what is a Pakistani?) led its elite to emphasise the Islamic character of the state and Pakistan's non-Indianness by continued hostility towards India.
(b) The distribution of political power in Pakistan was lopsided – in favour of the army and the bureaucracy – and Pakistan's political culture did not favour

Table 1.1 *cont.*

mass or democratic politics. Hence Pakistani politics and foreign affairs relied on military solutions to political problems at home and Indo-Pakistani affairs abroad.
(c) Kashmir was not the key to Indo-Pakistani problems. The problems were structural and cultural. They were embedded in hostile mutual images that the elites on both sides had adopted prior to partition (1947).
(d) Pakistan and China formed an anti-status-quo alliance against India from 1962, if not earlier.
(e) Pakistan's elite sought powerful external friends to balance India, underwrite the Pakistan domestic elite structure and provide economic aid.
(f) India's aim was to insulate South Asia from interventionary pressures from outside the region, prevent violent internal changes and build a stable state system.
(g) There are civilisational pulls (linguistic and cultural) that bring South Asians together, but on the other hand, because of India's size, small South Asian states are likely to have psychological problems with living with a large country. Also, Indian democracy is an immediate threat to the security of authoritarian, unrepresentative regimes in South Asia.
(h) Compared with the North-East and the Middle East, the USA sees South Asia as a low priority area. Russian geopolitical reasons make South Asia important. Russia seeks to contain Chinese influence in Pakistan lest it spread to Islamic countries south of the USSR and affect the peoples of Central Asian republics.
(i) China has many interests in South Asia and it is the least predictable of the great powers: (1) it maintains good relations with smaller South Asian countries so as to pursue anti-Indian policies; (2) it supports Pakistan to keep high demands on India and maintain political and military pressure on India; (3) it supports tribal groups in India's north-east to maintain pressure on the Indian union; (4) it encourages violent upheaval by the left in India.

6. R. W. Bradnock, *India's Foreign Policy Since 1971*, RIIA (London: Pinter, 1990).

(a) 'although India has undoubtedly sought a pre-eminent leadership position in South Asia, its ultimate good has been self-protection rather than aggressive or territorial expansionism'.
(b) With its immediate South Asian neighbours India has pursued 'almost entirely' political rather than economic interests.
(c) Faced by Islamic pressures in Pakistan and Afghanistan, and Sri Lankan and DMK Tamil separatism, which impacts on Indian internal security interests, India has abandoned non-violent conflict resolution and non-interference.
(d) 'The characterisation of India as a regional bully is misplaced, but during the 1980s it often showed little awareness of the difficulties its much smaller neighbours faced in relationships with what to them is a dominant power.'

preservation of law and order among the Indian subjects, and the British authorities kept the population generally pacified and disarmed. It relied on a small, centralised, political, military, police and intelligence machinery to run the country.[15]

Another of its missions was to develop economic relations between Britain and India in a manner that facilitated the transfer of Indian wealth to Britain. According to a press account, the chief executive of 'Windsor Inc.' is the British monarchy, whose hereditary possessions include 'gifts and plunder from the corners of the British Empire'.[16] This way British rule in India had political and economic functions. Another mission for the British government in India was to develop and utilise the Indian army and Indian facilities to advance British military operations outside India. Here India functioned as a base of operations for the advancement of British imperial defence interests in the Middle East, South Africa, South-East Asia and China, and in the fight against Germany in the First World War.[17] India functioned as the linchpin of the British Empire. Indian soldiers provided muscle under British command against its international enemies. All these missions developed in the international context of rivalry between the British Empire and other empires from the 1600s.

After the Second World War a new global setting emerged. This had a tremendous impact on the political and strategic affairs of the Indian subcontinent after 1947. Even though Britain played a valiant role in the war against Hitler, her economic and military position had weakened considerably because of the war. As a result the structure of global power relationships changed significantly. 1945 saw the ascendancy of US and Soviet power; prior to the Second World War these countries had not occupied centre stage in world politics. The Second World War also saw the beginning of the breakdown of European empires and the projection of nationalism onto the world stage. Japan's industrial and military development in the late 1800s and its expansion into Asia and the Pacific reflected the force of nationalism. It was not until later that nationalism emerged in India and China. With the resurgence of nationalism in the anticolonial struggle, the European empires began to crumble. However this point should not be overstated. The political force of nationalism entered the global picture at the end of the Second World War even though nationalist movements had come into being earlier.[18] After the Second World War, Asian nationalism was not strong enough to affect global power relations, although it was a factor in the erosion of the European empires in Asia.

While great-power relations developed independently of nationalism, Indian nationalism had an impact on the future of the British raj. The Indian revolt against British authority and the latter's loss of motivation to carry on in India[19] produced a radical change in the structure of power in the subcontinent, and 1947 saw the emergence of a number of a new states. In transferring power to the Indians and others, the British were obliged to break up their Empire into separate parts. They had already detached Burma[20] from the Empire in 1937; Ceylon[21] had always been treated separately from India and it gained its independence in 1948 in the wake of independence for India and Pakistan.

The territorial and strategic unity of the India subcontinent was fragmenting at precisely the point when China was moving in the opposite direction. Between the mid-1800s and the early 1900s, internal fragmentation, power struggles and civil war between competing political and military factions were features of Chinese political life. This was followed by a process of unification under a central communist and nationalist authority. In contrast, in the subcontinent it was the exact reverse. Fragmentation in subcontinental political affairs (up to 1600) was followed by a process of unification under Britain's rule between 1600 and 1947. Partition reversed the process of unification; it restored the earlier pattern of fragmentation, in this case with India and Pakistan as separate states. With the transfer of power by Britain in 1947, and the break-up of the territorial and strategic unity of the subcontinent, competitive strategic and political ideologies emerged among the Indian and Pakistani political elites. The differences between the two were sharp and fundamental.

PATTERNS AND TRENDS

A number of salient patterns and trends in South Asian international relations (1947 to the 1980s) have shaped the behaviour of and relations between India and her neighbours. This book studies the following.

First, India has emerged as a regional power. It has demonstrated its ability to preserve the Indian Union. It has successfully asserted its right and duty to create a regional order (Nehru in the Himalayan kingdoms; Indira Gandhi, Morarji Desai and Rajiv Gandhi in the rest of South Asia). The trend in Indian policies has been to secure India's regional pre-eminence, while the trend among South Asian states other than Pakistan has been reluctantly to accept the framework of Indian regional policies.

Second, Pakistan has relied on a number of methods to reduce India's dominance in South Asian and international affairs, including an arms race to reduce the gap between Indian and Pakistani military power; building international and regional diplomatic and military alignments to corner and pressure India on the principle that 'the enemy of my enemy is my potential friend'; encouraging insurrection in Indian border provinces so that India's balkanisation weakened it and cut it down to size, all the while projecting the view that Pakistan was the defender of Indian Muslims and the guardian of the subcontinent against Indian hegemony. There was convergence in the interests of India's neighbours in promoting Pakistan's strength and diplomatic position as a line of pressure against India.

India's smaller neighbours were no doubt concerned about the dangers of Indian hegemony. However South Asian crises – in Bangladesh (1971), Sri Lanka (1984–89), Nepal (1988–89) and the Maldives (1989) – reveal that Pakistan's arguments had limited appeal to South Asian states. To them, India's size and big brother attitude is a problem but Indian support is also necessary to enable them to cope with internal and external problems. Moreover the change in the international scene – expressed by major shifts in US–USSR, USSR–China, US–China relations during the 1970s and 1980s, the break-up of the USSR in 1991, and the emergent detente between the People's Republic of China and India – has reduced Pakistan's opportunities to manipulate the great powers and India's smaller South Asian neighbours to act against India. Under these circumstances, the trend points to a diminishing Pakistani ability to develop anti-India coalitions in the international and regional spheres.

Third, the distribution of power (broadly defined in terms of a country's economic strength; its scientific and technological growth; its capacity to solve internal, economic and social problems; its political unity and capacity to accommodate conflicting pressures, and so on) has always favoured India. However, narrowly defined, 'power' implies military power. Despite its size, India did not have a military advantage from 1955–60, when Pakistan had the edge in tanks and aircraft. Since that time, however, the region has seen the development of an asymmetrical distribution of military power in India's favour. Today, neither Pakistan nor a combination of South Asian states could defeat India by military means. The lopsided distribution of power – broadly or narrowly defined – is likely to last for the foreseeable future. This trend has been in place since 1971, when India defeated Pakistan in the Bangladesh war of independence.

Fourth, as noted earlier, in East–West affairs and in US foreign policy the strategic importance of Pakistan has declined in the post-Cold-War world, and since the Afghanistan war and the demise of the USSR. With the decline of the former Soviet threat, the United States' need for Pakistan in its intelligence activities against the USSR have diminished and Pakistan's utility as a front-line state has declined. Now India is acquiring this status as the new frontier against the expansion of Islam.[22] With the collapse of the USSR as a communist and military threat to Western interests, and with a major shift in Indo–Russian ties, the Russian factor in Indian foreign affairs no longer irritates the United States. These changes in the international and the regional context seem irreversible. They are helping Indian policies and leaving Pakistan on the margins of US thinking.

Fifth, the history of war in South Asia indicates that South Asian elites see war in Western terms: it is a continuation of politics by other means. But wars are neither frequent nor inevitable.[23] Table 1.2 outlines the incidence of war, military crises, terrorism and civil strife in South Asia between 1947 and 1995.

Sixth, the history of alliances in South Asia (Table 1.3) shows an enduring pattern since 1949. This contradicts the thesis of non-alignment of South Asian states. South Asian alliances mostly involve India as a partner, except where large external powers enter the partnership, as in the US–Pakistan and Pakistan–China relationships. These alliances demarcate the framework and create opportunities for interstate bargaining. Such bargainings are dynamic. In some the consultative process and the relationship has been strengthened – for example between India and Nepal, India and the United States, and India and China. In others they have weakened – for example Pakistan and the United States, Pakistan and China – or the consultative process and relationship are still being formulated – for example India and Sri Lanka. The trend in South Asia shows a dynamic evolution of relations, but the pattern shows differing types of relationship.

Finally, South Asia has seen a new trend, namely the emergence of the problem of 'soft states'. Such states have a number of features: porous borders with ethnically driven border-crossing and subnational/transnational social and military conflicts; mass migrations; a high concentration and monopoly of governmental power; a high concentration/monopoly of economic power in state and non-state hands; and the rise of drug and arms cartels and private armies with a capacity to subvert the state and/or by-pass it in certain circumstances. In soft states there is both a high concentration of state and private power,

Table 1.2 Incidence of war, military crisis and terrorism

Year	Location	Parties involved	Nature of event
1947	Punjab and Bengal	Hindus, Muslims and Sikhs	Communal violence
1947–48	Kashmir	Pakistanis, Kashmiris and Indians	Tribal invasion of Kashmir and war between India and Pakistan
1962	Himalayan frontier	China and India	War
1965	Rann of Kutch	Pakistan and India	War
1965	Kashmir and Punjab	Pakistan and India	War
1971	East Pakistan (Bangladesh) – the Indo–Pakistani border was a secondary military theatre	Pakistan army, Indian army, Indian intelligence and Bangladeshi guerrillas	Civil war leading to the Indo–Pakistan War
1984	Indian Punjab	Sikhs, Indian Military forces and Pakistani forces	Insurgency and separatism
1984	Jaffna, Sri Lanka	Sri Lankan Tamils, Indian Tamils, Sinhalese, and Indian and Sri Lankan governments	Insurgency and separatism
Mid-1980s	Chittagong hill tracks	Chakma tribals, Bangladeshi military forces and Indian intelligence	Insurgency and separatism
1987	Indo–Pakistani western border	India and Pakistan	Military crisis
1987	Himalayan frontier	India and China	Military crisis
1989–90	Kashmir	Kashmiri, Indian and Pakistani military forces	Insurgency and separatism
1989–90	Assam	Assamese hill tribes	Insurgency

Table 1.3 Alignment patterns in South Asia, 1947 to the mid-1990s

Period	Allies	Enemies (public or secret)*	Common interests of allies
From late 1940s/early 1950s to present	India–Sikkim India–Bhutan India–Nepal	China China China	• Fear of China's expansionism. • Need to codify a cooperative but subordinate relationship between India and the Himalayan kingdoms
From early 1950s to present	Pakistan–USA	India, USSR	Containing Indian power and Soviet influence
From mid-1950s to present	Pakistan–China	India, USSR	Containing Indian power and Soviet influence
From early 1950s to 1990	India–USSR	China, USA, Pakistan	Strengthening each other's international and South Asian position

* This refers to the common enemies of the allies.

and a high incidence of social conflict that generates internal strains. A soft state is not necessarily weak, but rather the monopolies that dominate its institutions confront powerful and competitive internal non-governmental countervailing forces where different sides are involved in a high-risk political game. These monopolies are like well-organised 'forbidden cities', as in Imperial China, and are able to manage domestic and international challenges to their authority and power. Their existence points to the value of studying the domestic structures of South Asian states in addition to relationships among the states.

With this general background, in the chapters that follow we will define the structure of power in South Asia, as well as the interests, values, perceptions and strategies of the interacting parties, and the issues that are thrown up by the relationships. The next chapter addresses theoretical concerns; it also provides the theoretical underpinning to this book.

2 The Structure of Power in South Asia: Literature Survey and Research Design

South Asian international relations require an understanding and explanation of the history of war, diplomacy and politics in the region since 1947. General theoretical models of great power dominance and lesser power subordination do not help us understand the structure of power in South Asia, and the historical pattern and trend in the formation of this structure. The first section of this chapter provides a summary of the main Western approaches to regional international relations. It presents the similarities and differences between our work and the literature. The second section outlines our research design, and the third offers an overview of the origins and history (process and pattern) of development of the structure of power in South Asia.

In Chapter 3 we shall investigate the pattern of 'polarity' and 'alliances' of three kinds of state within South Asia from 1947 to the 1990s, but it will be useful to describe here the three state types.

(1) *India* is the largest country in the region in terms of tangible measures of power, for example possession of military and economic strength, and population and land size. But it has not necessarily and continuously been the dominant power in terms of intangible measures of power, namely an ability to organise alliances, secure consent and authority, manage threats, shape the distribution of power within the region, and minimise or exclude foreign interference or external pressures on India and the region.

(2) *Pakistan* is a lesser power than India in terms of the tangible measures listed earlier, but it is also an essential player in the South Asian structure. Its position rests on a number of capabilities: (a) to form international alliances that help it to maintain near military parity with India; (b) to maintain military, diplomatic and political pressures on India's border areas; (c) to engage in an arms race with India; (d) to project its self-image as the guardian of the Muslims of the subcontinent; and (e) to project its self-image as the defender of South

Asia states against Indian expansionism and hegemony.

(3) *Other lesser South Asian states* (Nepal, Bhutan, Bangladesh, Sri Lanka and the Maldives) have particular foreign policy orientations and positions in the South Asian system; they differ from Indian and Pakistani approaches to diplomatic and military affairs. They share Pakistan's concern about 'Indian hegemony', but unlike Pakistan they are either in alliance with India (Nepal, Bhutan, Bangladesh, Sri Lanka) or, in the absence of a formal alignment, they rely on methods and strategies that differ sharply from those of Pakistan vis-à-vis India. For instance Pakistan is relying on an arms race to seek security; others are not. Pakistan seeks military and diplomatic parity with India; others do not. Pakistan seeks to encourage India's balkanisation, and to cut it down to size if parity cannot be achieved by Pakistani arms-race and alliance activities; others do not, as India's break-up could lead to the internal fragmentation of these states, and a strong India is a guarantee of their territorial and regime security.

Given this threefold classification of South Asian states, in Chapter 3 we shall assess the polarity (indifference, hostility) and alliances between India and Pakistan between India and the smaller South Asian states, and between Pakistan and the smaller South Asian states.

By doing this, we intend to demonstrate the role of the three types of South Asian state in the formation and development of the South Asian power structure. This broadens the focus of our analysis of the literature. The conventional approach views South Asia essentially as a story of Indo–Pakistani rivalry.[1] By broadening the analysis we will show the conceptual and empirical richness and complexity of South Asian international relations. Our approach has merit because it enables the reader to assess the South Asian power structure as well as the role and interests of all the units in the system of states.[2]

WESTERN PARADIGMS IN THE STUDY OF SOUTH ASIA

The literature reveals the presence of a number of competing paradigms that are relevant to the study of the history of South Asian international relations. In our judgement none of these necessarily or sufficiently explains or understands the system or the structure of power that emerged in South Asia between 1947 and 1995. Each paradigm contains a kernel of truth, but each is conceptually and empirically weak or incomplete. None of them provide a blow-by-blow account of the history of the development of a system of states and a power structure;

they were not intended to do so. None of them thoroughly address the five main academic issues that are central to the assessment of the system of interstate relations. These issues relate to:

1. The *organising principles* (norms) in the South Asian system of states and their power structure.
2. The *distribution of military and economic capabilities* (power) among South Asian states.
3. The *characteristics* of the units (states, bureaucratic organisations and leaders involved in South Asian affairs) of the South Asian system – their internal and external *orientation*, including the relationship between threat perceptions and polarity and threat perceptions and alliances.
4. The *pattern of behaviour* of each unit and of the system as a whole.
5. The *pattern of regional and international alignments and turning points in shifts in alignments* in the history of South Asian international relations.

Table 2.1 provides an outline of the competing paradigms, followed by a commentary on each paradigm.

RESEARCH QUESTIONS

The literature outlined in Table 2.1 show sharp differences on salient points. This section highlights areas of agreement and disagreement among academic practitioners as they concern South Asia. Once the controversies are defined, it will be easier to set out our research design and approach. Several major disagreements are noteworthy in the literature:

First, *is the South Asian regional subsystem unipolar or bipolar?* Buzan makes the case for bipolarity: the South Asian security complex is defined by Indo–Pakistani rivalry; there are just two major states and one defining rivalry. Even the 1971 war did not alter the bipolar structure of power in South Asia:

> Although Pakistan was certainly weakened politically by the loss of its pretension to Islamic exclusivity, its military strength was not much affected, and its leaders quickly left behind any inclinations they might have had to defer to Indian hegemony. Despite its many troubles, Pakistan has remained both strong enough and wilful enough to sustain bipolarity.[3]

Table 2.1 Competing paradigms of South Asian regional security

Author	Paradigm	Determinants
Barry Buzan 'Regional Security', Centre for Peace and Conflict research, Copenhagen, Working paper no. 28, 1989.	Regional security complexes or subsystems of regional security	(a) Geographical and cultural proximity; geopolitical and historical roots are a key factor. (b) Security interdependence with a high concentration of shared (mutual) rivalry (fear) or shared interests (trust, cooperation, harmony); the interdependence is durable, not necessarily permanent. (c) Regional security complexes act as mediators between international system and states. (d) Power and pattern of amity, indifference and enmity among states produces security.
S. P. Cohen (ed.), *The Security of South Asia* (New Delhi: Vistar 1988), ch. 15	Regional/local military balance(s) of power that are susceptible to external (global) great power actions; regional security structure; regional arms control and stability; India–Pakistan power sharing.	(a) Arms race. (b) Alliances. (c) Arms control arrangements. (d) Confidence-building measures. (e) Political and military rivalry between India and Pakistan. (f) Small states' insecurity and fear of Indian hegemony.
M. Brecher, The New States of Asia (New York: Oxford University Press, 1966), ch. 3	Subordinate subsystem of southern asia that faces danger of instability and disintegration.	(a) Geographic proximity. (b) At least three actors. (c) Recognition by others as a distinct region, community or segment of global system. (d) States in the region see themselves as part of region.

Author	Paradigm	Determinants
		(e) Units of power in subordinate states' systems are weaker – using a sliding scale of power compared with power held by states in the dominant system. (f) Changes in the dominant system have a greater effect on the subordinate systems than the reverse.
L. J. Cantori and S. L. Spiegel, *The International Politics of Regions* (Englewood Cliffs, NJ: Prentice-Hall, 1970).	Regional international relations; subordinate (regional) state system is the intermediate unit of analysis between 'nation-state' and 'dominant system'. (There are three levels of analysis: dominant, subordinate and internal.) Each subordinate regional state system has core, intrusive and peripheral sectors.	(a) Geographical proximity. (b) Role of 'intrusive systems'. (c) Economic, political and social interactions that are intense, continuous and organised. Four variables – level of cohesion, nature of communications, level of power and structure of relations (alignments) – define the homogeneity/heterogeneity of a subordinate state system.
R. Vayryren, 'Regional Conflict Formations: An Intractable Problem of International Relations', *Journal of Peace*, vol. 21, no. 4 (1984).	Regionalism and fragmentation of international order; regional subsystems; regional conflict formations; regional power centres.	(a) There is a single capitalist division of labour and a fragmented political and cultural system. (b) The penetration of the capitalist world economy of regions is uneven and hence there is homogeneity because of capitalism and heterogeneity because of differences in the level of development of regional subsystems. (c) In dependent and homogeneous regional subsystems, where economic logic prevails, conflicts and other processes are primarily externally inspired.

Table 2.1 *cont.*

Author	Paradigm	Determinants
		(d) In autonomous, heterogeneous and geopolitical subsystems internal causes are more probable.
S. M. Walt, 'Testing Theories of Alliance Formation: the Case of Southwest Asia', *International Organization*, vol. 42, no. 2, (spring 1988).	Alliance strategies: balancing threats, or bandwagonning; detente.	'States balance against different kinds of perceived external and internal threats and not just against power alone.'
R. Vayrynen, 'Economic and Military Position of the Regional Power Centres', *Journal of Peace Research*, vol. 16, no. 4 (1979).	Regional power centres	(a) Actor that exerts a regional hegemony akin to the global dominance of an imperial power, but at a subsystemic level (b) Possesses strong military capability.
	Domestic development of region centres: gradual development of productive forces and the emergence of an industrial sector usually stronger than in the subordinate neighbouring countries; increased economic development, increased dependency on capitalist (first world) economies.	Three stages: (a) Export of raw materials and agricultural products (import of manufactured/semi-manufactured goods). (b) Import-substitution stage: • establishment of the local industrial base and domestic production. (c) Export-led growth: • alliance of state, foreign and domestic capital and TNCs; • symbiosis of army and state coercion to maintain national security or stability; • economic and military strength coincide and reinforce each other.

R. Vayrynen, however, makes a different case. He distinguishes between a feudal pattern of interaction and regional power centres with spheres of influence: 'Usually such power centres sit at the top of the hierarchy of an identifiable regional subsystem. Indonesia, India, pre-revolutionary Iran and Nigeria may serve as examples of this tendency'.[4]

Second, *what is the core concept in the study of regional security issues?* Here the contrast is between the work of S. P. Cohen and B. Buzan. To Cohen, 'power' and a power balance are central concepts. He sees the Indo–Pakistani arms balance and its maintenance as the central issue in South Asia, that is, the prevention or containment of an Indo–Pakistani military imbalance and Indian dominance.

Compared with Cohen, Buzan's scope is broader and more sophisticated. To Buzan, the core concept is 'security', which is broader than 'power'. Security requires a discussion of the distribution of military capabilities *plus* the pattern of amity (alliances), indifference and enmities. Security/insecurity is the product of this combination. By combining assessments of the distribution of power and the patterns of amity/enmity, the analyst is enabled to assess the structure of regional subsystems. This cannot be done by studying military balance charts or regional arms races, technological changes and military budgets. Buzan's work enables us to discuss regional security structures; Cohen's work has a bilateral (India–Pakistan) focus, which is not regional. Cohen's approach, by neglect or by design, removes the issue of regional security structure or subsystem from academic discussion.

Third, *when was the South Asian regional subsystem formed, and if it changed, when was this?* The issue of timing is critical. Two alternative approaches may be used to address the question. In the first, Buzan maintains that the 'South Asian complex sprang into existence almost fully formed in 1947'. He sums it up as follows: 'The South Asian security complex... has displayed a durable bipolar structure for nearly four decades. Its continuity resides in the primacy of India and Pakistan within the subcontinent, in the continuation of that treatment of each other as major rivals.'[5] Here, the 1947 partition was the basis of bipolarity and enmity between India and Pakistan, and post-1947 developments have not changed the regional security complex created in 1947. Indo–Pakistani rivalry is the critical and decisive element in the definition of the regional subsystem. Here Buzan and Cohen are in agreement.

The second hypothesis is implicit in Vayrynen's study of causation in regional conflict formation. The issue has three components. The first requires a determination of the timing and circumstances of the *origin of regional conflict formation*. The second requires a determination of the timing and circumstances of *regional security-subsystem formation*. Here the subsystem possesses qualities such as organising principles, distribution of power, unit characteristics, patterns of behaviour of units and the regional subsystem, and patterns of alignment. These qualities enable the analyst to explain and predict the inner workings of the regional subsystem. The final component requires a determination of the timing and circumstances that explain and predict *regional subsystem change*. In sum, the scholar must be able to provide a research design that explains the process and the underlying imperatives behind regional conflict formation, regional security-system formation (with elements of both conflict formation and cooperation formation) and regional subsystem change. Unless all three components are assessed, the issue of regional security structures is not likely to be meaningfully and fully addressed.

In the absence of agreement among scholars about regional security paradigms, our approach is to adapt competing views to develop our options for hypothesis development and testing. In our judgement, Vayrynen is the most open-minded on the topic of regional conflict formation and system change. To him causation may be external, regional or local.[6] Ayoob, on the other hand, stresses external causation in South Asia, and Vayrynen is critical of Ayoob's overemphasis on this.[7] At the theoretical level, Buzan is open-minded about external and internal causation, but his judgements of the South Asian security complex show a bias. To him Indo–Pakistani bipolarity began in 1947 and therefore the dominant source of causation is local, that is, it is centred on India and Pakistan.

Fourth, *How many 'security interdependencies' exist in South Asia and what is the hierarchy of importance of each interdependency?* Security interdependency means that two states make a hostile or friendly pairing and their behaviour is regularly interactive. The conflict or friendly relationship formed is durable and permanent. Buzan and Rizvi see only one strong security interdependency in South Asia, namely India–Pakistan.[8] However, if we take Buzan's concept of 'pattern of amity, enmity and indifference' and apply it to the South Asian scene from 1947 to the 1990s, the evidence reveals multiple security interdependencies – within South Asia, and between South Asian states and external powers (Table 2.2).

The impact on the regional subsystem and the international system of the interactions within each security interdependency may vary, depending on the salience of the issues between the members of each

Table 2.2 Interstate relations in South Asia

Security interdependency	Example
1. Hostile–hostile	India–Pakistan wars (1947–8, 1965–71)
2. Hostile–indifferent and powerful	Pakistan–India (in the 1980s–1990s)
3. Friendly–friendly	India–Nepal Treaty (1950)
4. Hostile–friendly	India–Nepal, 1988–9 trade embargo and subsequent agreement
5. Friendly–friendly	India–Sri Lanka in the 1950s
Hostile–hostile	India–Sri Lanka from the mid 1980s to 1989)
Friendly–friendly	India–Sri Lanka Accord (1987)
Friendly–indifferent	India–Sri Lanka after the withdrawal of the IPKF from north–east Sri Lanka

interdependency, and on the security agenda of the powers in the international system. An investigation of the presence of multiple security interdependencies casts doubt on the alleged dominance of Indo–Pakistani polarity in South Asia. Buzan distinguishes between higher and lower level security complexes. The great powers that impact on regional security subsystems are members of the higher security complex, and local powers are members of the lower security complex. Higher-level security complexes impact on lower-level security complexes, but not vice versa.

This intuitively sound distinction needs to be tested in the South Asian case. Our analysis shows that the distribution of military and economic capabilities in South Asia became asymmetrical in India's favour over time. The number of security interdependencies grew over time and thus a hitherto dominant security interdependency, namely the Indo–Pakistani one, lost its importance in both the South Asian regional subsystem and the international system. Under these circumstances, no security interdependency can enjoy a dominant position in South Asia and the impact of the 'higher' on the 'lower' has decreased over time. The hypothesis is that *the larger the number of security interdependencies, the greater the likelihood that no single security interdependency will dominate the regional subsystem.* Secondly, *a large number of these interdependencies and asymmetries in the distribution of military and economic power increase the opportunities for the possessor of asymmetrical regional power, namely India, to manage the regional agenda*, to divide and rule, form temporary or permanent alliances, secure negotiating partners on different issues, intervene by other methods (economic warfare, military action, clandestine measures, psychological warfare), and generally bring about effective management. Thirdly, if the *power and the interests of members of a 'higher security complex' change, substantive changes in the external setting are likely to reinforce the aforesaid happenings.* As Buzan rightly points out, 'power' and 'security' are relative. Reduced intrusiveness in regional affairs increases the impact of a regional power. To recap, in these circumstances the patterns of amity, enmity and indifference are likely to contain a multiple matrix of interstate relations.

STABILITY VIA REGIONAL MILITARY AND DIPLOMATIC CONFLICT AND COOPERATION FORMATION

According to Henry Kissinger, 'History so far has shown us only two roads to international stability; domination or equilibrium.'[9] By adapting the works of Buzan, Vayrynen, Cantori/Spiegel, and Walt, we intend to show that regional stability is not dependent on strategies of domination (imperialism, hegemony) or equilibrium (balance of power); that stability requires strategies that manage interstate conflict. Security and stability is possible in a unipolar regional subsystem provided regional conflict formation and regional cooperation formation has occurred.

In this context, Box 2.1 summarises and integrates the main scholarly concepts and traditions that explain and predict regional security structures. We have borrowed and discarded select elements from the scholarly concepts and traditions under review. This is to clarify issues. Box 2.1 also helps us understand the history of conflict in South Asia; it requires an open-minded search for internal, regional and external causation in regional conflict and regional subsystem development. Vayrynen's approach makes better sense in assessing the attitudes and policies shaping the Pakistan–US alignment (1951–62), the Pakistan–China alignment (1955–62) and the India–USSR alignment (1949–71).

Box 2.1 shows that alliance activities in South Asia have elements of both 'balancing', and 'bandwagonning', but at times neither despite the presence of threats. This conclusion departs from Walt's main conclusion and theory. Consider the following.

> **Box 2.1 Walt's theory and South Asia[11]**
>
> *1. Balance of power theory: imbalance of power causes an alliance against the most powerful state. Evidence and analysis of three cases*
>
> (a) From 1947–54 India was bigger than Pakistan in population and economic, technological and military potential, but the actual military strength of the Indian army was not greater than that of Pakistan. However Pakistani decision makers feared India even though the fact of comparative military strength at the time did not justify that fear, and this led the Pakistani elite to seek an alliance with the United States. Here a perceived or potential 'imbalance of power' and an 'imbalance of threat' shaped Pakistan's actions. The pattern of Pakistan's alliance behaviour fits in well with the balance of power theory.
>
> (b) India signed treaties with Himalayan kingdoms – Nepal, Bhutan and Sikkim. For the 'weaker' Himalayan kingdoms this was bandwagonning, that is, acceptance of a subordinate status. Note that the imbalance of power and fear of Indian domination did not lead the Himalayan kingdoms to seek alliance with outside power(s) against India.
>
> (c) Ceylon (later Sri Lanka) signed a defence pact (1948–56) with Britain. It feared India's domination. This indicates an alliance activity that was motivated by both balance of power and balance of threat considerations.
>
> *2. Balance of threat theory: imbalance of threat causes an alliance against the most threatening state. Evidence and analysis of two cases*
>
> (a) Pakistan felt threatened by Hindu and Soviet expansionism and sought unsuccessfully (1947–51) to develop an alliance with the United States and Muslim countries in the Middle East. Here Walt's theory is not validated.
>
> (b) From 1947–49 India did not seek an alliance against Pakistan, even though it invaded Kashmir in 1948, and Jammu and Kashmir were partitioned into Pakistani Kashmir and Indian Kashmir with a UN-supervised ceasefire line. According to Walt, Pakistan was India's most important rival. Indian leaders saw Pakistani leaders as misguided, and rivals, but Indian elites still did not seek an external alliance to check Pakistani's ambitions. Indian's behaviour in this period does not validate Walt's imbalance of threat theory.

First, from 1947–54 – that is before the US–Pakistan military pact established a linkage – Pakistan sought an alliance with the United States because it feared an imbalance of power would result from 'Hindu imperialism and Soviet expansionism'. Pakistan's actions were motivated by its concern to balance India's threat. It saw a threat to its existence, its ideology and its regime's interests from democracy and secularism. Hence the quest for a US alliance was motivated by three interacting motives: external security, ideological security and regime security of Pakistan's elites. Here the analyst needs to explain the relationship between Pakistan's external alliance activity, with its internal political/power context, and the pattern of internal alliance activity.

Second, India was initially indifferent to Pakistan's threat despite Pakistan's hand in the use of force in Kashmir in 1947–48; India saw a Pakistani threat to Kashmir but it started external alliance activity only after the pattern of Pakistan's external and internal alliance activities crystallised in the early 1950s. The point here is that a 'bigger' (more powerful) state (for example India) may perceive threats from a 'smaller' irredentist neighbour (for example Pakistan), but it may not necessarily seek an alliance against such a neighbour. But if an international power such as the United States weighs in on a local dispute, such as when the United States supported Pakistan's case on Kashmir at the UN from 1948 onwards, it may seek an international power such as the USSR as a diplomatic ally, such as when Nehru and Radhakrishnan sought and obtained Moscow's support on Kashmir in 1949–51.[10]

This discussion reveals four interesting hypotheses. First, as stated above, *alliance formation activities in South Asia have elements of both 'balancing' and 'bandwagonning', but at times neither, despite the presence of threats in the perception of decision makers. Furthermore a country may employ the tactic of bandwagonning, which is motivated by a policy of balancing.* For example India made concessions to the USSR in the areas of disarmament and Korean War policies (1949–51). This is a sign of bandwagonning – a sign of India's pro-Moscow tilt and the dilution of non-alignment. This tactic was justified by the need to have Moscow on India's side in South Asian and international affairs so as to deal with Indian policy concerns about Pakistan, China and the United States. Here an integral link between balancing (the aim) and bandwagonning (the method) is indicated. This is in contrast with Walt, who assumes that the two strategies are mutually exclusive. Our hypothesis also contrasts with Walt's theory that threats produce balancing rather than bandwagonning alliance activity.

Second, *not all threats lead automatically to alliance building; rather the relationship between threats and alliances is driven by particular or local factors*. The nature of the threat, how it is perceived by the ruling elite and the availability of policy options are critical variables. When Pakistani forces invaded Kashmir in 1947–48, Nehru, India's prime minister and the key decision maker in India's Kashmir policy, saw this as a threat but his strategy was twofold: to treat it as a matter of local aggression that required a local military response; and to appeal to the UN – the world community. (Walt's balance of threat theory predicts that the alliance partner is a single power in a threatening situation.) Only after the UN had failed to accommodate Indian threat perceptions, only after Pakistani alliance activities had revealed the emergence of a Pakistan–US alignment in Kashmir affairs, and only after an emerging military–civil bureaucratic coalition had militarised Pakistani decision making, did India seek an alignment with a major power – the USSR. This pattern of Indian behaviour points to a need to refine Walt's balance of threat theory and make it context-relevant. The refinement lies in the following hypothesis. *A satisfied and a bigger country (India) is likely to avoid external alliance activity with a great power as long as a military threat is perceived to be localised and containable by diplomatic, military and political measures. However it is likely to engage in external alliance activity with a great power (the USSR) when a smaller but irredentist state (Pakistan) is seen as having succeeded in linking with a higher security complex.* Here balance of threat theory needs to tease out the relationship between the key players' threat perceptions and leadership style, their policy options and policy responses (whether a unilateral inaction/action or bilateral alliance approach is sought), and the relationship between a higher and a lower security complex. Table 2.3 refines Walt's approach.

In sum, India–Pakistan conflict formation was the result of several changes in the South Asian strategic and political scene by the mid-1950s:

1. The formation of the US–Pakistan military alliance.
2. The consolidation of the dominant position of the civil and military bureaucracy in Pakistan.
3. Indian counteralliance activity, leading to friendly relations with the USSR in the early 1950s. These elements produced an organised pattern of conflict in Indo–Pakistani relations after 1954. We call this conflict formation.

Table 2.3 Walt's theory revised

Problem	Solution
1. Perceived or potential imbalance of power, and imbalance of threat	Pakistan sought alliance with the United States against communism and India (the most powerful state in South Asia in Pakistani elite thinking), and Pakistan intervened against Indian interests in Kashmir and elsewhere (e.g. Junagarh).
2. In 1953–54 Pakistan's external power increased as a result of its alignment with the United States, as did the internal power of the civil–military oligarchy, which was aligned to the United States. It led India, although more powerful than Pakistan, to perceive an imbalance of power and an imbalance of threat.	India sought a defacto alliance with the USSR to balance the US–Pakistan challenge to Indian interests.
3. 1 and 2	Indo–Pakistani (not regional, South Asia-wide) conflict formation

Sources: Compiled by the authors using S. M. Walt's and R. Vayrynen's works. For information about the policies of the United States, the USSR, India and Pakistan, see S. S. Harrison, *The Widening Gulf* (New York, The Free Press, 1978); S. Gopal, *Jawaharlal Nehru* (Cambridge, Mass: Harvard University Press, vols. 1 and 2, 1976 and 1979 respectively; and vol. 3, Delhi: Oxford University Press, 1984); E. Reid, *Envoy to Nehru* (Delhi: Oxford University Press, 1981); M. S. Venkataramani, *The American Role in Pakistan 1947–58* (New Delhi, Radiant, 1982); K. Arif (ed.,) *American–Pakistan Relations*, vol. 1 (Lahore: Vanguard Books, 1984).

The process of Indo–Pakistani conflict formation developed from communal chaos in 1947 to organised interstate conflict by 1954. It was paralleled by another kind of alliance activity, which bring us to our third hypothesis.

Parallel to the process of conflict formation in Indo–Pakistani affairs (1947 to the present) was a process of regional cooperation formation in South Asia. The latter was driven by India's interest in developing diplomatic, economic and military relations with its smaller South Asian neighbours. As well there was a recognition by the small South Asian states (except Pakistan) that there was no meaningful alternative to bandwagonning in relation to India. With the exception of Pakistan, India's smaller neighbours have traditionally chosen the strategy of bandwagonning. But at times they have also tried to balance India's power by seeking the support of international power(s) outside the region. For example, after 1962 Nepal sought to balance India by developing its China connection, but still it failed to escape Indian intervention in 1989–90. Following its independence in 1948, Ceylon (later Sri Lanka), tried to find external security partners – Britain (1948–56), China (1960–70), Israel and the United States (1980s), ASEAN (1980s) – but its quests ended in failure. In these cases strategies of balancing are the exception, not the rule, and when used, they have failed. In sum, there is overwhelming evidence of the use of a bandwagonning strategy by India's smaller neighbours, except Pakistan, and limited evidence of attempts to rely on a balancing strategy. This hypothesis challenges Walt's theory that bandwagonning is rare.[12]

Figure 2.1 charts the process of regional conflict formation and co-operation formation. Our assumption, contrary to Buzan's, is that in 1947 there was near chaos in Indo–Pakistani diplomatic and military affairs, as well as in both countries' internal affairs. In 1947 the Indo–Pakistani relationship was tentative, ambivalent and limited. There were elements of communal violence, mistrust, territorial irredentism, attempted detente-making, ideological and religious conflict, and limited war in 1947. That is, Indo–Pakistani conflict formation in a stable, predictable form had not yet occurred in 1947. Bilateral interstate polarisation was not inevitable in 1947 as it was in 1954 and thereafter. Secondly, in South Asia from 1949–51, regional cooperation formation occurred when India signed security pacts with the Himalayan kingdoms. Finally, the establishment of India–USSR links from 1949–51 by Nehru and Stalin represented India's balancing strategy vis-à-vis the United States. These developments produced conflict in India's relations with the United States in the early 1950s, as well as cooperation with the USSR.

The fourth and final hypothesis concerns imbalance of interests. To recapitulate, Walt is right to emphasise the inadequacy of the balance of power theory and the utility of the balance of threat theory. Buzan is right to emphasise the inadequacy of the power theory and the utility of regional security complexes; the latter are geographical, historical and policy entities with intense and predictable conflictive and friendly links and interactive processes. We intend to build on these distinctions by proposing further refinements.

Polarity and alliances (alignments) are usually studied in a unidimensional way. In the South Asian context from 1947 to the 1980s,

(1)	(2)	(3)	(4)
Near chaos	Indicators of stable regional conflict formation	Indicators of stable regional cooperation formation	Consent and integration
	Types of activity • Limited confidence-building measures • Normalisation talks • Balancing • Intrigue • Hostile propaganda • Arms race • War and subversion • Crisis: escalation and de-escalation	*Types of activity* • Bandwagonning • Open borders • Free trade • Friendship treaty • No war expectation • Extensive people-to-people exchanges • Extensive intergovernmental exchanges	
	Example: India–Pakistan, India–China *Structure of power* Feudal (bipolar) or multipolar	Example: India–Nepal, India–Bhutan *Structure of power* Unipolar	
	Distribution of power is asymmetrical. Opposition to hegemony is high; however, the conflict relationship is stable. The trend is to avoid general war.	Concessions are asymmetrical. There is a high degree (but not total) consent on the part of the weaker/smaller states.	

Figure 2.1 Regional conflict and cooperation formation in South Asia

the pattern of amity (friendship) and enmity was portrayed by Western scholars (B. Buzan, Leo Rose, G. Rizvi, S. P. Cohen) as in Figure 2.2.

Table 2.4 lists the issues/interests that defined the enmities/friendships of key South Asian players.

The representation of alignments in Figure 2.2 and Table 2.4 is very simplified. In reality there are elements of friendship and enmity in each relationship, but circumstances define the respective weight of each. A relationship may shift along a spectrum that ranges from *harmonious relations* (total agreement exists), to *difficult relations* (enmity and mistrust exist, but are manageable and negotiable), to *indifferent relations* (benign or malign neglect occurs) to *enmity* (a desire to destroy or weaken the enemy is the norm). The nature of the relationship depends on the compulsions and opportunities that the protagonists face. Furthermore, even if, say, the relationship is overtly one of enmity, an element of cooperation may be present, and vice versa. These

```
                        USSR
                       /|\ \
                      / | \ \
                     /  |  \ \ PR China
                    /   |   X
              USA -/----|--/-\------ India
                   \----Pakistan-----
                    \   |   /
                     \  |  /
                      \ | /
                   Smaller South Asian States
```

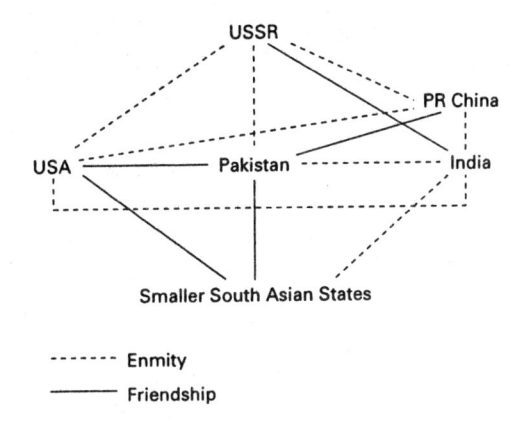

‑ ‑ ‑ ‑ ‑ ‑ Enmity
─────── Friendship

Figure 2.2 Simplified model of public enmities and friendships in South Asia

Table 2.4 Public enmities and friendships in South Asia

Countries	Relationship	Interest/issues
Pakistan–US	Friends	• To contain communism (Soviet and Chinese) • To oppose Indian hegemony • To secure military parity between India and Pakistan
Pakistan–USSR	Enemies	• See Pakistan–US
Pakistan–smaller South Asian states	Friends	• Fear of Indian hegemony
Pakistan–China	Friends	• To contain India
Pakistan–India	Enemies	• To contain Indian expansionism • To contain Pakistani adventurism
India–USSR	Friends	• To contain Pakistani adventurism; support for India on the question of Kashmir • To contain Chinese influence in the area • To contain US influence in the area
India–China	Enemies	• To maintain the diplomatic and military position on the Sino–Indian border

continued on page 38

Table 2.4 continued

Countries	Relationship	Interest/issues
		• To contain each other's international and regional influence
India–US	Enemies (strategic affairs)	• To contain each other's regional and international influence
India–Pakistan	Enemies	As for Pakistan–India
India–smaller South Asian states	Enemies	• To contain Indian hegemony • To contain development of foreign (anti-Indian) influences among smaller neighbours of India
USSR–China	Enemies	• To contain each other's influence
USSR–US	Enemies	• To contain each other's influence

relationships are driven by the issues and interests of the policy communities. Our hypothesis is that *enmities and friendships are defined by interests of the core (regional), intrusive (global) and peripheral (regional and global) players; that interests are revealed by the crisis and non-crisis behaviour of players; that crises reveal ambivalence (real dilemmas, vacillation) in the definition of interests of the policy players; and that interests may change in response to changing domestic and external imperatives (constraints and opportunities) of the players*. In this perspective, Figure 2.3 depicts the parallel issues/interests that divide countries or unite them. The issues/interests and elements of division and cooperation are revealed by the behaviour of each player. Figure 2.3 thus stresses the utility of studying *combinations* of public enmities and secret friendships as well as public friendships and secret enmities in each relationship in a historical fashion. The evidence in support of Figure 2.3 is outlined in Table 2.5.

Figure 2.3 and Table 2.5 modify Buzan's framework substantially. With our expanded framework the analyst is required continually to probe and test the duality of friendship and enmity in each interstate relationship. Our framework expects the analyst to search out ambivalent and changing interests of policy constituencies (among core, peripheral and intrusive players) in a regional subsystem or security

```
        USSR ----------------- PR China
          /  \               /  |
         /    \             /   |
        /      \           /    |
      USA ============ Pakistan ---------- India
       |              |                |
       |              |                |
       '------- Smaller South Asian States -------'
```

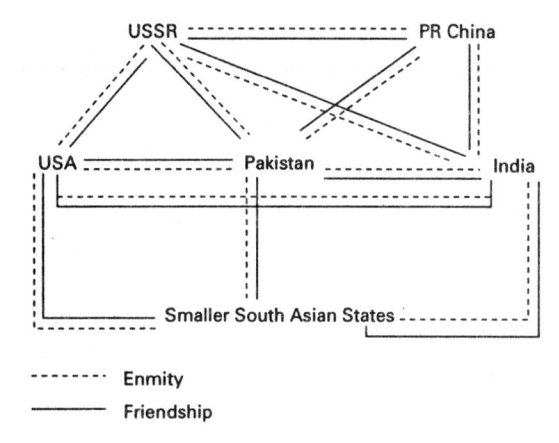

-------- Enmity
———— Friendship

Figure 2.3 Complex model of enmities and friendships in each relationship in South Asia

Table 2.5 Dual elements of friendship and enmity in South Asian international relations

Countries	Relationship	Interests/issues
Pakistan–USA	Friends	• Allies against the USSR in Cold War • US gave arms and diplomatic support to Pakistan on the question of Kashmir (1950s–1970s) • Allies in Afghanistan affairs
	Enemies	• US restrained Pakistan's war-like behaviour in the 1980s in Kashmir • Pakistan ignored US interests in the nuclear sphere
Pakistan–USSR	Enemies	• Opposed each other's international positions on Korea, disarmament, India, Kashmir, Afghan issues
	Friends	• Both sought to protect Pakistan's territorial integrity against Indian military pressure in the 1965 and 1971 wars

continued on page 40

Table 2.5 continued

Countries	Relationship	Interests/issues
Pakistan–smaller South Asian states	Friends	• All opposed Indian hegemony
	Enmity or indifference	• The smaller states seek Indian aid and want to develop cooperative relations with India to improve their well-being
Pakistan–China	Friends	• See Pakistan–China in Table 2.4
	Enmity or indifference	• China failed to oppose India militarily in the 1971 crisis
Pakistan–India	Enemies	• See Pakistan–India in Table 2.4
	Friends	• Civilisational pulls emphasise Indianness • Both seek and are developing confidence-building measures • Both wish to avoid war over Kashmir
India–USSR	Friends	• See India–USSR in Table 2.4
	Enemies	• The USSR sought to contain development of Indian strategic power (nuclear, missiles, space) and prevent Indian military expansion into West Pakistan, and later to prevent Indian political domination of Pakistan.
India–China	Enemies	• See India–China in Table 2.4
	Friends	• Both seek a serious normalisation dialogue • Both wished to avoid the

The Structure of Power in South Asia

		USSR's anti-China collective security arrangement
India–US	Enemies	• See India–USA in Table 2.4
	Friends	• The US has continually aided Indian economic development (1947 to the present) and Indian military development (1962 to the present) in a circumscribed manner
India–Pakistan	As for Pakistan–India above	As for Pakistan–India above
India–smaller South Asian states	Enemies	• See India–smaller South Asian states in Table 2.4
	Friends	• India aided Bangladesh in 1971 • India fought Tamil separatists in the 1980s and JVP insurgents in 1971.
USSR–China	Enemies	• See USSR–China in Table 2.4
	Friends	• Both recognised the utility of limited cooperation
USSR–USA	Enemies	• See USSR–US in Table 2.4
	Friends	• Both recognised the utility of arms reduction and cooperation in the post-Cold-War era

complex. In our approach the analyst must study historically the patterns and shifts at three levels: the distribution (balance/imbalance) of power (from balance of power theory); the distribution (balance/imbalance) of threats (from Walt's theory); and the distribution (balance/imbalance) of interests (from our analysis).

In this context Buzan's approach is deficient in two ways. First, it has no analytical mechanism to explain significant changes in the power structure within a region; his framework does not require continuous probing and testing of changing interests, changing distributions of power and changing threat perceptions among the players. Second, Buzan's research method does not explicitly require a search of patterns of amity and enmity in the relationships of regional and international players on salient issues such as territorial disputes, diplomatic and military rivalries, ideological disputes and economic and other issues.

In sum, from Buzan and others we need to discover the pattern of distribution of *power* and the pattern of *alignments* that shape a regional security structure. Walt can indicate the pattern of distribution of *threats* that explain the balancing/bandwagonning strategies of countries. Vayrynen can show the process leading to *regional conflict formation*. Our critique of Buzan should help define the fabric of amity and enmity that is driven by commonalities and differences in each dyad; this is measured by studying the pattern of behaviour of the dyad members on salient issues. Finally, we need to introduce the notion of regional cooperation formation to build-up Vayrynen's theory of regional conflict formation.

HISTORY OF THE DEVELOPMENT OF THE POWER STRUCTURE IN SOUTH ASIA: A GENERAL OVERVIEW

There are many reasons for studying South Asia. The region is large in size – its population is around a billion and growing and represents about a fifth of all humanity. The region has variety – it contains seven states with diverse political, economic, cultural and military histories and different levels of development in each sphere. It is home to all the major religions and two major fundamentalisms: Islamic and Hindu. The region has a variety of ethnic groupings, and ethnic and religious subcultures have an impact on domestic and regional political, and economic and military affairs. South Asia is a microcosm of the subcultures and trends in the world today, whereby ethnic and religious differences are on the ascendant.

The region has problems – ethnic and religious conflict, Indo–Pakistani cultural and military clashes, strains in relations between India and her neighbours, problems of internal social and economic underdevelopment, drug and arms trafficking are entrenched in different parts of the region, and the region is replete with many malcontents in the policy and societal spheres. These characteristics affect the affairs of states as well as their economic and social well-being.

The region has a history of war and there is a dynamic pattern of belligerency, war preparation, crisis making, crisis avoidance, confidence building, arms control and conflict resolution activities. There are two nuclear powers within the region and many in the neighbourhood – China, Russia, Kazakstan, the United States in the Indian Ocean and the Gulf region, and potentially Iran. The region has emerged as a regional centre of nuclear proliferation and nonproliferation dynamics. It is also a major centre of the theory and practice of non-alignment in a unique global setting of bipolarity and multipolarity, and, according to some, of unipolarity after the collapse of the USSR.

The region has always been an arena where great power competition has been played and managed. After 1947 it also showed that weaker members of the international system are able to participate in the great powers' games. The policies of India and Pakistan reveal the importance of cultural, strategic, diplomatic and economic bridge building in East–West, South Asia–Gulf, South Asian–Indian Ocean and South Asian–South-East Asian relations. India has functioned as an important interlocutor for the West in the Third World and in the non-aligned movement; Pakistan has functioned as a broker for the West in relation to moderate Muslim countries in the Middle East and the Gulf areas and in relation to China.

These reasons ought to have inspired a serious Western study of South Asian strategic and diplomatic affairs and contributions. Unfortunately, since 1947 Western policy considerations have retarded the development of study of the region. Consequently several traits in Western behaviour have created a negative burden. What are these?

First, from a fixation against Nehru and Indian non-alignment, the dominant Western attitude among policy and academic practitioners since 1947 has been one of neglect and indifference towards the South Asian subsystem and its dynamic pattern of alliances and polarity. This happened because the South Asian states, with the exception of Pakistan, were of no use to the West in East–West rivalry.[13] Here Western strategic interests and perceptions shaped academic neglect and academic disorientation. That is, practical policy concerns interfered with the development of South Asian diplomatic and strategic studies. These circumstances created a negative and emotional baggage that has inhibited serious academic work on the changing power dynamics of the region, and its implications for the development of a regional security structure.

Second, because of the region's poverty and material weakness, its colonial history and an apparently obsequious and defensive political style, the West developed an attitude of superiority towards the subcontinent. Here cultural and economic differences shaped the outlook of the political and academic elites of the West.

Third, because of Pakistan's strategic orientation in the Cold War era and Western mistrust of India as a wild card in international and regional security affairs, as well as a mistrust of Indian power ambitions, the West has placed excessive importance on Indo–Pakistani affairs and especially on the problem of the Indo–Pakistani military imbalance.[14] Hence India's positive role in regional and international security affairs was underestimated until the early 1980s. At that time Indian power and political will emerged and vital considerations led Indian and Western elites to take each other seriously.

Despite this negative legacy, two competing approaches have emerged about India's role. The first is represented by Sisir Gupta's writings. He saw a process of unity of the subcontinent under British rule, followed by territorial fragmentation and disunity following the British departure, and then he considered the possibility of a stable or cooperative state system in the area.[15] This view stressed the civilisational pull or the 'Indian subconsciousness' of South Asians, including South Asian Muslims.[16] This Indianness could, according to Gupta, lead to cooperative interstate relations under two conditions.

1. If India was powerful enough to integrate the region on the basis of civilisational pull.
2. If the South Asian states were roughly equal.

Without these conditions, even with a policy of Indian non-intervention, the psychological problem of small states' insecurity vis-à-vis a large neighbour can not be overcome, according to Gupta.[17] Gupta was pessimistic about India achieving the first condition. Thus he thought that India must learn to live with problems.[18]

The second approach is that of Rose and Kumar. Their work stresses the theme of intraregional disunity as a result of Indian strategic ambitions and the negative reactions of India's neighbours. These authors highlight several elements in South Asian international relations.

First, present-day India, Pakistan and Bangladesh were at the core of an integrated (under British political and military authority) South Asian foreign policy system up to 1947. Afghanistan, Nepal, Tibet, Sikkim, Bhutan and Sri Lanka were peripheral territories in British Indian security affairs up to 1947. Up to 1947 British India's foreign policy was outward looking. It was concerned with defending imperial interests in the Indian subcontinent as well as in adjoining colonies.[19] This policy probably owed its proper beginnings to Lord Curzon.

Second, since 1947 South Asian states have been inward looking and their position and interests within the region have been the primary focus of their foreign policies.[20] Third, according to Rose and Kumar:

> it has been the interrelationship between India and Pakistan that posed the major security problem for both countries and, indeed, for the subcontinent. Pakistanis long maintained that India would never accept the results of partition, and were determined to reunify the subcontinent. It has been argued that Pakistan's security policy must be based on this unfortunate 'fact of life' even in other disputes (e.g. with Afghanistan), and that external balances to India's superior resources and capacities are essential to Pakistan's survival.[21]

The perspective on security issues in Nepal, Bangladesh, Sri Lanka, and Bhutan is similar to that of Pakistan in that the major problem for each is their relationship with India rather than with external powers. All except Bhutan have sought to use external powers as counterbalances to India.[22]

One fact little noted outside the region is that all of the South Asian states except Pakistan have already been brought within the matrix of an Indian security system which is regional rather than international in scope. In some cases, this is through formal agreements; in others through the unilateral extension of the Indian system to neighbouring states.[23]

The above explanations are embedded in two entirely different policy and scholarly traditions. Sisir Gupta has studied India's relations with its neighbours in a multiple context: (1) an asymmetrical distribution of resources and area that is in India's favour; (2) interventionary pressures by the great powers on India that work against India; (3) Pakistani policy towards India that is driven by irredentist ambitions; and (4) India's weakness in the international system. The Rose–Kumar approach ignores the second, third and fourth of Gupta's elements; and by focusing on the first element their analysis concentrates on the problem of Indian hegemony.

The controversy inherent in the two lines of thought requires debate and systematic analysis. Our aim is to do just this as both approaches have a common concern: stability and common security in India's relations with her neighbours. However, in our view neither corresponds completely to the actual pattern and process of development of the South Asian system of states and to India's diplomatic–military behaviour since 1947. Hence the following pages first offer a critique of the two traditions and then provide an outline of the history of the South Asian system of states.

Sisir Gupta's *framework of the South Asian states' system* may be analysed in the following way. The aims of the key players varied.[24] India wanted to create a cooperative and a stable state system in South Asia through regional self-help. It wanted a credible security system in Asia and a cooperative coexistence system in the world. On the other hand the Western powers wanted to find ways of making India and Pakistan cancel out each other's power, so that Western power, not Indo–Pakistani power, would protect South Asia and the Indian Ocean area. Pakistan wanted to balkanize, weaken and marginalise India and create Indo–Pakistani parity. Gupta's premise is that the world political system was unable or unwilling to ensure peace and security in South Asia. Furthermore the great powers would not leave India alone. Gupta identified the motives of the players in South Asia. Pakistan was anti-status quo; it wanted to gain Kashmir, either by force or by diplomatic means. India was status quo. China (1950s–1960s) was anti-status quo. The United States (1950s–1960s) was anti-status quo inasmuch as it supported Pakistan's claims to Kashmir. The USSR (1950s–1980s) was status quo inasmuch as it did not favour a change in the territorial status quo in the subcontinent.

Finally, Gupta characterised the South Asian situation in 1947 in the following way. First, civilisational pulls existed. The Indianness of South Asians, including Pakistani Muslims, was a part of the South Asian political setting. Second, South Asian states are of unequal size and even without Indian interference, small states feared Indian hegemony. Third, the incidence of social and military conflict in the region was high. Fourth, interstate relations were disorganised. Finally, Indian's power to integrate the region did not exist.

Compared with Gupta's analysis, Leo Rose took a benign view of the great powers' activities in South Asia, and a less benign view of Indian activities. He emphasised the following.[25] India sought paramountcy in cooperative relationships in an India-led regional security system. Its methods included hardline diplomacy against 'external interference', and bilateral diplomacy. The main determinants were Indian geopolitical strategic interests and the security of land frontiers in the Himalayas; moral and ideological principles were unimportant. The reaction of India's neighbours varied. There was general suspicion about Indian hegemony, but responses varied. Pakistan opposed Indian hegemony and sought to secure Indo–Pakistani parity. Nepal and

Bhutan worked towards a cooperative relationship (bandwagonning). Sri Lankan and Bangladeshi policies varied between bandwagonning and balancing activities.

In its quest for a stable regional political system, India relied on a combination of restraint and intervention. India was reluctant to upset the territorial status quo, but it intervened in cases of extreme provocation and threat to India's interests. The key determinant was its perceived interests vis-à-vis menacing behaviour by hostile neighbours. The reaction of India's neighbours varied. With the exception of Pakistan, India's neighbours approved of positive Indian interference (when it suited their interests) and disapproved of hostile Indian interference (when it did not suit their interests). Pakistan has been uniformly critical of all Indian interventions.

Finally, with regard to the concept of a regional economic system with India as a focal point, the policies of the external powers varied. The United States stressed the value of regional economic interests. An example of the preferred method was the Indus River agreement between India and Pakistan under World Bank auspices. The USSR sought a broader regional economic grouping that would include the USSR, Iran and Afghanistan. Iran and Iraq, too, wanted a broader economic grouping but without Soviet involvement. India's neighbours feared Indian economic dominance because of India's sheer size and proximity.

There is a similarity between the views of Gupta and Rose. Both are concerned with the development of a stable regional system in South Asia. Gupta calls it a stable state system based on 'cooperative coexistence' and regional self-help. Rose, on the other hand, differentiates between a regional security system, a regional political system and a regional economic system. Both recognise the problem of insecurity in the relationship between India and its smaller neighbours.

But beyond these similarities, the differences between the two are significant, as follows:

Gupta: There is a corelationship between Indian security and that of its neighbours.

Rose: There is tension between Indian security and that of the smaller neighbours.

Gupta: India's aim is a power balance in Asia, not an Indo–Pakistani arms balance.

Rose: An Indo–Pakistani arms balance is the crux of the South Asian security question.

Gupta: Pakistan's aim is to secure institutional parity in the subcontinent. This is not in India's interest.

Rose: Such institutional parity is desirable and it is the aim of the US–Pakistan relationship to secure this objective.

Gupta: India deals with three levels of statecraft in the modern international system: South Asia, Asia, and the international system. Western powers should encourage the local/regional powers to be responsible for the development of Asian security through self-help. Regional security structures ought to be the result of cooperative self-help and not the result of Western balance-of-power interventions.

Rose: Is silent on India's behaviour towards the Asian and international levels.

Gupta: The West's aim is to help develop Indo–Pakistani parity so that the two countries cancel out each other's power potential.

Rose: Does not comment on this aspect of Western policy.

Gupta: India wants a regional status quo but the United States and the former USSR want a global status quo, and to prevent the extension of China's influence into Pakistan and the Middle East. Towards this end, the superpowers are willing to satisfy Pakistan's anti-status-quo urges in relation to India.

Rose: Is silent on this point.

Gupta: There is an underlying civilisational unity among South Asian peoples and states. But no state is powerful enough to integrate the region by civilisational or power means and there is a problem with India's size, that is there is the psychological problem of living with a large neighbour that occurs even if the neighbour is noninterventionist. This is inevitable; hence India must learn to live with its problems.

Rose: Says nothing about these aspects.

Gupta: The United States encouraged the Sino–Soviet conflict (especially under Henry Kissinger) so that it might play the role of balancer in the region. After the Pakistani civil war of 1971 the United States was willing to rebuild Pakistan with China's help, and it readopted its old policy of Indo–Pakistani parity so that the power potential of the two would be neutralised in mutual animosity.

Rose: Is silent on this aspect of US policy.

There is a general fit between Gupta's approach and the history of South Asian international relations. However his analysis lacks a tight and continuous link between concepts and historical data. Hence it is pre-theory, not theory. Such pre-theory is valuable as it enables us to reconstruct the story of South Asian international relations. Our discussion of the pattern and process of change in regional conflict formation and alliance formation relies on the following chronology.

1947–48: There was near chaos in South Asia. There was partition, mass killings and mass migration. The governments were free of colonial rule but they were all weak entities.

1949–51: (1) Redistribution of political power occurred inside Pakistan. The civil–military oligarchy gained internal power, and advocates of democracy and non-alignment lost power.
(2) Cold War attitudes effected a shift from indifference to a pro-Pakistan tilt in US thinking and policy in South Asia.

1949–51: (1) India's discomfort in Kashmir caused an Indian tilt towards the USSR in select diplomatic issues.
(2) Indian treaty relations with Himalayan kingdoms were affirmed. A cooperative but subordinate state system emerged in the Himalayas.

1955–60s: China–Pakistan amity emerged.

1955–71: Changes in the distribution of threats, interests and policy ideas created instability in Indo–Pakistani relations and war broke out. The 1971 war acted as agent of stability in South Asian international relations because it created a stable military imbalance in South Asia.

1971–1990s: The change in the distribution of power caused a reassessment of the threats and interests of key players.

These trends came about as a result of several developments:

1. Following its experiences with Pakistan and the United States in Kashmiri affairs and with China in Himalayan affairs, India determined to increase its military, economic and diplomatic weight rather than rely on peaceful diplomacy, international goodwill and fortunate circumstances to advance its interests.
2. Pakistan failed to gain its anti-status-quo objectives by force with US and Chinese help.

3. In spite of the massive amount of aid it gave to Pakistan, the United States failed to achieve an Indo–Pakistani balance of power.
4. China too failed to realise its aim to neutralise Indian power.

To sum up, the key elements in the development (change, as well as improvement) of the pattern of South Asian power relations passed through three main phrases. The next chapter explains this history.

3 Polarity and Alliances in South Asia, 1947 to the Mid-1950s

There are three types of relationship among South Asian states today. The first is the enduring conflict between India and Pakistan. The second resulted in India bringing the Himalayan kingoms into line. The third can be characterised as 'difficult', with elements of competition/hostility and cooperation in different spheres, Indo–Sri Lankan and Indo–Bangladeshi affairs being the best examples.

The theme of this chapter is that polarity (enmity), alliance (friendship) and difficult relationships are to be found in the following spheres of South Asian political, diplomatic and foreign activities:

1. In the domestic structures of South Asian states as these affect the countrys' foreign and military policies towards neighbours.
2. In relations among South Asian states, relations between India and Pakistan, India and its smaller neighbours, and Pakistan and the smaller South Asian states.
3. In the dealings between South Asian states and great powers that have major interests in the region.

The emergence of these patterns of polarity, alliance and difficulty points to conflict formation and cooperation formation and the development of a 'regional security complex'. These patterns provide structure, regularity, predictability and explanatory reasons for South Asian international relations. The emergence of these patterns in an important region of the modern international system deserves academic scrutiny and policy attention because these did not exist immediately after British India was divided into several territorial units in 1947 and 1948. The methods of each pattern vary. *Where friendships exist*, the methods rely on negotiation, compromise and compensation, and occasional political intervention to settle controversies. *Where conflict exists*, the methods seek confidence building and containment of conflict. In South Asia a relationship of conflict is a dynamic process. It requires a balance between three contradictory processes: (1) war preparation because of the mistrust between India and Pakistan; (2) to avoid the danger of a costly and unproductive war, both develop confidence-building measures; (3) both engage in psychological warfare to fan internal controversies and external pressures. In a *relationship of difficulty*, different methods – military and diplomatic pressure, sanctions, negotiations, compromise and compensation – are used to move from a difficult to a cooperative relationship.

In all these relations the objectives vary. In a relationship of friendship the objective is to create a stable and cooperative state system. In a relationship of conflict, the objective is to form a stable, predictable process of competitive coexistence. In a difficult relationship the objective is to move from a competitive coexistence relationship to one of cooperative coexistence. In all three, attention to the other side's perceptions, interests and strategies is a constant feature in the policy process.

How did the South Asian states achieve these patterns of relations in about 50 years? What kinds of diplomatic, military and ideological struggles were fought, and by whom, to shape a South Asian system of states under difficult conditions? In our judgement the pattern of alliances and enmities was established in South Asia from 1947–55. This chapter therefore concentrates on this period.

Finite phases and associated themes define the development of a South Asian system of states. Summarised below are the themes and relevant periods, and each theme is discussed in a section of this chapter.

First, the general diplomatic and military situation in South Asia in 1947–8 was conflictual and unstable. A structure of power did not exist. But this phase did not last long.

Second, when Jinnah assumed power in Pakistan he found that the country's internal situation was his main problem.[1] Jinnah, however, had a firm strategic concept: to put pressure on India and to achieve Indo–Pakistani parity by force and diplomatic pressure. The problem with Pakistan's domestic structure was resolved by the development of an internal civil–military coalition that favoured an aggressive forward policy towards Kashmir and India. Here Pakistan's internal political situation, Jinnah's strategic ideas and Pakistani elite interests indicated an intimate connection between domestic political structure and foreign policy. This theme has dominated Pakistan's Kashmir policy and India policy since the early 1950s.

Third, Jinnah's strategic concept was not sufficient to shape an Indo–Pakistani balance of power. In the first phase (1947–8) the United States and other great powers were mostly indifferent to South Asian diplomatic and strategic issues. But when the West found Pakistan to be an attractive strategic partner in the Cold War, US policies produced a US–Pakistan alignment and an ambivalence towards India. The United States supported Indian democracy and economic reconstruction, but it checked Indian diplomatic aims in Kashmiri, Indo–Pakistani and international affairs. This pattern of alignment and polarity in US policy was formed in the early 1950s and continued to dominate US relations with India and Pakistan up to the 1990s. Convergent US–Pakistan interests solidified Indo–Pakistani enmity and stalemated Indo–Pakistani relations. In addition, this alliance shifted the balance of power in Pakistani politics in favour of Pakistani civil–military bureaucracy.

Fourth, as a result of several changes – the situation in Kashmir, the emergence of the Pakistan–US strategic alignment, the restructuring of Pakistan's internal power elite, which favoured military expansion and an anti-democratic policy framework, and the situation in Tibet – a shift in India's policy occurred. In 1949 India moved away from a policy of equidistance between itself and the major powers (the United States, the USSR and China) towards active involvement with all the powers, but with a pronounced tilt towards Moscow. Beneath the activism was an expectation that Indo–Soviet relations were likely to be friendly but those with the United States and China were likely to range between difficulty and conflict. This phase and pattern of behaviour revealed a subtle and fundamental restructuring of Indian foreign policy, even though its public posture was to remain non-aligned. Here the theme was, and is, that Indian foreign policy was/is sensitive to the relationship between four elements: the situation in Kashmir and other Indian border provinces; the nature of the US–Pakistan connection; the nature of Pakistan's domestic power structure; and the pattern of great power relations. Mutual rivalries in the latter provided India with diplomatic opportunities to shape the pattern of alignments and polarity between South Asian states and the external powers. Here India's approach to foreign affairs was both active and reactive to external developments. This approach started in the late 1940s and continues today.

Fifth, by 1954–5 the foreign policy and strategic interests of Pakistan, the United States and China had converged. The convergence between the United States and Pakistan, and between China and Pakistan, affected diplomatic relations and the distribution of military power between India and Pakistan from 1955–60. Out of the new situation came an infusion of foreign military aid into the subcontinent, and an arms race between India and Pakistan. In the mid-1950s the balance of military power favoured Pakistan. By the early 1960s it had started to shift towards India, and by 1971 a military asymmetry in India's favour had been established, and this has been maintained.[2]

Finally, the 1965 and 1971 wars led the key external players to rethink their policies towards the subcontinent. The adjustments concerned the definition of interests, threat perceptions and geostrategic ideas that had shaped the US–Pakistan and China–Pakistan alignments. The realignment process started in 1965 and continued throughout the 1970s and 1990s. By the early 1980s, India and the United States had started to tilt towards each other in the political and economic spheres.[3]

The China–India relationship, too, underwent a process of bilateral normalisation, and there was a realignment in US–Pakistan and China–Pakistan relations. This continued after the Soviet decision to leave Afghanistan and the ending of the Cold War. In sum, changes within South Asia, as well as in the international sphere, changed South Asian alignments between the 1970s and the early 1990s. We now turn to a definition and assessment of each phase.

The situation in 1947–8 had the following characteristics. First, no state in the subcontinent was strong enough to integrate the whole region. India and Pakistan were divided in diplomatic, military and ideological terms, and India lacked the diplomatic skill and military power to direct regional developments. At the same time, no outside power had the inclination or the capacity to control the subcontinent after 1947 in the way that the British had done earlier.

Second, India is larger than the other South Asian states, and hence it was perceived as dangerous by its smaller neighbours. Irrespective of the pattern of Indian behaviour, this asymmetry of size was by itself enough to produce a sense of small-state insecurity. This was a normal reaction.

Third, small states frequently suffer from the problem of regime insecurity, which is disguised and projected as state insecurity. Among many South Asian states the ruling power structure was narrow at the top, and in several cases it lacked broad popular support. India and Sri Lanka had a democratic political system but the decision makers were few in number. Pakistan was run by a civil–military oligarchy with a theocratic and irredentist bias. Nepal, Bhutan and Sikkim were monarchies. The Maldives were unimportant and not a political model of any kind. India was a political model, a pole of attraction for several reasons: the Indian political struggle brought down the British in a key part of their Empire; India had a preference for non-violent political change; and it took steps after independence to broaden the political process despite the defects in its democratic practices. So even in the absence of Indian intervention, its democratic model was a threat to a majority of its neighbours; it threatened regime survival and power. Indian democracy and elections were a reminder to its neighbours of their undemocratic behaviour and their narrow political base.

Fourth, South Asian states, including India, were militarily and economically powerless but they were culturally secure and diplomatically ambitious, especially India and Pakistan. From 1947 India's aim was to insulate itself and the region from interventionist pressures from outside, especially from the United States and China. Pakistan's aims differed: it wanted to secure itself with assistance from outside the region by aligning itself with the United States and China; to develop an Indo–Pakistani balance of power; and to increase its interventionist pressure on India. During the Nehru years, India's aim was to prevent dramatic changes in South Asian international relations so that a cooperative state system with Indian primacy could be formed. Pakistan tended to use violent means when necessary to diminish Indian power and increase its own.

Finally, the South Asian states recognised the need to achieve internal stability and internal development, but the priorities varied among the governments. For India, a peaceful environment was paramount.[4] For Pakistan the primary concern was to stabilise the civil–military oligarchic rule in domestic affairs and to expand its alignments with friendly powers; internal economic and social development and a peaceful regional environment were secondary aims.[5]

In other words, following Britain's withdrawal from South Asia there were significant signs of activity and polarisation in the diplomatic, military and ideological approaches of South Asian states.

1947 was an important year because it revealed the presence of contending Indian and Pakistani strategic approaches to regional and world affairs; it also indicated the absence of a structure that showed a distribution of power and a pattern of diplomatic and military alignments among South Asian states. Consequently elite and societal attitudes and approaches were competitive, but there were no mechanisms to mediate, moderate or contain the Indo–Pakistani conflict. South Asian states displayed parochial orientations rather than interstate relationships. Pakistan looked to the United States and Britain for support because of its anti-India orientation. Ceylon (in 1948) looked to Britain because of its traditional ties with London and its mistrust of India. The Himalayan kingdoms looked to India for political and economic support because of its historical and cultural links with its northern neighbours. In other words, most of the decision makers did not have well-defined diplomatic and military policies because the external environment was fluid and the main preoccupations of governments were internal.

The second phase was a critical turning point. Five major alignments occurred from 1947–52. These came about as a result of converging and diverging threat perceptions, policy ideas and interests of the key states that were active in South Asian affairs. The process of conflict formation, particularly in Indo–Pakistani and Indo–US affairs, began in this phase, as did the process of alliance formation, particularly in Indo–Soviet and Indo–Himalayan kingdom affairs, and the reorientation or restructuring of diplomatic strategies by Pakistan, the United States, India and the USSR.

THE FIRST ALIGNMENT

The first alignment occurred within the Pakistani government. A fundamental shift in the distribution and location of political power in Pakistani politics had a major effect on Pakistan's foreign and military affairs. It also consolidated the pattern of conflict between India and Pakistan. Table 3.1 shows the attitudes of the dominant players in the ongoing internal power struggle within the Pakistani establishment in each subperiod. The winners in the internal power struggle were Jinnah and G. Mohamed.

THE SECOND ALIGNMENT

The second major alignment occurred in Western, especially British and US, attitudes and policies towards Pakistan during the 1949–51 period. Table 3.2 summarises the winning arguments and the evolution of Anglo–US thinking with respect to Indo–Pakistani affairs.

Table 3.2 reveals the cluster of ideas and forces at work inside the US government at the time. The British High Commissioner in Delhi opposed Caroe's ideas. The US government ignored warnings by Nehru, US ambassador Chester Bowles and others against granting military aid to Pakistan. The players in Table 3.2 won the policy debate.

Table 3.1 The first alignment: Pakistani government, 1947–51

Period	Dominant player	Policy idea/strategic concept	Threat perception	Elite interest
1947–48	M. A. Jinnah	Political authoritarianism in internal affairs is necessary. Unfreeze Kashmir issue by military means. Seek US alliance to strengthen Pakistan.	Provincialism and democracy threatened Pakistan. Hindu and Soviet imperialists threatened Pakistan.	Centralised powers and oligarchic rule were necessary. Western alignments could help the Pakistani political, military and economic elites.
1948–51	Liaqat Ali Khan	A mix of authoritarianism and democracy is necessary. Unfreeze Kashmir issue by diplomatic means. Consider Pakistani non-alignment.	As Jinnah.	Pakistan's internal problems could be managed by democratic means. Indo–Pakistani normalisation process could help Pakistani interests.
1951–	Ghulam Mohamed	Political authoritarianism in internal affairs is necessary. Unfreeze Kashmir issue by diplomatic and military pressures on India. US alliance strengthened Pakistan.	As Jinnah.	As Jinnah.

Sources: A. Kapur, *Pakistan in Crisis* (London: Routledge, 1991); S. J. Burki, *Pakistan, A Nation in Making* (Boulder: Westview Press, 1986); K. B. Callard, *Political Forces in Pakistan, 1947–1959* (Hong Kong: Cathay Press, 1959); A. K. Ray, *Domestic Compulsions and Foreign Policy: Pakistan in Indo-Soviet Relations, 1947–58* (New Delhi: Manas Publications, 1975).

Table 3.2 The second alignment: shifts in Anglo–US ideology and policy, 1949–54

Period	Dominant player	Policy idea/strategic concept	Elite interest
1949–51	Sir Olaf Caroe	British Tory geopolitical thinking: the Gulf is important because of oil and the Soviet threat. A close accord is needed between the Gulf states and the great powers whose interests are engaged in the Gulf; a 'northern screen' along the Soviet border is needed to contain the USSR. Pakistan is in the inner circle of the Gulf/Southwest Asian defence against the USSR; India is on the fringe of the defence periphery. There is no natural interdependence between India and Pakistan. Pakistan is in the first line of defence and it is up to India to mend its differences with Pakistan so as to strengthen mutual defence.	Caroe–Pakistan elite convergent interest is revealed.
September 1951	Gen. Hoyt Vandenberg, US Air Chief of Staff	US Cold War collective security ideas: 'we have an eye on bases in Pakistan'.	Caroe–Pakistan elite–US elite convergent interest is revealed.
December 1951	H. Bryroade, assistant secretary of state for Near East, South Asian and African affairs	Bryroade appreciated Caroe's approach to Pakistan. Caroe had been sent to the United States on a tour sponsored by the British Foreign Office.	As above.

March 1952		US committed to idea of military aid to Pakistan.	As above.
November 1953	Vice-President Richard Nixon	Nixon favoured a US–Pakistan military alliance not only against the USSR but also as a 'counterforce' to Nehru's India. His aim was to check Indian hegemony in the region.	As above.
1953	H. Baldwin, New York Times	US needs to oppose Middle Eastern nationalism, communism and Nehru's anti-Westernism.	As above.
February 1954	US and Pakistan governments	US–Pakistan military alliance is a guarantee for international and regional security. Pakistani air bases were useful against Soviet targets. Pakistani military manpower would be useful against communist targets and this would offset the costs to the United States of using GIs.	As above.

Sources: Compiled by the authors using Selig Harrison, *The Widening Gulf* (New York: Free Press, 1978), pp. 263–7; and Olaf Caroe, *Wells of Power* (Westport, Conn.: Hyperion Press, 1979; published in 1951 by Macmillan, London).

THE THIRD ALIGNMENT

The third major alignment concerned India's foreign policy. A number of developments affected India. First, Kashmir was invaded by a government-supported Pakistani movement and this led to de facto partitioning of the principality. Second, India felt that the US government's attitude on the Kashmir issue favoured Pakistan.[6] Third, Nehru's visit to the United States in October 1949 was disastrous and the leaders of both countries managed to upset each other.[7] Fourth, Pakistani and US government elites viewed each other as strategic partners in an anti-communist and anti-India context after 1949. The visit of Pakistan's Prime Minister Liaqat Ali Khan to Washington in early 1950 was a sign of a warming of the relationship. Fifth, the Chinese takeover of Tibet by force increased the concern within India about Himalayan defences.[8] Sixth, there was an ideological left–right split in the composition of the Indian elite, with Nehru leading the 'leftists' and Patel the 'rightists'. The split polarised Indian foreign policy attitudes.[9] Finally, Nehru, Krishna Menon and S. Radhakrishnan, who were key figures in Indian foreign affairs at the time, sought to improve India's relations with Moscow for a number of reasons.[10]

The shift in Indian's foreign policy orientation in the early 1950s is a little understood development in Western studies of South Asian diplomatic affairs. Because of its critical importance as a turning point, it deserves serious academic investigation. From 1949–52 Nehru and the Indian ambassador to Moscow, Radhakrishnan, brought about a tilt towards the USSR. It was driven by an Indian concern to have the USSR on India's side in the Kashmir issue and generally in world affairs, especially those relating to Korea, China, disarmament and the UN. Here lies an untold story. Although pieces of the story are revealed in the Indian foreign policy literature, more is probably buried in Indian and Western archives. The following section first provides the specific context of India's USSR policy changes, and then identifies the element of realignment in Indian policy.

Background to the third alignment: India and the USSR, 1949–52

This shift occurred in the context of three issues in Indian foreign affairs. The first concerned India's approach to Kashmir and Pakistan. Between 15 August 1947 and 24 October 1947 the key Indian decision maker was the prime minister, Nehru. His main policy idea or strategic concept was to view the Kashmir issue with detachment. His interests were multifaceted: to maintain his dominance over Kashmiri policy, and fight the opposition of Indian rightists who favoured a stronger military stance; to maintain British and Lord Mountbatten's support for his leadership; and to build his image as a democrat, a friend of Pakistan and a peaceful statesman. From 1947–8 Mountbatten, the first governor-general of India, was the other key player in Kashmiri affairs. His main policy ideas or strategic concepts were twofold: to 'stop the fighting and stop it now' and that a Kashmiri plebiscite was necessary.[11] At that time the affinity in Indian decisions about Kashmir was between Nehru and Mountbatten rather than between Nehru and other Indian leaders.

After 24 October 1947 Nehru's orientation towards Kashmiri affairs changed and several nuances appeared in his policy. His new policy ideas and strategic concepts were to: (1) defend Indian-held Kashmir militarily but not to take military steps to liberate Pakistani-held Kashmir – Nehru rejected the advice of his military commanders who felt able to retake all of Kashmir in a matter of weeks; (2) hold on to Indian Kashmir by political and diplomatic measures; (3) avoid a war with Pakistan over Kashmir; and (4) announce a willingness to have a Kashmiri plebiscite.[12]

The second issue concerned Tibet and China. In 1949–50 the key Indian players were Nehru, Krishna Menon and K. M. Panikkar. Their main policy ideas and strategic concepts were: (1) to contain China through a policy of friendship; (2) a belief that invasion of India by China was unlikely,[13] and (3) despite Nehru's advocacy of friendship with China he had private misgivings about its military intentions.[14] The aim of the key players was to project the image of Nehru as an East-West mediator and an advocate of an Asiatic federation led by India and China. The Nehru line on China was controversial in India at the time. In 1950 Sardar Patel was the Indian home minister and a rival of Nehru. He felt that India must concentrate on two fronts – Pakistan and China – simultaneously.[15] He emphasised the value of building Indian foreign relations on realistic lines and not on the basis of false expectations.

The third issue concerned Nehru's attitude towards Soviet and Chinese communism. Following Indian independence Nehru became concerned about Soviet expansionist tendencies. The following report by the State Department outlines the multifaceted nature of Nehru's approach to the USSR.

Despite Nehru's gradually increasing dissatisfaction with the Soviet Union, he has been prone to look for excuses for Soviet behaviour and policies even when he has found them blameworthy and to hold the Western powers at least partially responsible for the unfavourable direction which Soviet foreign policy has taken. In a conversation with Assistant Secretary of State George McGhee in March 1951, Nehru said that the USSR is what it is today largely because of the way the nations of the world isolated it during the early years of its existence.

During this conversation, Nehru agreed with Assistant Secretary McGhee that the Soviet Union had aggressive and expansionist designs, but declined to comment on the suggestion that collective action is necessary to combat the forces of aggression. In a confidential conversation with Ambassador Bowles in November 1951, however, Nehru reiterated the view that the USSR is presently an aggressor, suggested that it had become an imperialist nation on the same pattern as the Czarist regimes, and even went so far as to state that he fully understood the American position of balancing Soviet forces in Europe.[16]

In 1949 Nehru saw value in developing Indo–Soviet ties but Stalin was hostile to India and Nehru was concerned about the Soviet authorities' poor diplomatic treatment of the Indian ambassador to Soviet Russia, Madame Pandit, his sister. Against this background, in 1949-50 Nehru's main strategy was to seek an India–China accord to strengthen India's diplomatic position and engage with the commmunist world. He argued that China should not become a Soviet plaything and should not be isolated from world affairs. In April 1949 the State Department noted:

> Nehru was keenly desirous that Indian–Chinese relations should not suffer because of the Communist victory. If anything, he apparently thought Indian friendship was more important than ever, in order that China should not become isolated from the rest of the world as had the Soviet Union. He was anxious that China should not become 'a mere plaything of Russia.' According to an Embassy despatch, Nehru remarked that he felt 'that the Chinese civilization is so individualistic and differs so greatly from that of other countries, including the USSR, that the government established by the Chinese Communists will not be merely an extension of Russian influence.[17]

The interest of Nehru's supporters was to project an image of him as a builder of Asiatic international relations with China and India as the core powers. Small states were unimportant in Nehru's approach. According to Nehru, 'they occupy a position subordinate to India and China, they would have no choice but to organize around the two larger countries.' This view was expressed in April 1949.[18]

From 1950–52 Nehru privately felt that Indian border defences in the Himalayas must be guarded against Chinese intelligence, military and infiltration activities. This revealed a concern with border security and it contradicted Nehru's public posture on China. The following State Department report explains Nehru's actions.

> Despite Nehru's repeated assertions that China is not presently an aggressive force in Asia, he is said to be deeply disturbed by the recurrent reports of Communist intelligence and military activity as well as infiltration along the Himalayan border areas. In September 1950, while discussing the possibility of Comunist aggression in Asia, Nehru said: 'We are well aware that if aggression should come it would be from the East and not from the West.' Two months later, in a reference to the McMahon Line (which purports to define India's northeastern boundary), Nehru declared before the Indian Parliament: 'We will not allow anyone to come across that boundary.'
>
> After the invasion of Tibet, the Indian Government appointed a military commission to study the defense problems of northern and eastern India, and as a result of the commission's recommendations, additional check posts have been established along vulnerable border areas. The government also made a secret survey of northeastern India to check possible routes through which Communist troops could enter India. Early in 1952, the Indian Army dispatched a number of excellent officers into Assam to strengthen the Assam Rifles and to institute closer security measures all along India's northeastern frontiers. At roughly the same time, notwithstanding Nehru's official attitude of non-interference in the internal affairs of other countries, he sent an Indian military mission to Nepal to reorganize the army of the mountainous kingdom lying between India and Tibet. In addition, India agreed to supply light arms, automatic weapons, and uniforms for 10,000 Nepalese troops and to aid in the construction of militarily usable roads and airfields in Nepal. In the latter part of April 1952, Nehru visited the Indian protectorate of Sikkim and other possibly vulnerable regions along the Indo–Tibetan border.[19]

In March 1951 Nehru argued that, unlike the USSR, China did not presently have aggressive and expansionist designs. China was a potentially expansionist force but it lacked the capacity to be aggressive. Nehru appeared to rely on diplomatic methods to entice China towards an accord with India.[20]

The shift in Indo–Soviet relations occurred in the context of these attitudes and issues. The friendly Indo–Soviet alignment crystallised during 1949–52.[21] It occurred in phases. During April–July 1949 Nehru felt that a psychological approach to the Soviet leadership was needed. Nehru also wanted to project himself as a spokesman for world peace and as an East–West mediator. In September 1949 Dr Radhakrishnan, the new Indian ambassador in the USSR, sought world peace and peaceful coexistence and improvement in great power relations. Building on his credentials as a Professor of Philosophy at Oxford University he sought to promote himself as a spokesman of humanity, and of course he urged better Indo–Soviet relations. Radhakrishnan felt it was important to understand opponents' views so as to develop a settlement on common understanding.

While Radhakrishnan emphasised that Indian policies were independent, Stalin remained sceptical. To him the Indian government was still under the influence of British imperialism, and Lord Mountbatten, the first governor-general of India, was a symbol of British influence. However Stalin felt that flexibility with the Nehru government was appropriate. Here the Soviet interest was to explore the prospect of an accord with the West and to use India as a bridge builder. In 1951 Radhakrishnan raised the Kashmir issue with Stalin. He argued that the USSR should be concerned about Kashmir's future if only because it shared a common border. The geostrategic argument attracted Soviet attention and in January 1952 the USSR used its first veto in India's favour at the UN Security Council. This signalled Stalin's interest in finding common ground with India and using it to advance Soviet interests in the international sphere. Gopal calls this a turning point in Indo–Soviet affairs and Indian foreign affairs. He maintains that the 'Soviet administration ... recognised [Radhakrishnan's] crucial role in building Indo–Soviet understanding; and so did Nehru'. This indicates that Nehru took the credit for building this accord even though he was not the architect or executor of the policy. Table 3.3 outlines the policy debate that led to the development of the Indo–Soviet alignment. Table 3.3 indicates the existence of a sharp ideological and policy struggle within the upper echelons of the Indian government. In the absence of evidence contradicting Gopal's view of his father's achievements, it appears that (B) and (C) represented the winning argument, (A) was

Table 3.3 The third alignment: the cluster of ideas and forces, 1949–52

(A) Bajpai, Pandit and Nehru

- 1949: Mrs Pandit, Indian Ambassador to Moscow, stopped promoting Indo–USSR relations because of her and Stalin's attitudes.
- Nehru had ambivalent attitudes about the USSR and the West.
- Bajpai, head of India's Foreign Office, complained about the Soviets' 'unconfiding character'.
- Bajpai, and to an extent Nehru, opposed Radhakrishnan's Korean policy.
- Bajpai opposed Radhakrishnan on grain imports from the USSR.

(C) Nehru and Radhakrishnan

- Both agreed that the United States was more bellicose than the USSR.
- For the same reasons as Radhakrishnan and Krishna Menon, both pushed for China's entry to the UN.

(B) Radhakrishnan and Krishna Menon

- Both pushed for a treaty of friendship between India and the USSR.
- Both objected to Nehru's support of UN resolutions against North Korean aggression because it was a 'decision of one bloc'.
- Both pushed for China's entry to the UN to weaken Sino–Soviet ties and strengthen India's position in Asia.
- Radhakrishnan downplayed the danger of Soviet aggression.
- Radhakrishnan proposed a global deal to end the Cold War.
- Radhakrishnan thought that Stalin was keen on reaching an understanding with the Western powers.

(D) Nehru

- Nehru accepted the UN resolutions charging North Korea with aggression.
- Up to 1951 Nehru did not ask for Soviet support on the Kashmir issue because it would severely 'tilt' Indian nonalignment.

Sources: S. Gopal, *Jawaharlal Nehru*, vol. 2 (Cambridge, Mass: Harvard University Press, 1979); S. Gopal, *Radhakrishnan* (London: Unwin Hyman, 1989).

the losing one, and as a result of the ascendency of (B), the Nehru line in (D) changed in favour of (B). This change contributed to a decisive shift in Indo–Soviet relations and Indian foreign policy. It revealed that Nehru could be swayed by the advice of his ideologically determined colleagues (Menon and Radhakrishnan), but not that of his senior officials, especially Bajpai and his sister, Madame Pandit. In our view Nehru was ambivalent at both the ideological and the policy level, and this seemed to cancel out his private views and make his policies vulnerable to pressure from his associates if this was well timed. Ideologically Nehru admired Western values and privately he was concerned about Soviet and Chinese intentions. But at the policy level he thought Washington was immature and bellicose and the USSR wanted peace. Dissonance existed between Nehru's inner and privately expressed ideological convictions and his policy assessments concerning the motives and capacity of the great powers. At the same time these split images were vulnerable to domestic and external pressures and international events. Because the Nehru/Indian decision-making unit was crowded with diverse personalities, competing ideologies and assessments of the problems and strategies for their solution, Nehru seemed to lack space to manoeuvre even though to the outside world he alone carried weight. In this alignment others actually counted more than Nehru. As a result of these events and pressures, in 1952 Nehru accepted a tilt towards the USSR in Korean and disarmanent affairs, and towards gaining Soviet support for the Indian view on Kashmir, thereby giving the Kashmir issue an international and a geopolitical slant. As he had opposed this course of action up to 1951, his action revealed that reversal of his non-aligned ideology was open to persuasion by his closest advisers and by the prospect of bringing Moscow to Delhi's side.

THE FOURTH ALIGNMENT

The fourth alignment concerned India's relations with the three Himalayan kingdoms – Nepal, Bhutan and Sikkim. Here orientations occurred within the context of a history of treaty relations between British India and these kingdoms. The treaties showed the existence of a cooperative and subordinate system that diminished the independence of the kingdoms. The pattern of Indian behaviour from 1949 onwards was to expand and deepen relations with the three countries because of changes in China and Tibet, the rise of democratic India and internal changes in each kingdom. In other words, India adapted the British colonial government's approach to the Himalayan kingdoms to suit Indian policy concerns and interests. The relationships were not one-sided – there was an element of mutual consent and mutual gain even though the distribution of power favoured India.

These treaty relations had a unique character. They offered room to manoeuvre (choice) for the smaller, weaker players, but on the other hand India, the larger, more powerful player, was required to exercise restraint. The expectation of restraint was important given Nehru's patronising attitude (noted earlier) that small states did not count in Asian affairs. They did not, inasmuch as India's objective was to lock them into a subordinate relationship, but on the other hand they did count to the extent that the kingdom's political interests and economic well-being were advanced via the treaty relations. So Indian policy and the treaties had elements of subordination and accommodation. In such a cooperative relationship diplomatic persuasion by the subordinate parties and occasional interventionary pressure by India were the preferred methods of action. This mode of behaviour differs from *machpolitik*.[22] The requirement of consent by the weaker partner, was the moral justification for this pattern of alignment. Secondly, despite the presence of contentious issues in bilateral relations with India, the behaviour of the Himalayan kingdoms revealed a faith in bandwagoning rather than non-alignment, isolationism or balancing behaviour in relation to India. They expressed a faith in the utility of a system of treaty relations that offered protection and advantage to them. Table 3.4 outlines the pattern of treaty relations that governed British India's and India's relations with the Himalayan kingdoms.

Box 3.1 presents the main characteristics of India's relations with the Himalayan kingdoms. Historically, relations have fluctuated from cooperation to mistrust, depending on how the elite and public opinion in the kingdoms have assessed the nature of Indian behaviour in periods of stress or crisis, but on the whole they have functioned more on the side of cooperation than mistrust. Whether the Indo–Himalayan kingdom relationship in high or low on the cooperation/mistrust scale depends on an interplay among three variables: the nature of India's behaviour; the balance of power and the debate within the policy establishments in the Himalayan kingdoms; and the effect of the international environment on the country concerned. These variables should be studied because although the pattern of Indian behaviour in this part of the world is fairly predictable, reactions to it vary, depending on the strength of the other two variables.

Table 3.4 Pattern of treaty relations with the Himalayan kingdoms

Period	Player	Main features of treaty
1923	Britain–Nepal	Nepal was constitutionally independent but it acknowledged British influence over Nepal's foreign relations and external trade.
1865–1910	Britain–Bhutan	Bhutan accepted British control over its foreign affairs. Britain saw this as implying suzerainty over Bhutan.
1890–1893	Britain–Sikkim	British–Chinese treaties recognised British protection of Sikkim in return for Sikkims waiving its claim on the Chumbi valley.
1948	India–Sikkim	An agreement was signed to adhere to the provisions of the Britain–Sikkim treaty.
1949 (August)	India–Bhutan	India recognised Bhutan as a semi-sovereign state. It undertook not to interfere in the internal administration of Bhutan. Bhutan agreed to be guided by Indian advice in its external relations. Arms could be imported 'from or through India' as long as Bhutan did not endanger Indian security. India was to pay an annual subsidy to Bhutan.
1950 (December)	India–Sikkim	Treaty affirmed British India–Sikkim relationship, declaring Sikkim an Indian protectorate with autonomy in its internal affairs. India was obliged to defend Sikkim and it had the exclusive right to develop Sikkim's economic and military infrastructure. Sikkim was not allowed to deal with foreign powers. Indian troops were allowed to be stationed on the Sikkim–Tibet border.
1950 (July)	India–Nepal	It restated the principles of the 1923 Treaty (substituting India for Britain). The treaty spoke of 'everlasting peace and friendship' between the

Table 3.4 *continued*

	two countries. Each acknowledged the principle of sovereignty, territorial integrity and independence of the other state. It emphasised the urge to expand bilateral diplomatic relations. Nepal was required to import arms 'from or through' India. Nationals of the two countries had reciprocal privileges in residence, property ownership and trade. Nepalese soldiers were permitted membership, including the officer ranks, of the Indian armed forces. Security threats were to be dealt with through mutual consultation. (The last clause was revealed in 1959.)

Sources: C. H. Heimsath and S. Mansingh, *A Diplomatic History of Modern India* (New Delhi: Allied Publishers, 1971); *Keesing's Contemporary Archives*, vol. VII (London: Keesing's Publication, 1948–50), pp. 10157–58, 10176, 10933, 11147.

Box 3.1 Elements and characteristics of cooperative and hostile relations between India and the Himalayan kingdoms

Cooperative but subordinate relations:

- Indian support for ruling families and the public in the kingdoms enabled them to avoid the fate of the Tibetans.
- Indian economic aid increased the well-being of the peoples in the area.
- Indian aid strengthened the territorial and border security of these areas against Chinese pressures.
- Indian policy strengthened bilateral ties without making weak neighbours into helpless satellites.
- Indian aid developed the weak states' internal infrastructure and communications.
- India's conditional assertion of the principle of non-interference in internal affairs of the kingdoms, combined with a 'duty' to defend the area, created a principle of good neighbourly policy.

Hostile relations:

- The patronising political and diplomatic style of Indian governments indicated insensitivity to local sentiment.

- Indian intervention (diplomatic, economic and military) affected regime interests and public opinion in the Himalayan areas.
- India's opposition to the involvement of foreign powers in Himalayan areas when it could affect Indian interests was seen as a sign of domination.
- Indian military occupation or presence outside indian borders was seen as domination.

Historically, India's behaviour in the Himalayan areas reveals a constant pattern of stimulus and response. This pattern has several characteristics. First, 'India has been reluctant to intervene in the internal affairs of these countries except in the event of an extreme threat to India's interests.[23] This is also true of Indian interventions against Pakistan (the 1965 and 1971 wars) and Sri Lanka (the mid-1980s). Indian threat perceptions show a low tolerance of hostile foreign (especially Chinese) influences in the Himalayan areas.

Second, the interventions have been limited and proportional to the threat. They have been driven by political purpose rather than by territorial design or economic gain. The interventions have not produced territorial conquests or permanent military occupation, nor have they caused economic ruin of the weaker country. Interventions have been temporary and mutually beneficial.

Third, reactions to Indian interventions have varied. When an Indian intervention was seen as helping the ruling establishment and/or an international ally (for example the United States) the intervention was encouraged or tolerated. When not, it was criticised. What counts is not the fact of Indian intervention, but the interests of India's neighbours and the great powers involved in the area at the time the intervention occurs. Such interests govern the variations in the reactions to Indian intervention.

Finally, a constant in the pattern of relations is that the Himalayan kingdoms have never relied on an arms race with India in their quest for survival and the security of their regime or state; nor have they seriously tried to bring the great powers to their side against India in security and foreign affairs. There is a contrast between the security behaviour of Pakistan and that of the Himalayan kingdoms. However there are a few exceptions. Nepal flirted with China under King Mahendra and King Birendra from 1960s to the 1980s. Sikkim was involved with the United States in the 1970s. Sri Lanka sought the alliance of the United States, Singapore, Pakistan and Israel from the 1960s to the mid-1980s. Despite these exceptions the kingdoms did not seriously try to restructure the pattern of treaty relations with India.

Indian political behaviour in the 1949–50 period changed the character of treaty relations with the kingdoms. Compared with the earlier British influence, India's influence over Nepal increased from the 1950s onwards.[24] Under Nehru the belief that Nepal was a part of the Indian security zone was explicit in 1949 but became public only in 1959. The protectorate status of Sikkim continued in the 1950 treaty as under the Britain–Sikkim relationship, but the 1950 treaty opened up Sikkim to Indian penetration in an extensive and enduring way. By 1975 Sikkim's status had been transformed from a protectorate to a member of the Indian Union. This illustrate India's political will and its determination to change the constitutional or legal basis of political relations according to its national interests. India continued the British pattern of treaty relations with Bhutan on the principle of non-interference and respect for Bhutan's isolation. However, with the emergence of a unified communist China in 1949 (the People's Republic), and with the takeover of Tibet in 1950, the changed external context created an incentive for Indo–Bhutanese cooperation to avoid the takeover of this strategic Himalayan area.[25]

In sum, the pattern of extension of British Himalayan treaty relations by India had several undercurrents: (1) India's determination to create a security zone in the Himalayans, and to create a strong Indian union, revealed its political will and a strategic dimension in Indian diplomacy; (2) China's forceful takeover of Tibet and the rise of a unified and ambitious political authority in China revealed India's response to significant external changes; and (3) Indian independence revealed the appeal of democracy in South Asian and Third-World politics. Each undercurrent had a positive and a negative side. First, India's political will reassured its neighbours as it ensured protection of the areas and regimes; concerned on the other hand, Indian balkanisation could also lead to the break-up of the smaller states. Second, the rise of China might have been a blow against Western imperialism, but it also increased pressures in the Himalayan areas. Finally, Indian democracy was an attractive idea as it meant a commitment to peaceful change, but on the other hand mass politics challenged the right and power of the narrowly based ruling elites in the kingdoms. Here India's ideals clashed with the interests of the elites.

All four major alignments discussed in this chapter were definitive and enduring. The first has dominated Pakistani political and military affairs since the early 1950s.[26] The second has influenced US–Pakistan and US–India strategic relations since the mid-1950s, even though US attitudes and policies have wavered between total loyalty to an ally and ambivalence.[27] The third alignment lasted from the early 1950s to the late 1980s, until the collapse of the USSR. The fourth alignment continues.

THE FIFTH ALIGNMENT

The fifth and final alignment of this period concerns China and Pakistan. Here some background is required. During the early 1950s the public focus in South Asian and in Asian affairs lay in the resurgence of China and the development of Sino–Indian relations. These two countries were the first to sign a peaceful coexistence agreement in 1954.[28] Nehru's public posture highlighted China's importance in Asian and world affairs and the value of Sino–Indian friendship. Nehru had a complex view of China that was articulated to Western ambassadors in Delhi. It included a number of assessments. First, the PRC was emerging as a great power and this factor was changing the entire Asian and indeed global balance. Second, China was likely to cooperate with the USSR for a while but then, given Chinese nationalism, it was likely to go its own way, that is, a Sino–Soviet split was likely. India's China policy was meant to make clear to China that the USSR was not the only friend of China. On this basis India adopted a cautiously friendly attitude towards China while maintaining a security watch in the Himalayas and disapproving of some Chinese actions. Finally, India's links with China would enable it to influence Chinese behaviour and participate in Sino–Soviet affairs.[29] The US establishment – Dean Acheson, John Foster Dulles and administration officials – however, felt that Nehru's India was misguided in its China policy. This view contributed to the US mistrust of India in Asian affairs. Furthermore India's diplomatic ambitions, political style and political will were seen to justify the US view that India was likely to be the successor to Japanese imperialism in Asia and that US allies ought to contain India's influence in international affairs.[30]

In the early 1950s a pattern of alignments dominated South Asian affairs: (1) India and the United States had a difficult relationship – there were elements of friendship as well as conflict; (2) India and China were publicly friendly; (3) the United States and Pakistan were publicly friendly; (4) India and the USSR had become secret friends by 1952, and were publicly friendly by 1955; (5) the United States and China displayed open enmity; and (6) the United States and the USSR were open enemies.

But this pattern of alignments had another, secret dimension without mention of which our study would not be complete: it concerned the gradual development of Sino–Pakistani agreement on a number of crucial issues. First, with the establishment of the PRC in 1949 Pakistan approached the issue on a *realpolitik* rather than an ideological basis. It did not want India to claim the main role on the China question and it hoped to win Chinese support for Pakistani claims to Kashmir. Pakistan recognised China in January 1950 and called for Chinese representation in the UN and the Security Council. Second, Pakistan had a balanced policy on the Korean war. It condemned North Korea but not China as the aggressor and refused to accept economic sanctions against China. China approached Pakistan in terms of Chinese interests and not on ideological grounds. Even though Pakistan's alliance activities (US–Pakistan, 1954; SEATO, 1954; and the Baghdad Pact, later CENTO, 1955) threatened China with encirclement, China pursued other angles and had other reasons for establishing a relationship with Pakistan: it sought relations with Muslim Middle Eastern countries via Pakistan; it sought links with Pakistan because of uncertainty over China–India relations; it recognised the caution in Pakistan's China policy; and it hoped that Pakistan would be semi-autonomous in its external behaviour and not simply a US satellite.[31]

In sum, since Jinnah's days Pakistan had pushed hard for an alliance with the United States, but having secured it, it cast a wider diplomatic net in the early-to-mid-1950s to build a link, or at least a policy option, with China. At the same time, even though Chou En-lai was making full use of Nehru's pro-China policy, personality and policy issues started to cloud the Sino-Indian relationship in the mid-1950s. Both Nehru and Chou had strong egos. India and China were diplomatic rivals in Asia. Both represented great civilisations. The Sino–Indian Himalayan border (the McMahon Line) was not simply an undefined or undemarcated boundary – China had strategic interests in the Sinkiang region and the Sino–Indian border issue played a part in Sino–Soviet power rivalry. In this context the Sino–Pakistani relationship emerged, reflecting shared interests rather than ideology. In the early 1950s there was no military or economic purpose for this relationship. Rather it showed a sense of mutual attentiveness and a drive on both sides to develop cracks in international (US–Soviet, Sino–Soviet) security relations as well as to build on the deep divide between India and Pakistan. The Sino–Pakistani alignment reflected the following: (1) China and the USSR were public friends and secret enemies; (2) Pakistan and the United States were public friends but, despite US–China animosity at the time, Pakistan and China were also likely partners because of their common concern to contain and divide India; (3) Pakistan had the potential to function as a bridge to extend China's influence in the Middle Eastern countries – the USSR's southern neighbours and an area of vital interest to the United States – where oil security and the containment of commmunism were the norms of US and Pakistan foreign policies.

This was the background against which the Chinese government started to acquire intelligence about Pakistan's political leaders in the early 1950s. According to an informed study, Harold Holt – later prime minister of Australia and allegedly a Chinese spy for most of his career – was asked to report to China on Pakistani affairs. This was in 1952.[32] Clearly China was thinking ahead even as Nehru and Chou were proclaiming the dawn of the *Hindi–Chini bhai bhai* (Chinese and Indians were brothers) era.

In 1954-55 China was going through an intense internal power struggle that involved Mao, Chou and Lin Piao.[33] Despite this preoccupation, Chou was able to participate actively in the Bandung conference (1955), which marked his emergence onto the world stage as an effective statesman and set the scene for the build-up of the Sino–Pakistani alignment. Two elements shaped this, and both were decisive and enduring in their effect on Indo–Pakistani and Sino–Indian affairs and on China's relations with India's other neighbours. The first element was that Chou, unlike Nehru, was flexible in recognising the right of a country to enter into collective security arrangements at the Bandung meeting; this way Nehru's emphasis on peaceful coexistence was undermined. Secondly, as Rushbrook Williams notes:

> Following on the Bandung Conference, when the nations of Asia, under the lead of China, by whom India was momentarily overshadowed, drew up a charter of peaceful co-existence amidst scenes of wild enthusiasm and speeches of brotherly amity, Karachi received – as I have been assured on unimpeachable authority – a private message from Peking. The Chinese People's Government assured the Government of Pakistan that there was no conceivable clash of interests between the two countries which could imperil their friendly relations: but that this position did not apply to Indo–Chinese relations, in which a definite conflict of interests could be expected in the near future. No more cynical expression of realpolitik can be imagined.[34]

The Chinese initiative sealed the Sino – Pakistani relationship on an anti-Indian basis. This was also in line with the anti-Indian stance of key personalities in the US government, for example Richard Nixon. Thus by the mid-1950s, Pakistan, with its anti-status-quo learnings, had two international allies; and India, a status quo country, a friend of Moscow and a diplomatic rival of the United States and China in world affairs, was diplomatically on the defensive, internally preoccupied and the object of external pressure.

SUMMARY

The patterns of polarity and alliance in South Asia were firmly set between 1947 and 1955. The geographical centres of the core relationships were northern India, the Chinese border areas and the Kashmir area. The political centres were Karachi, Delhi, Washington, Moscow and Beijing. The distribution of military and economic capabilities between the key players was not the key determinant of these core relationships. Rather threat perceptions, elite interests and strategic ideas drove the process of conflict formation and alliance formation. The interests of the great powers were asymmetrical. During this period US interests had a strategic content. The United States sought Soviet and Chinese containment, Gulf oil security, containment of Nehru and India, and US bases in Pakistan. Chinese interests too were broad based. They sought to guard China's interests vis-à-vis the USSR, to extend Chinese influence into the Middle East via Pakistan, and to contain Nehru's India. Stalinist Russia had an ideological view of Nehruvian and Gandhian India, seeing it as a part of the British Empire even after 1947. Initially Stalin saw no strategic value in India or Pakistan but he valued the link with the Communist Party of India. Later he realised that there were diplomatic and strategic opportunities to extend Soviet influence via India into the Third World and the United Nations. This focus became pronounced in Soviet foreign affairs after the US-led alliances in the Middle East and Pakistan brought the United States into the Soviet backyard.

Events in this period had several aspects. First, the pattern of alliance and polarity was the result of activities of key personalities, their perceptions, their definitions of national interests and their ideas. This was a small, secretive and highly charged world. These players determined the pace and level of activism and intervention. Second, strategic interests and outlooks were important; ideologies were not.

Despite Nehru's concern about Soviet communism and aggression, and despite Nehru's pro-Westernism, the Indo–Soviet alignment emerged. The Sino–Pakistani alignment emerged despite the Pakistan's opposition to communism and its alignment with the United States. India and the United States differed sharply over world and South Asian affairs, even though both were democracies. Both the USSR and China were communist but they were divided in their approach to South Asian affairs, and each other. Likewise democracies were not allies in South Asia, nor did differences in the political values of elites inhibit alliance formation. These situations illustrated the irrelevance of ideology in explaining the South Asian pattern of alliance and polarity.

Third, Caroe and US policy makers pushed for Pakistani involvement in Western defence matters because of Middle East oil security and of the need to check the USSR and India. The search for collective security under US leadership rested on the idea of encouraging and maintaining divisions between Pakistan and India and Pakistan and the USSR. This indicated the working of an important strategic principle, namely the key players sought to divide power and influence in the region by organising power struggles in the area as long as these resulted in stalemate rather than war. All the alliances rested on the principle that the enemy of my enemy is my potential friend.

Fourth, the key players sought advantages and involvement in regional affairs by means of alliance rather than unilateral action. Finally, the United States showed a low tolerance of activities by India that challenged its international position, but an accommodation of activities by a regional ally that were anti-status quo. China was the exception to this approach during this period. Its rhetoric indicated a high degree of tolerance for a change in the international status quo as well as a wish for change in the existing regional situation.

The pattern of conflict and cooperation that had emerged by 1955 created the framework for the subsequent restructuring of South Asian international relations in the 1955–71 period. The history of the arms race, and war and military crises involving India, Pakistan and the great powers occurred within the context outlined in this chapter. It is to a discussion of these aspects that we now turn.

4 Arms Race, War and Crisis in South Asia, 1955–71

This chapter identifies seven major themes in international relations in the subcontinent from 1955–71. It assesses the key variables that led to war in this period and discusses the consequences of South Asian wars in shaping the structure and texture of regional international relations. Our conclusion is that each war changed the kaleidoscope of variables that were present at the time war was initiated. The main players showed ambivalence in their war behaviour. Along with the changing distribution of military power, South Asian war experiences reveal a pattern of ritual confrontations and deadly encounters.[1]

The period from 1955 to 1971 saw the arms race between India and Pakistan taking concrete shape, the Cold War entering the subcontinent, and wars and crises between India and Pakistan (1965 and 1971) and India and China (1962). South Asian international relations during the period make an interesting case study of a five-power strategic game. Had it been a US–Pakistan versus India–USSR story, it could have been studied as a straightforward extension of the Cold War into South Asia. In this case the emphasis would be placed on a study of the behaviour of the bloc leaders (the two superpowers) and their clients. There would be some justification for doing so as the literature refers to India as a Soviet client and Pakistan as that of the United States. However, in our view, this is misleading because the diplomatic and strategic activities in the region were multifaceted – they involved two regional players (India and Pakistan) and three external players (the United States, the USSR and China). The weaker (India and Pakistan) had freedom of choice vis-á-vis the stronger; and the stronger faced constraints because of their internal and external difficulties. Moreover, because of the five-power interactions (with each power having domestic, regional and international difficulties and opportunities), the US–Soviet Cold War was not the sole or primary determinant of the policies of the United States and the USSR; indeed two detentes – US–Soviet and US–China – were in play in the subcontinent during this period. So the Cold War paradigm is not especially helpful in understanding South Asia's international relations at that time.

The international relations of the region centred on five cold wars: between, (1) India and Pakistan – here the Cold War became hot in 1965 and 1971 and then reverted to normalcy; (2) the United States and the USSR; (3) the USSR and China; (4) the United States and China; and (5) China and India, where it became hot in 1962 and then returned to cold. These wars were never purely bilateral affairs. There were varying degrees and intensities of interactions involving others. The policy actions of the five players were focused on third parties' interests within bilateral relations. Because of the intense and continuous engagement of the multiple interests of the players in the region, albeit a secondary region in the international system, the diplomatic and military behaviour of the players provides valuable insights into their attitudes and policies towards South Asia as well as the other powers.

During crises in this period the players' behaviour showed activism, interventionism and ambivalence. The subcontinent seemed to turn away from its proclaimed faith in the peaceful development of the region, towards a recognition of the utility of coercive interstate diplomacy and repression of internal affairs in the management of internal and external crises. The military machine became central to the process of creating regional order, adjusting bilateral relations into a predictable (but not necessarily harmonious) form, and forcing or inducing a change in the pattern of behaviour and thinking of policy elites with anti-status-quo learning. Coercive diplomacy became an essential instrument in interstate behaviour. The players were not inclined to war, but neither did they shy away from the use of force under given circumstances, for example if the risks were manageable, if the use of force was driven by a concern to develop a regional order and punish undesirable behaviour, and if the danger of losing by not fighting was greater than the danger of fighting.

In conventional wisdom, crisis and war imply instability and disorder. Our reading of South Asian crises and wars is that they were driven by strategic and political purposes. This validates the classical view of war, that is, wars may be fought for good or bad reasons but there is no such thing as an accidental war.[2] So the actions of the players in starting, conducting and finishing a war or a crisis in the region would indicate continuous political control over the war or crisis. South Asian wars reveal a process of deliberation, whether or not we judge the reasons to be good or bad. Moreover each crisis produced a sense of caution among the players and caused rethinking about the future. If fear of losing an advantage, fear of external domination and anxiety about a state of weakness triggered the outbreak of war, fear of punishment induced caution among South Asian strategic players. The South Asian wars and crises provided the players with valuable lessons. The point is that in a situation of persistent hatred, war may be necessary to introduce regional order and good government:

1. In the absence of fear of military reprisal, intercommunal passions (for example between Hindus and Muslims) cause uncontrolled or unorganised social conflict, anarchy, communal violence or ritual confrontations.
2. Successful war that is motivated by concern with regional order and good government results in:
   – a modification of behaviour;
   – the prevention of bad behaviour;
   – attitude modification (a rethinking of hatred or conflicting social and political attitudes and interests).

THE THEMES

The arms race as a policy tool in South Asia

The Indo–Pakistani arms race took shape during this period. Previously the two countries had relied on local war in Kashmir, international alliance activity and bilateral political or psychological warfare to manage their rivalry. After 1955 both sides recognised the utility of arms build-up and war preparation in their policies. Out of the arms build-up came the capacity to wage war. According to traditional theory, wars occur because (1) evil-minded governments cause war and (2) unfair peace conditions cause war.[3] In both instances, arms availability enables war.

This period was historically important because three elements combined to produce an explosive situation. First, India perceived Pakistan's civil – military oligarchy as evil-minded. Second, Pakistan considered that India had cheated Pakistan out of Kashmir following partition. Third, the availability of arms made war an option. As a result of this combination, the Indo–Pakistani social conflict was escalated by policy decisions into organised military clashes; ritual cultural and diplomatic confrontations became deadly fights. The shift from unorganised and inconclusive social conflict between Hindus and Muslims (1947–54) to organised military conflict between India and Pakistan (1955–71) was facilitated by the arms race. The diplomatic rivalry between China and India was defined and managed by the 1962 war and the consequent China–India arms race. Enmities were expressed by a pattern of arms build-up among these states, and in turn rivalries were regulated by the wars that followed the enmity and arms build-up.

Learning the value and war and war avoidance

The period is noteworthy for the high incidence of war, as well as the beginning of a trend against war. After the 1971 Bangladesh war, crises and interventions did occur between India and her neighbours, but crisis diplomacy rather than war diplomacy became the norm. The Indo–Pakistani arms race continued after 1971 but it did not lead to war. The South Asian wars increased the incentive to rely more on psychological warfare and low-risk intervention, although at times there were high-risk crises (as in 1987 and 1989–90). While the war experiences of the 1960s changed the distribution of power in the region, they also changed the distribution of threat perceptions and the interests of the players in the region. As a result, the behaviour and attitudes of the conflicting parties changed after 1971.

The transformation of Indian policy and attitudes

Up to 1955 the pattern of polarity and alliance (Chapter 3) showed India to be militarily passive and diplomatically reactive in regional affairs except in its relations with the Himalayan kingdoms, and with the USSR with regard to Kashmir and world affairs. The number and strength of India's enemies seemed poised to contain Indian strength in the mid-1950s. However, following the announcement of the US–Pakistan military alliance in 1954 India's strategic policies changed decisively and it started to engage Pakistan in an arms race. It took the war into Pakistani territory in response to Pakistan's decision to wage war in Kashmir in 1965. It militarised the East–West Pakistan social and ideological divide by aiding Bangladeshis in their fight against Pakistani repression; in the process it brokered the division of Pakistan in 1971. It determined to inhibit Pakistan's ambitions to create an Indo–Pakistani military parity that was to India's disadvantage. Thus the peaceful Gandhian approach and Nehru's faith in a policy of 'no war with Pakistan' were abandoned.

The shaping of the US–Soviet and US–China detentes

South Asia was one of the areas where the United States and the USSR learned to avoid direct confrontation, and they learned to transform their Cold War into policies of competitive coexistence and, in part, cooperative coexistence. They eventually came together because of their common desire to contain China.

This detente occurred in a secondary zone of superpower conflict. It was less significant than the superpower detente in arms control and atomic energy that began to take shape in the mid-1950s and continued thereafter. The US–Soviet detente in South Asian affairs was replaced by the US–China detente from the late 1960s to 1971. Still, the fact that it had occurred showed that two competitors could find areas of agreement; that the interests of the capitalists and the communists could be reconciled. The fact that the United States had switched its detente relationship from the USSR to China by the late 1960s showed that the United States was more concerned with the Soviet problem than with that of China. These shifts showed subtleties and flexibility in US policies and the desire among ideological rivals to find areas of agreement.

The context of the first detente was the on-going European, Middle East and Asian cold wars. This detente centred on the common fear of the superpowers that China was likely to extend its influence to the Middle East via Pakistan, that China could encourage a revolutionary situation to develop in East Pakistan, where the leftists had a pro-Chinese orientation, and that Indian security and its peaceful democratic approach were threatened by Chinese pressures in border areas and by its nuclear programme. In the 1962 border clashes both superpowers rallied to India's side and provided military aid for India's defence. Pakistan's relationship with China caused a rift between President Kennedy and President Ayub Khan in the 1960s (this changed later when President Nixon and his adviser, Henry Kissinger, favoured a US–Pakistan–China alignment in order to exert pressure on the USSR in the early 1970s.) Detente also existed with respect to nuclear affairs: both superpowers put pressure on India to join the Nuclear Non-Proliferation Treaty (NPT), which was adopted in 1968, and both sought India's non-nuclearisation. The US–USSR detente had three effects. First, it showed that superpower accommodation could occur in a secondary zone and that the Cold War was not universal, inevitable or irreversible. Second, this detente meant a commitment to India's economic and political development and the use of India as a point of contact and exchange between the two Cold War superpowers. Finally, the detente indicated limits to the superpowers' support for India: India was not allowed to break up West Pakistan or to go nuclear. (The US–China detente will be discussed later.)

Pakistan's failure to balkanize or balance India and liberate Kashmir

During this period Pakistan failed in all its aims with regard to India: it failed to gain Kashmir by force, to achieve military parity, and to balkanise India. The 1965 war was orchestrated by Bhutto and the Pakistan army to liberate Kashmir by force. It reflected an awareness that Pakistan's military and psychological advantages would probably be lost if it failed to intervene in Kashmir. However India's decision to attack Pakistan itself, rather than to limit military action to the Kashmir theatre, led to the failure of the Pakistani military campaign and isolated the hawks inside Pakistan. The fear of Indian retribution opened the door to introspection in Pakistan. It started an internal debate about Pakistan's war aims; about the military effectiveness of the Pakistani army; about the readiness of Kashmiris to rise in revolt against India; about India's political will to retain Kashmir; about the limited support among Pakistanis for the government's Kashmir policy and the war option; about East Pakistan's isolation and vulnerability to Indian attack; and about the reliability of Pakistan's allies in a crisis. In sum, the 1965 war cracked the traditional faith in the war option in Pakistan; it also put into doubt the Pakistan leadership's premise that it had internal support for a policy of hostility towards India as well as for using force to liberate Kashmir. It polarised Pakistani politics and society and strategic thinking within the government.

India learnt many lessons from the 1965 war. It determined to avoid a situation in the future where the great powers were in a position to dictate the terms of ceasefire between India and Pakistan, as occurred in Tashkent. 'No more Tashkents' became the new slogan. It determined to win any war in two or three weeks, that is, before military spares ran out and before the great powers could enforce a ceasefire through the United Nations Security Council. It determined to teach Pakistan a military lesson should it be tempted to use force to settle the Kashmir issue, and it resolved to acquire a military advantage against its irredentist neighbour as a long-term insurance for India.

These lessons were applied to the 1971 war even though it differed in purpose, location and effect. The 1965 war was initiated by Pakistan in Kashmir with the aim of liberating Kashmir by force. In 1971 the initiative lay with the Bangladeshis and the Indians, and the military activity centred on East Pakistan. In 1965 the military and diplomatic encounter was inconclusive. In 1971 it was deadly and conclusive in four ways. First, it was a military fight between India and Pakistan that destroyed Pakistan's unity and the War occurred in East Pakistan, not Kashmir. Second, it was a social and a military conflict between East and West Pakistan. Third, it was a fight between two ideologies and interests, between the civil–military–economic oligarchy in West Pakistan and the mass-based advocates of democracy, pluralism and provincial autonomy in East Pakistani affairs. Finally, it was a fight between two major alliance systems – US–China–Pakistan versus USSR–India. In 1971 Pakistan lost all four battles. Furthermore, the oligarchy was humbled in the eyes of the Pakistani population as well as the world community. This reinforced the mood of introspection that had emerged in Pakistani affairs after the 1965 war and Pakistan's political and military orientation became inward, not openly expansionist. After 1971, Pakistani anti-status-quo activities in Kashmir were quelled by its military weakness and by fear of Indian punishment; and following the loss of East Pakistan its repressive tendencies lost an outlet.

However the Indo–Pakistani wars of 1965 and 1971 did not eliminate Kashmir from Pakistan's agenda: thoughts of irredentism remained in Pakistan after 1971, but militarily it was subdued and active in only a clandestine way. Kashmir remained Pakistan's unfinished business of partition, a legacy of the past. It reappeared on the policy agenda in the latter half of the 1980s. By then Pakistan had learnt to manage its internal political situation following the consolidation of power by President and martial law administrator Zia-ul-Haq. Pakistan had regained its military strength and confidence on the basis of the arms aid it received for its defence as a frontline state against Soviet-controlled Afghanistan. Because of this Pakistan was able to change its military and diplomatic strategy in the mid-1980s however the memory of the 1965 and 1971 wars remained fresh and Pakistan did not seek general war with India. Instead it sought a diplomatic peace offensive, combined with a policy of increasing its interventionist pressure in Punjabi and Kashmiri affairs, and a policy of nuclearisation to equalise the unequal distribution of Indo–Pakistani military power.

China's failure to contain India or stimulate an Indian revolution

China and India moved quickly towards a peaceful diplomatic relationship during 1949–54, but beneath the surface there existed a layer of mutual suspicion and rivalry in their respective approaches to South Asian, Asian and world affairs. Nehru projected China and India as the pillars of Asian security; he felt that the smaller countries did not count and were likely to fall into the sphere of influence of other big powers.[4] Nehru also stressed Asia's importance in the modern international system.[5] China, on the other hand, welcomed Nehru's thoughts of Asianism and the place of China in it, but at the same time the Chinese leaders had a different set of preoccupations: to escape the US containment net; to make China into an international presence; to safeguard Chinese territorial security and strategic interests in its border provinces; to extend China's influence in its neighbourhood; to manage its rivalry with Moscow; and generally to advance the Maoist view of revolutionary reform of the global power structure through the projection of anti-status-quo positions in world and regional affairs.

All this meant that while Nehru's India and Maoist China converged on the ideology of peaceful coexistence, the mental outlooks of the leaders and the two states' interests diverged. For China, peaceful coexistence was a tactic; for Nehru it was a belief – in retrospect, a mistaken one – that peaceful coexistence between two rival powers was possible. China saw the Himalayan kingdoms as a part of the Chinese sphere of influence,[6] Nehru saw them as a part of the Indian sphere. Thus, shortly after China's forceful takeover of Tibet, a Himalayan battleground emerged that engaged the two powers even as both were smiling at each other and proclaiming eternal friendship. Chinese security requirements in Tibet and Sinkiang put China on a collision course with India on the McMahon Line, and the controversy led to a limited war in 1962. In this case the security imperative had precedence over friendly diplomatic relations with India. Conflicting interests had also led China to incline towards Pakistan in the mid-1950s, to embrace Pakistan's position on the Kashmir controversy, and to reach a boundary settlement that led to the transfer of Kashmiri territory from Pakistan to China despite Indian objections. These activities reveal convergence of interests between China and Pakistan and a divergence of interests between China and India in the 1950s; patterns that were taking shape in parallel with the public friendship between China and India.

The pattern of Chinese strategic behaviour during the period under review shows that Chinese behaviour was driven by *realpolitik* and not primarily by ideological concerns. In hindsight its activities against India and in Pakistan's favour reveal ambivalence and a concern for Chinese interests in the region; they were rational in relation to Chinese goals. When the 1962 war brought in the United States and the USSR on India's side, China wisely ordered a unilateral ceasefire. When the 1965 war broke out between India and Pakistan, China threatened to open a second front in Sikkim, but actually it did nothing to support Pakistan militarily during the crisis; caution and ambivalence characterised Chinese crisis behaviour. China's arms supply to Pakistan started in 1966, after relations between India and China had become hostile. This was meant to strengthen Pakistan's military pressure against India and reduce India's military capability against China. However, although this policy raised the costs of Indian defence, India was nonetheless able to mount a defence against both Pakistan and China. In the 1971 war China gave some diplomatic support to Pakistan but China's concern, like that of President Nixon and Henry Kissinger, was to secure the territorial integrity of West Pakistan. Had China been faithful to its ideological convictions it would have sided with the liberation forces in Bangladesh; but it did not. Indeed in the late 1960s China advised pro-Chinese leftists in East Pakistan to cooperate with the military regime in Pakistan.[7] In the 1971 war China did not support the cause of Bangladeshi revolution, nor did it threaten India militarily. China's behaviour in the 1965 and 1971 crises was a case of diplomatic posturing and military non-involvement.

As a result of its outwardly fierce but inwardly cautious and shifting pattern of strategic behaviour, China failed in all its basic aims towards India other than to acquire some territory by force in the Himalayas; the latter was China's only tangible and significant gain. But this gain was offset by the loss of sympathy of the Indian government and the Indian people for Chinese interests and policies. China also failed to build West Pakistan into a meaningful line of pressure against India, and it failed to excite rebellion in Indian border provinces. What it did was sufficient to arouse Indian suspicions and force India to adopt countermeasures, but its pressures were not enough to destabilise India. Maoism failed in India, and the pro-Chinese communists were discredited in Indian party politics as a result of the 1962 war.

China's criticism of Indian hegemony fanned diplomatic rifts between India and her neighbours but did not materially change the power structure of the region. There is no doubt that China harmed India's international influence in the Afro–Asian world and among its smaller neighbours, but here again the balance sheet was mixed. It showed to India the transient value of influence based on Nehruism rather than on economic and military strength, and it enabled India to take corrective measures. Chinese pressure created an inducement and a cover to accelerate Indian military and political development in the border areas. This period is important for the study of China–South Asian relations because it revealed the full pattern of China's orientation in subcontinental affairs as well as the limits of Chinese power in the region.

The failure of the US aim to contain India

The literature usually stresses the United States' affinity with democratic India. However, to understand South Asian international relations it is necessary to appreciate that the United States has acted to contain Indian diplomatic and military power. This is a fixed element in US foreign affairs that came into being during the Cold War and it continues into the post-Cold-War period. So even though South Asia is marginal in US foreign affairs, the Indo–US relationship has been a difficult one because of differences in strategic outlook and interests. The depth of official US opposition to Indian power and ambition is revealed by a declassified US government document that portrays Nehru's India as a successor to Japanese imperialism in Asia.[8] Since the late 1940s US containment of India has taken many forms.

1. From 1948 onwards, supporting Pakistan's position on Kashmir.
2. By 1949, mobilising international opinion against Indian diplomatic activities.
3. After 1954, seeking Indo–Pakistani military parity, which would cancel Indian power and keep India preoccupied with Pakistan. This was done by continually rearming Pakistan so as to balance Indian arms.
4. From the 1960s to the present, checking India's nuclear development by exerting international and unilateral pressure.
5. Checking Indian military activities that threaten Pakistan, as in the 1965 and 1971 wars.

US policies towards India have therefore been multifaceted and they were in full play in the period under review. The US alliance with Pakistan, its arms supply policy to India and Pakistan, its crisis behaviour in the 1965 and 1971 wars, and its nuclear non-proliferation policy in relation to India in the 1960s individually and collectively point to systematic opposition to India's quest for autonomous diplomatic and military power.

But even though its strategic concept was pursued with relentless energy, the US failed to achieve its basic aim. It may have raised the diplomatic and financial costs of developing Indian autonomy, but it failed to modify the pattern of Indian strategic behaviour and strategic thought; on the contrary it reinforced it. Indeed it may be said that US opposition to India helped India to focus more clearly on the issues and to take suitable countermeasures. The contrast between US and Indian strategic approaches became clear during this period. The United States wanted Indo–Pakistani parity; India sought and acquired military imbalance as the basis of Indo–Pakistani relations. The United States wanted Indian denuclearisation and adherence to the NPT; India sought and acquired a nuclear weapons option. The United States wanted India to make concessions to Pakistan on Kashmir; India refused. In sum, the United States was able to arm Pakistan but could not enable an arms balance with India. Even the best and brightest of the US strategists, Richard Nixon and Henry Kissinger, failed to check India in a war that engaged all the great powers in subcontinental power politics and led to the break-up of Pakistan and the creation of a new state by violent means.

VARIABLES IN SOUTH ASIAN WARS, 1960s TO 1971

The above themes have underlined the trends in South Asian international relations during the period in question. Now we assess the key variables in each war, and their importance. The discussion is divided into two subperiods: 1954–65 and 1966–71. Each war (1962, 1965 and 1971) had a defining quality. Each encounter shaped regional power relationships; and the winners and losers were determined by the results of war. South Asian wars are a rich source of information about the threat perceptions, interests and power of the key players, whereas peacetime alignments do not reveal the critical differences in their strategic behaviour.

The following are the key variables in the 1954–65 subperiod that led to three wars (between India and China in the Himalayas in 1962, India and Pakistan in the Rann of Kutch in 1965, and India and Pakistan in Kashmir and across the international border in 1965).

Variables in the India–China war, 1962[9]

1. China feared being ignored and contained by the US–Soviet detente in South Asia.
2. The United States and the Soviet Union were more willing to invest in India's internal development than in that of China, and to invest in India's policy of bilateral alignment with the United States and the USSR.
3. China did not mind hurting India because of its advocacy of US–Soviet detente.
4. The Chinese leaders were irritated by Nehru's egoism and arrogance towards China and India's challenge to China's military and diplomatic positions in the Himalayan kingdoms.
5. Indian hospitality to the Dalai Lama threatened China's hold over Tibet.
6. Chinese strategic interests in Sinkiang required access through Aksai Chin.
7. India's military policy towards China, the push of its police and military personnel into contended border areas, India's friendship with the USSR and increasing Sino–Soviet differences in the latter half of the 1950s were also aggravating factors.

All these developments led China to launch a full-scale war across the Himalayan border. The inevitable consequence was that India suffered a major military and diplomatic defeat.

Variables in the Rann of Kutch war, 1965[10]

1. Pakistanis hated Indians.
2. There were territorial differences in the Rann of Kutch.
3. Pakistan wished to probe India's determination to resist border incursions in Kutch as a prelude to a military campaign in Kashmir.
4. Pakistan believed that India was internally weak and ready for a crushing blow.

These considerations led Pakistan to initiate the Kutch military action. India's response was slow and it confirmed Pakistan's view of Indian weakness.

Variables in the India–Pakistan Kashmir War, 1965[11]

1. The Pakistani elite, especially Z. A. Bhutto, favoured the use of force to settle the Kashmir dispute; the timing was right because

Nehru's death was followed by a new, untested and weak leadershkip.
2. Hatred of Hindus was in full play, with a widespread belief among Pakistanis that Indians were intransigent and cowardly.
3. Pakistan's international alliances created an expectation of support from the United States, China and modern Muslim countries in a war with India.
4. There was confidence in Pakistan's military prowess and power gained through modern military aid.
5. There was a fear that India was likely to change the military balance against Pakistan as a result of the arms build-up, and the opportunity to strike was limited.
6. There was an expectation that the oppressed Kashmiris were ready to revolt against Indian rule and that Pakistani intervention was needed to spark off the revolt.
7. Pakistan's failure to gain Indian concessions on Kashmir in the Bhutto–Swaran Singh meeting (1963–64) was seen as a reason to rely on force rather than diplomacy to settle the Kashmir issue.

These calculations led Pakistan to start the 1965 war in Kashmir. India's calculations differed:

1. India's political will to thwart Pakistan's aggression had to be demonstrated.
2. India was a status quo power and it needed to show its determination to maintain the Indian Union, by force if necessary.
3. There was confidence in the new Indian military machine.

These calculations led India to attack Pakistan across the international border. The result was a military stalemate followed by ceasefire and Soviet mediation at Tashkent.

Variables in the Bangladesh war, 1971[12]

1. The hatred between West and East Pakistan led to the Bangladesh revolt against Pakistani authority and declaration of independence in April 1971.
2. India was determined to encourage Bangladeshi autonomy in Pakistani affairs.
3. India believed that without its military aid East Pakistan could become a Vietnam in India's backyard and drain India's economic and social resources.
4. Several major international alignments were engaged in this war:

The Sino–US rapprochement supported Pakistan against India and the USSR; Chinese pressure on India not to fight was relentless; the USSR and India had an interest in containing China's influence in the region. These alignments created risks as well as opportunities for India.
5. India was determined to assert its status as a major force in the region and to be the architect of the settlement, that is, no repeat of Tashkent to give the USSR prestige as a mediator. India's enhanced military strength gave it the opportunity to develop a winning strategy.

A combination of these variables led India to intervene militarily in this war. Both India and Bangladesh were successful. The US–China–Pakistan coalition was defeated and the war revealed the inability of this coalition to develop a winning strategy.

How did these wars affect strategic relationships in the five-power South Asian diplomatic–military game? Our contention is that periods of peace in South Asia were nonetheless periods of instability. In the 1955–71 period India was the largest South Asian state but the distribution in terms of our fivefold scale did not favour India. It was not defenceless but the winning coalition seemed to consist of the United States, Pakistan and China, not India and the USSR. The results were simmering social or ideological conflict, diplomatic rivalries, military crises, arms races and, eventually, war.

So the first part of our theory is that the asymmetry that favoured the anti-status-quo forces (China against India, US–Pakistan against India) led to instability and war. The second is that each war revealed ambivalence in the policy behaviour of each player. This highlights the constraints under which the players, including the superpowers, laboured. As each war progressed, the policy concerns of the players showed the true pattern of behaviour, choices and interests of each player. Each South Asian war offered good insights into the motives and capabilities of each player; it tested their declarations and public positions. This knowledge enabled the protagonists to learn lessons about their friends and enemies, and about their choices and limitations in the future. The third is that the prospect of general war passed after 1971 because Indian and Soviet diplomatic and military behaviour created an asymmetry of power in favour of the status quo forces. Hence the existence of a war option by a status quo power (India) had a stabilising effect.

The following discussion tests our theory. The data outlines the peacetime asymmetries, wartime ambivalences and the results of deadly encounters. The process of change is sequential and linear in the South Asian case.

Before 1971 the distribution of power favoured the anti-status quo, irredentist coalitions. After 1971 there was a shift in favour of the status quo coalition and a sharp reduction in the authority of the irredentist coalition. After 1971, competition continued in strategic relations among the key players in South Asia. Crises and pressures continued to emerge in their relations with each other, but despite these, their relations evolved towards increased stability and security.

India–China war, 1962

Threat perceptions
Before the outbreak of the war of 1962, peacetime threat perceptions had a skewed distribution among the players. For India, China was not expansionist or aggressive. Furthermore the Indian government felt that it was protected by the global balance of power. It also felt that the border dispute could be managed by diplomatic means, but that India needed to strengthen its border defences and its security position in the Himalayan areas.

United States' threat perception differed from India's. China was both expansionist and aggressive and the two Asian countries were rivals. For the *USSR*, China was an adventurist in world affairs, ambitious in Asian affairs and antagonistic to Soviet interests and to activities that sought to reduce US–Soviet tensions. These fundamental differences led to the Sino–Soviet dispute, beginning in the mid-1950s. For *Pakistan*, India was aggressive and China was peaceful and friendly. For *China*, India was aggressive and a threat to good neighbourly relations with the other South Asian countries and with China.

These concerns produced three different strategies. The first sought to contain Indian power and influence and to create an Indo–Pakistani diplomatic and military balance in the subcontinent. Pakistan, the United States and China were the main participants in this strategy. The second sought to contain Chinese power and influence in South Asia, South-East Asia and the Middle East. The United States, the USSR and India participated in this strategy. The third sought to create an Indocentric policy that would subordinate the state system in South Asia. This was an Indian strategy that had limited support from the USSR and limited consent from the Himalayan kingdoms in the form of treaty relations.

These diverse attitudes indicated a lack of common theory or philosophy that could be translated into a strategic concept. Nevertheless these diversities were actively pursued by the players. Hence they created a disequilibrium in the diplomatic and military affairs of the region. The first set challenged India's right and ambition to function as a regional power and to take its place in the world order. It also sought to neutralise Indian power and prestige by keeping India engaged in a relationship of conflict with Pakistan.

The second set challenged China's ambition to function as a great power and to gain international influence in Asia and, in competition with the United States and the USSR, in the Middle East and Eastern Europe. The third challenged the small states' sensitivity about regime security, state sovereignty and the danger of Indian hegemony and intervention in their affairs. These were the primary factors in play in the region when the 1962 war broke out. They required strategies to contain Indian and Chinese power by the great powers outside the region. However they did not require a check on the anti-status-quo stance of Pakistan, China and the United States in subcontinental affairs.

Peacetime alliance relationships before 1962
Before the 1962 war the pattern of enmity and alliances in South Asia was also skewed in a number of ways, as follows:

1. The United States and Pakistan openly became military and diplomatic allies from 1954 onward.
2. China and Pakistan became secret diplomatic allies from 1955 onward. Later they developed a military relationship as well.
3. India and the USSR became diplomatic allies from 1949/52 onward. Later they developed a military relationship as well.
4. India and the Himalayan kingdoms became diplomatic and military allies; these relations had a treaty basis and this indicated long-term friendship.
5. The United States and China displayed open enmity until 1972.
6. The USSR and China were openly friendly at the time. The Sino–Soviet Friendship Treaty governed their public relationship. But with the beginning of differences in the mid-1950s we can infer the existence of secret enmity between the two.
7. The United States and the USSR were enemies in that they were the main Cold Warriors. But in South Asia the two functioned as secret friends because of their parallel interest in containing Chinese influence in the region, extending to the Middle East via South Asia.

This pattern of alliance and enmity was complex and skewed to advance the interests of one South Asian state (Pakistan) and two external powers (the United States and China). The first and the second alignment sought to contain and neutralise Indian power and influence within South Asia. Even though there was no formal convergence in the foreign policies of Pakistan, China and the United States (as the two latter states were openly hostile to each other), the three held a common motive, and each had the capacity, in different ways, to exert pressure on and contain India. The third alignment, however, helped India's diplomatic position on the Kashmir issue at the United Nations, and furthermore it represented a Soviet investment in India's political and economic well-being. It gave India diplomatic strength in its difficult strategic and diplomatic relationships with the United States and China. The fourth alignment showed that South Asia was not simply an Indo–Pakistani fight. Rather it revealed the existence of a system of cooperative and subordinate relationships between India and the Himalayan kingdoms. The fifth and sixth alignments reinforced the seventh. It enabled the formation of the US–Soviet detente in South Asia; the subcontinent became an area of superpower cooperation during the Cold War. This detente was stimulated by their joint concern to contain a revolutionary China that challenged the international authority of the superpowers, interfered with their bilateral relations through its opposition to US–Soviet detente, and sought to revolutionise or pressure India in the border areas. This particular detente had a pro-India and an anti-China motive; it was behind the quick support that India received from the superpowers when the 1962 war broke out.

Peacetime elite and national interests before the 1962 war
These, too, showed great asymmetry. For *Pakistan*, the decision-making process in foreign and military affairs was dominated by a civil–military oligarchy. Its interest was to liberate Kashmir by force or to acquire Kashmir for Pakistan through pressure exerted by the United States and its associates at the United Nations and by other diplomatic means. Here, territorial irredentism was the driving element. Another key interest was to cut India power and prestige to size either by fanning Indian balkanisation or by seeking an Indo–Pakistani military and diplomatic balance. For *India*, the decision-making process was dominated by Nehru and a small coterie of advisers in foreign and military affairs. Their interests were multiple: to find a peaceful solution to the Kashmir problem either by integrating it into the Indian Union by consent of the Kashmiris or by Indo–Pakistani agreement; to strengthen border

security; to advance Nehru's and India's international diplomatic position; to show that Indian democracy worked in border areas also; to participate in the US–Soviet–Chinese diplomatic game as a major player despite its internal economic and military weakness; and to seek security via internal development and not primarily by military means.

For *China*, the decision-making process was dominated by Mao, Chou En-lai, the party and the security apparatus of a centrally controlled China. China's aims were multifaceted: to secure the McMahon Line in the Himalayas and to guard Chinese security interests and prestige in the area vis-à-vis India and the USSR by diplomatic and military measures; to use Nehru and later discard him to enable China to break out of the diplomatic isolation imposed by the United States and the Western world; to escape from such isolation by using Pakistan as an outlet, a window of opportunity and a base to extend Chinese influence into South Asian and Middle Eastern affairs; to strengthen Pakistan militarily and help it to develop into a continuous line of pressure against India, to contain Indian influence in South Asia, and to divert Indian military pressure away from the Himalayas and towards Pakistan.

For the *United States*, the decision-making process was complex. It involved a number of Republican and Democratic administrations and a number of competing domestic bureaucratic and Congressional players and interests. Still, two main strands of national interest may be discerned in the history of US–India relations. One primary interest was to contain the development of Indian strategic power and foster the development of an Indo–Pakistani balance. The second was to help Indian economic development and foster Indian democracy as an alternative to China in Asian affairs.

For the *USSR*, the decision-making process after 1949 centred on the personality of Stalin and his successors. It was at the highest level, in contrast with US diplomacy towards India where mid-level forces shaped the policy process. Even before the Sino–Soviet dispute emerged in the mid-1950s, the Soviet aims were to support the Indian case on Kashmir in the UN with Soviet vetoes, and to keep India on the Soviet side in international security and diplomatic affairs. Another aim was to help strengthen the infrastructure of heavy industry in Indian economic development. After the mid-1950s these aims were reinforced by the Soviet need to develop India as a diplomatic counterforce to China; that is, Sino–Soviet differences reinforced Soviet–Indian relations in a positive way.

Finally, the Himalayan kingdoms (Nepal, Bhutan, Sikkim) and Sri Lanka were preoccupied with their own bilateral relations with India rather than with global power politics. Their preoccupations were with the relationship between domestic politics, economic development and foreign affairs, and bilateral issues and problems with India.

These elite structures and interests in South Asian international relations showed a diversity, without a common theory or philosophy of international relations, among the players. In each case a close correspondence is indicated between closed elite and decision-making structures as well as deeply held foreign policy and military attitudes and policies. While the general approach of each country had a public expression, the decision-making process was secretive and immune from public scrutiny. This was true in the case of the democratic United States and India, communist USSR and China, and Islamic–oligarchic Pakistan. Furthermore the decision-making processes in peacetime had many marks of ritualistic confrontation in the external relations among the players.

Peacetime strategic concepts

In the South Asian world before 1962, each player had a clear strategic concept that defined its diplomatic and military behaviour. For the United States, an Indo–Pakistani diplomatic and military balance was necessary for regional security. This was also Pakistan's and China's strategic concept, but with one difference. The United States and Pakistan articulated it; China did not and there was ambiguity in the Chinese posture. India believed that foreign interference in subcontinental affairs was not tolerable if it seemed to harm Indian interests. This implied that a natural Indo–Pakistani imbalance should be allowed to emerge that represented the interplay of regional forces rather than of international ones. Another Indian concept was that ways must be found to secure Indo–Pakistani peace or normalisation by political and diplomatic measures. Undoubtedly this approach showed a belief in the stability of a cooperative and subordinate system of neighbouring states. The Himalayan kingdoms accepted the Indian concept; Pakistan did not and actively lobbied against 'Indian hegemony'. Sri Lanka appeared to be ambivalent about the Indian concept, neither accepting nor rejecting it. The USSR ostensibly supported India's primary position in the subcontinent, but Moscow's diplomatic behaviour during the South Asian wars (see below) showed a preference for Indo–Pakistani polarity rather than Indian predominance in the region. This suggests that Moscow's policy, as distinct from its posture, was ambivalent with regard to the Indian concept of an Indocentric state system in the area, including Pakistan.

These concepts showed a polarised distribution of policy attitudes. The US–Pakistan axis and China favoured an Indo–Pakistani struggle for balanced (equal or semi-equal) power rather than Indian dominance. By weighing in on Pakistan's side, the United States (openly) and China (secretly) saw themselves in the role of external balancers. This coalition favoured the anti-status-quo leanings in Pakistan's decision-making structure. The second set of attitudes was expressed by India. It sought cooperative coexistence among South Asian states under Indian leadership. So the Soviet position may be considered a third approach because of its partial convergence and partial divergence with India's approach. The fourth and final set was expressed by Sri Lanka. It was uncomfortable with the danger of Indian hegemony, but it was willing to work within the framework of the Indian quest for a cooperative and subordinate state system. In a way Sri Lanka's position differed from that of the Himalayan kingdoms in relation to India. Had Sri Lanka been able to find external partners it may have preferred to align itself with, say South-East Asian countries such as Singapore, but the absence of choice led to its quest for a relationship of uneasy coexistence with India. For the Himalayan kingdoms, however, their natural destiny lay with Indian material and diplomatic help, and with Indian goodwill and cooperation rather than security ties with extra-regional partners.

Peacetime distribution of military power before 1962
The distribution of military power was asymmetrical in the two military pairings that counted in the subcontinent – India and Pakistan, and China and India. According to informed estimates, Pakistan had a military edge over India from 1955–60 following the inflow of US arms into Pakistan.[13] China too had a clear military superiority over India, as the 1962 military encounter showed. During this period an overt India–China, India–Pakistan arms race did not occur, but there were limited military preparations on both sides in each pair and these were driven by their respective threat perceptions. For Pakistan, India was an enemy in every way – diplomatic, military and religious. China's military preparations were not driven by a concern with India as a threat, but rather because the United States, Taiwan and later the USSR were enemies. India foresaw problems with border defence in relation to China and it took limited measures to build a military infrastructure, but Nehru did not see China as a militarily expansionist state. Nor did Nehru see the Pakistan front as a critical issue that required Indian militarisation; Kashmir was seen as requiring local defence rather than

war between the two countries. But if there was no active arms race between India and Pakistan, in hindsight the evidence indicates the rise of an undeclared arms competition between India and Pakistan following the introduction of US weapons into Pakistan. This process started in 1955. In the period under review (1947–62), Pakistan's military edge remained, but by the early 1960s the asymmetry started to favour India in airpower, while Pakistan retained the edge in tanks. This period is therefore important as it marked the beginning of a controlled (not volatile) arms race in Indo–Pakistani affairs.

In terms of our five key indicators of power relations, these characteristics provided the context of South Asian affairs when China and India went to war in 1962.

Indo–Pakistani wars

Three major wars shaped the pattern of Indo–Pakistani bilateral relations as well as the structure of power relations in the subcontinent. The first war occurred in 1948, the second in 1965 and the third in 1971.

The 1948 war took the form of a tribal invasion, which was instigated by M. A. Jinnah, the founder of Pakistan. It was driven by a belief that Kashmir belonged to Pakistan because of the Muslim majority in Kashmir. This war led to the de facto partitioning of Kashmir into a zone held by Pakistan and another by India. It occurred before the Indian government settled down to the business of organising Indian authority in the border provinces. In 1947–8 the subcontinent was in a near chaotic condition, and the resettlement of millions of refugees in India and Pakistan was the immediate concern. India lacked effective governmental machinery in Kashmir as the Maharaja was still in charge and he had not decided whether to join India or Pakistan or to stay independent. Jinnah, on the other hand, had a clear strategic line on Kashmir – to gain Kashmir either by force or by Indian political concession and Pakistani pressure. In 1948 Nehru's strategic thinking was mixed and had contradictory elements. He sought Pakistani friendship without Indian concession. He sought Kashmiri consent and participation in the Indian political union, but also recognised its special status and the existence of a dispute between India and Pakistan. Finally, he sought to enhance his international reputation as a democrat and peacemaker by his willingness to have a plebiscite in Kashmir, and yet he sought to protect Indian interests. The 1948 Kashmir war did not occur within the framework of a well-defined system of states with accepted principles and practices, and there was no established structure by which to conduct interstate relations. The war occurred just as that process was getting started following the departure of the British.

The 1965 war dealt with the Kashmir dispute and it occurred in Kashmir itself, but the context and the process of this war differed from the one in 1948. It occurred in the context of an arms race between India and Pakistan that took shape following the introduction of US weapons into the subcontinent after 1954. Pakistani civil and military elites initiated this war, seeing an opportunity to seize Kashmir by force and fearing the loss of Pakistani military superiority as a result of Indian rearmament in the late 1950s. Activism and intervention marked Pakistani elite behaviour in Kashmiri affairs. In this war, India's political leadership changed its style and attitude. After Nehru's death in 1964, Prime Minister Shastri took a quite different line than Nehru's ambivalent approach to Kashmiri affairs. Nehru avoided war with Pakistan over Kashmir. His successor took the war to Pakistan by ordering the Indian army to cross the international border to relieve Pakistani military pressure in Kashmir. For Pakistan, Kashmir was disputed territory, hence it was fair game for military intervention and political subversion. For Pakistan, Indian military action across the international border was aggression. For India, Pakistani subversive action in Kashmir constituted aggression and this required an appropriate response. In war, the Indo–Pakistani border meant nothing to India in its military and diplomatic tactics. In the eyes of Pakistanis, Hindus were cowardly and weak. For Indians, this image had to be changed by military action. In 1965 there was a stalemate on the military battlefield that was resolved by diplomatic intervention by the UN Security Council and Soviet mediation at Tashkent in 1966. Territorial status quo was restored with the ending of the war, which had come to a grinding halt when military spares ran out on both sides.

The war, however, was a psychological turning point. It revealed India's determination to retaliate (something akin to the psychological effect of the 1967 Arab-Israeli war on Arab thinking), if Pakistan acted in a destructive and irresponsible manner. It also showed the Pakistani public that war was not a realistic option against India; and it highlighted to the great powers the dangers of Indo–Pakistani military conflict. For Indian military planners the 1965 war revealed a need to plan for a short war 'the next time' to avoid the problem of limited military spares and of great power diplomatic intervention to stop the fighting. In other words, any future war must be won before foreign suppliers could terminate the war by cutting off spares and before the world community could intervene diplomatically to prevent Indian military and diplomatic victory. On this occasion the great powers prolonged the Indo–Pakistani stalemate: by promoting a negative, continuous engagement between the two sides, Indian power and potential in the region and in the global diplomatic sphere was neutralised.

These lessons shaped India's military strategy in the 1971 war, although the context and nature of the confrontation was radically different. In 1971 the centre of military confrontation was in East Pakistan and it involved Indian, Pakistani and Bangladeshi forces (the Western Indo–Pakistani front was maintained by a holding operation). The 1971 war resulted from a long-standing social and political conflict between West and East Pakistan that came to a head in 1969–71. Following an upheaval in relations between the two sides, Bangladesh revolted against West Pakistan's political and military authority. The Pakistani army retaliated to curb Bangladeshi nationalism. The persecution produced millions of refugees, who moved to India and strained its social and economic fabric. The world community was largely indifferent at the time because the grand strategists in Washington – Nixon and Kissinger – were busy shaping a coalition with the Chinese against the USSR, and Pakistan's dictator, General Yahya Khan, was a go-between in the delicate negotiations with China.

As the Bangladeshi refugees who crossed into India were staying, and because Bangladesh seemed about to become a Vietnam in India's backyard, India acted to help the Bangladeshi guerillas fight the Pakistani Army, although in part the Indian action was self-serving and directed against West Pakistani elites. The result was the break-up of Pakistan and the emergence of Bangladesh, a new state in international relations since 1972.

The Pakistani army's defeat confirmed the fact that, although it was the strongest *political* force in internal Pakistani affairs and it determined the orientation of Pakistan's approach to India and other foreign affairs, it could not fight and win wars, despite its large military budget and international allies.

In each of the wars the distribution of the key indicators of power relations was skewed. We turn now to a discussion of the pattern of distribution in each war.

Peacetime threat perceptions
For Pakistan a general perceptions of threat remained constant between 1947 and 1971. Pakistani elites stressed the danger of Indian hegemony and expansionism, and they saw in Indian behaviour a desire to break

up Pakistan and to undo partition. Hindu India was seen as the main problem. This concern was forcefully articulated by Jinnah as early as May 1947 in a conversation with US embassy officers in Karachi. To quote from a US government document:

> On 1 May Mohammed Ali Jinnah, Leader of the Muslim League, received two American visitors at his Bombay residence. They were Raymond A. Hare, Head of the Division of South Asian Affairs, Department of State, and Thomas E. Weil, Second Secretary of the US Embassy in India. Jinnah asserted that under no circumstances would he accept the concept of an Indian Union since the Muslim League was determined to establish Pakistan. He sought to impress on his visitors that the emergence of an independent, sovereign Pakistan would be in consonance with American interests. Pakistan would be a Muslim country, Muslim countries would stand together against Russian aggression. In that endeavour they would look to the United States for assistance, he added. Jinnah coupled the danger of 'Russian aggression' with another menace that Muslim nations might confront. That was 'Hindu imperialism'. The establishment of Pakistan was essential to prevent the expansion of Hindu imperialism into the Middle East, he emphasised.[14]

Initially the United States was indifferent to Jinnah's special pleading, but from the early 1950s the US government began to accept the Pakistani worldview. As such this particular threat perception became the centrepiece of Pakistan's Indian policy as well as a basis of the United States' India policy. These perceptions were in play in the three Indo-Pakistani wars. They justified, in Pakistani thinking, Pakistani military intervention in Kashmir. Furthermore policy makers realised the need to reduce Pakistani insecurity by increasing the pressure on India (given its alleged intransigence). This was attempted by unilateral Pakistani moves, by securing international pressure against India and by seeking India's balkanisation. These strategies had the same purpose: to fragment India's power and its political will to challenge Pakistan's interests.

An expression of this threat perception was a strategy aimed at making Pakistan militarily strong enough to stop Indian expansionism and at protecting Muslims in the subcontinent. To promote these aims, military risks could be taken to induce or force India to concede Kashmir to Pakistan.

India's perception of threat was not embedded in a bilateral Indo-Pakistani focus in the way that Pakistan's India policies were. Rather it revealed a fear of the consequences for the Indian Union of a theocratic solution of the Kashmir issue, a fear of the implications of the US–Pakistan military alliance for Pakistan–India relations, a fear that the cost of increased militarisation would be detrimental to Indian developmental activities and priorities, and concern about the effect of a militant Pakistan on India's regional and international influence. Specifically, India viewed the US–Pakistan alliance of 1954 as tilting the balance of power in Pakistani politics towards the civil–military oligarchy; it increased Pakistani intransigence and militarisation in relation to India; and it worked against the prospect of Pakistan–India normalisation and accommodation. The USSR shared India's projections of the effects of the US–Pakistan military alliance as it also threatened Soviet military and diplomatic interests in its soft underbelly. China was indifferent to Indo–Pakistani concerns in the late 1940s, but by 1955 it had aligned itself with Pakistan's approach, despite its friendship with India.

In sum, the threat perceptions of the major players in these wars were not uniform. From 1947, Indo–Pakistani relations were intensely polarised and totally incompatible, and there was no common ground or area of agreement between them. The US government was indifferent until the early 1950s, when it lent its support to the Pakistani worldview. Thus US perceptions shifted from initial indifference to a positive convergence with Pakistan. This shift occurred in US government thinking as well as US mainstream academic literature published between the 1950s and 1980s.

For China, the shift was from indifference to positive support of Pakistan's views on India. So by 1955 both the United States and China had adopted a sharply anti-India and pro-Pakistani orientation. India's perceptions were the minority view in the comparative picture, but the USSR supported India. From initial hostility and indifference to India, by 1952 Stalin had veered towards the Indian position on Kashmir and Pakistan. By 1954–55 Stalin's successors were seeing Pakistan and the United States as a threat to Soviet security and diplomatic interests. Thus in a secondary zone of international conflict, interesting combinations of temporary friendships emerged based on the permanent enmity between India and Pakistan. An oligarchic, militaristic state (Pakistan) joined hands with an imperial democracy (the United States) and a communist state (China), while another communist state (the USSR) shared India's threat perceptions. The core of this structure consisted of conflicting Pakistani and Indian views but the external powers reinforced the policy elites in these countries by providing international legitimacy for Indo–Pakistani threat concerns.

Peacetime external alignments
Pakistan fought the 1948 Kashmir war without the benefit of external allies. It fought the 1965 and 1971 wars with the backing of a formal alliance with the United States and a de facto diplomatic alliance with China. Pakistani elites expected these allies to support Pakistani policies against India.[15] The United States provided Pakistan with modern arms after 1954, while from 1966 China provided military equipment that was more suitable for the rugged South Asian military environment. Finally, Pakistan had allies in the Muslim world: Iran, Turkey and Indonesia, in particular, sympathised with Pakistan and provided it with military aid.[16]

India fought the 1948 war alone but thereafter it gained the diplomatic and military support of the USSR. The story of the emergence of the Nehru–Stalin connection has been told by the son of the Indian ambassador to Moscow at the time.[17] By 1952 India had gained Moscow's diplomatic support on the Kashmir issue. This enabled it to ward off Western pressure on India to make concessions to Pakistan. So Western diplomacy at the United Nations became a permanent line of pressure against India, but Soviet vetoes helped India to escape international intervention on the issue of Kashmiri self-determination.

Furthermore, following the 1962 India–China war, Moscow established a military supply relationship with India, as did the United States. A pattern in the distribution of aid reveals two factors in the behaviour of these players. US aid was deployed against China. It included high technology items to enhance Indian air defence and develop India's mountain warfare capability. But at the same time US aid was limited in quantity and it was meant to enhance India's defensive capabilities in relation to just China. In comparison Soviet military aid was plentiful and had generous financial terms, and the equipment had defensive and offensive uses. Soviet equipment in India was deployed against Pakistan and, to a lesser extent, against Chinese targets. The US and Soviet aid to India therefore carried political messages for Pakistan and China.

From the 1950s onwards interest India had three conflict relationships – with Pakistan, with China and with the United States – and a friendship with the USSR in the 1965 and 1971 wars. In the 1971 war the alliance pattern was broadened as a result of the de facto alignment between India and Bangladesh; both, for different reasons, were locked into a temporary friendship against the Pakistani government. In addition, during these war India had friendly treaty relations with the Himalayan kingdoms. These did not directly affect the Indo–Pakistani military encounters but they enabled India to maintain a security zone in the strategic Himalayan areas. This meant a buffer existed in the event of China opening a military front to divert Indian military pressure against Pakistan in the two wars. This did not happen however. All this means there was a lively pattern of alignments (enmities and friendships) as well as continuous interaction between two sets of alignments that revolved around Pakistan and India.

The behaviour of the great powers in the Pakistani and Indian alliance systems reflected a dual track of enmity and temporary friendship. The United States and the USSR were formally and publicly members of the Pakistani and Indian alliance systems respectively, but because of the superpowers' enmity with China at the time they formed a temporary friendship in South Asia to contain China's influence in the region. This convergence of interests was revealed in US support for Soviet mediation to end the 1965 war.

This was the story in the 1950s and 1960s. But by the time of the 1971 war the international context had changed: the United States, under Nixon and Kissinger, had tilted towards China in an attempt to curb Soviet ambitions in different parts of the world. In the changed context Moscow forcefully supported India in the diplomatic and military spheres. Here the Sino–Soviet dispute reinforced Soviet military diplomacy in the 1971 war. On this occasion the United States and the USSR were not temporary allies, as in the 1965 war.

Elite/national interests
Pakistan's war behaviour in 1965 was shaped by its oligarchic power structure. This was dominated by a coalition of army generals and senior members of the civil bureaucracy. Their attitude to India was ethnocentric: Hindus were seen as weak and Muslims were deemed to be superior, and this produced overconfidence about military victory in Kashmir. Although President General Ayub Khan wielded the power, the civilian members of his government – especially his foreign minister, Z. A. Bhutto, and his civilian defence officials – pushed for war with India to resolve the Kashmir issue. The main interest of the ruling elite was to secure Kashmir by force as negotiations had failed to produce concessions from India.

In the 1971 war the internal political context of Pakistani decision making was radically different. In 1965 Pakistan's elite structure had been homogeneous; it was oligarchic and in control of Pakistan's internal affairs. In 1971 an intense power struggle divided Pakistan's oligarchic structure and polarised the decision-making process. The internal power struggle involved Bhutto and his political party, the People's Party of Pakistan. Bhutto had always been a member of the top political elite, but after the 1965 debacle he left the government and began to seek power for himself. Between 1966 and 1971 he conspired with likeminded Pakistani generals to bring down the Ayub government. In order to gain power, Bhutto advocated democracy in Pakistan even though he himself had Bonapartist tendencies.

The internal power struggle at the time revealed tensions between three lines of thinking. The first, led by Bhutto, sought democracy and civilian rule, that is, the ascendency of Bhutto under democratic conditions. The second, led by Pakistani generals such as Yahya Khan, sought continued military rule, also under democratic cover. The third, led by the Bengali leader Sheikh Mujibur Rahman, sought provincial autonomy in East Pakistan and democracy in Pakistani affairs. Because Bhutto and the army wanted to overthrow Ayub Khan, the two formed a temporary coalition against the latter. This led to his resignation in 1969 and the army's acceptance of democracy and national elections in that year. The elections produced a massive victory for Sheikh Mujibur Rahman. This meant that he was now in a position to rule Pakistan, and not simply East Pakistan. Because of their hatred of Bengalis and their fear of losing power, Bhutto and the army formed a temporary alliance to check Rahman and stall the democratic process. In these circumstances, Rahman and his party despaired of gaining power by constitutional means. They presented a demand for maximum autonomy. When this failed they declared independence. Then followed a murderous wave of repression of Bengalis by the Pakistan army.

Thus the 1971 war occurred in the context of intense volatility in Pakistan's elite structures as well as in its politics and society. In 1965 the decision-making structure was small, closed and ethnocentric; it enjoyed internal public support to secure Kashmir's accession to Pakistan by force through the exercise of the right of self-determination by the Kashmiris. In 1971 the situation was different. In 1965 the Pakistani army failed to gain Kashmir by force. The Kashmiris failed to rise in revolt against India when the opportunity arose, and this disappointed Pakistani advocates of the war option. Pakistan feared serious reprisals when the Indian army attacked Pakistan itself. In these circumstances, Pakistani public opinion became divided. Consequently the 1965 results opened up a debate (1966–71) in Pakistan about the utility and feasibility of Pakistan's war option in Kashmiri affairs. Finally, in 1971 Pakistan's social, political and military thinking had another agenda, that is, what were the goals, methods and timetable to secure democracy in Pakistan? What was to become of provincial autonomy in West and East Pakistan? What would the future of the Punjabis be? (They had dominated Pakistani affairs since the 1950s. What was to become of the different ethnic groups in Pakistan (Sindhis, Baluchis, Pathans, Bengalis, Muhajirs and Punjabis)?

For India, the 1965 war took place in a post-Nehru context. Shastri, Nehru's successor, was small in stature (physically and politically), untested in Indian politics and foreign affairs, and was working in a vacuum created by Nehru's demise. India's political and military orientation was to keep the status quo, but following its defeat in 1962 by China its political culture was nationalistic and inclined towards resisting aggression by forceful measures. Furthermore, after 1962 the Indian military had the capacity to engage Pakistan militarily and it was also keen to undo the damage of the defeat of 1962. Moreover Kashmir was a strategically and symbolically prized territory. The political elites' interest was manifested by Prime Minister Shastri and the Congress. Both had to prove their mettle and show that post-Nehru India was not likely to fall apart. One way of doing this was not to lose the war. The war would therefore have to be taken into the enemy's camp. Moreover there was a need to induce fear and a rethinking of Pakistani perceptions and interests. The Indian national interest was Indiacentric and directed towards defending Kashmir and stabilising relations with Pakistan by coercive diplomacy. Here elite and national interests converged. Both elements were mindful of the need to reassure Indian public opinion following the debacle with China. Both elements were mindful of the presence of Pakistan's international allies and the constraints these created for Indian military and diplomatic actions.

The context of the 1971 war differed from that of 1965. In 1971 Indira Gandhi, the prime minister, saw an opportunity to stride onto the regional and world stage. The Indian decision-making apparatus had a geopolitical focus, having absorbed the lessons of the 1962 and 1965 wars. There was an awareness of the implications for India of the great divide between West and East Pakistan. East Pakistan did not care about the Kashmir dispute; instead it was locked into its fight with West Pakistan. West Pakistan could not defend the East because of the distance between the two. By 1971 West Pakistanis were divided about the utility of wresting Kashmir from India by force. Finally, further demonstration of India's political will and coercive diplomacy could decrease both Pakistani irredentism and the appeal of the war option for the Pakistani army. There was also an urge to move fast to help the Bangladeshis as the global and Asian geopolitical environment was changing rapidly with the impending US tilt towards China in mid-1971, when Henry Kissinger secretly visited China. In the 1965 war India's aim was defensive. In the 1971 war its aim was to alter regional geopolitics by force and to create a new regional order based on Indian diplomatic and military preeminence.

The interests of the great powers, too, changed between the two wars. In 1971 the United States was engaged in grand diplomacy to bring China to its side in Soviet affairs. At the time China was preoccupied with an internal power struggle. It was alert to the need to fashion a new relationship with the United States, but was cautious about US involvement in South Asian diplomacy. The USSR actively supported India's war aims in 1971 – it opposed US and Chinese aims as it was locked into an intense rivalry with both.

In 1965 the United States and the USSR saw the Kashmir war as a local crisis that required regional conflict resolution. At that time the US–Soviet detente was in effect. It tilted their responses towards UN intervention, bilateral ceasefire and Soviet mediation; these were the principles of the detente. In 1971 the triangular US–Soviet–Chinese diplomatic and strategic game gave the regional war in South Asia an international flavour. Without the superpower detente in the background to stimulate regional conflict-resolution activity, the language of the 1971 war changed. The UN, ceasefire and mediation were no longer buzzwords. The new thinking had a radically different tone: the breakup of Pakistan (partition by force); military intervention and the surrender of the Pakistani army to the Indian army; and the outmanoeuvreing of the American grand strategists by the elite of a poor country. 1971 saw a new language of strategic discourse between India and Pakistan and between India and the great powers.

Strategic concepts

During this period the main players in the region demonstrated a variety of concepts in their diplomatic and military behaviour. Pakistan came into existence on the theory of Muslim separateness. In projecting it, Pakistan had enjoyed the support of the British government. After 1947 this theory was developed into a view that the defence of Pakistan was necessary to safeguard the homeland of Muslims in the subcontinent; that Islam was in danger and needed military defence; that the state and the army were the backbone of the new Islamic society in Pakistan; that the cause of Pakistan was just, and hence its use of force against India and Kashmir was just. Finally, defence of Pakistan and defence of Muslim separateness required parity between

India and Pakistan so that Indian power and expansionism could be contained.

Pakistani views had a number of implications in modern studies of war, state and society, religion and politics and regional security studies. The theory of Muslim separateness implied a belief in religion as the basis of organisation of political power in Pakistan and in the organisation of relations between India and Pakistan. If Muslims are separate and in a minority, and if Indians are more numerous and expansionist in the Pakistan view, then conflict is inevitable between India and Pakistan because it is inevitable between Hindus and Muslims. This implies a faith in the cynical view of international relations. Secondly, a combination of 'Islam is in danger' and 'Muslims are a minority' themes justified the use of force because of the just cause; this pointed to the theory of just war. It meant that if the cause was just, the use of force to intervene against Indian interests and Indian sovereignty was just and defensive rather than aggressive. This theory undermined the injunction against aggression in the theory of modern war and international law. Finally, the doctrine of Indian hegemony reflected a faith in the Pakistani concept of parity as the basis of regional security rather than the Indian concept of responsible and defensive (non-expansionist) use of force to achieve regional order.

Pakistani's concepts were opposed by India, whose main strategic aim was territorial defence and border security. This meant defence of the Indian Union and an injunction against territorial expansionism beyond its borders. In addition, India envisaged strategic frontiers or a security zone in the Himalayas south of Tibet. Finally, India rejected the concept of Indo–Pakistani parity as the basis of Indo–Pakistani peace. Parity would cut India's ambition to be taken seriously as a responsible regional and international voice. It was rejected also because it appeared to reward wrong Pakistani theories and hostility vis-à-vis India.

For the period under review, mainstream US academic and policy thinking adopted Pakistan's concepts as the basis of stability and security in the subcontinent. Here Pakistani and US experts were in accord. Between 1955 and 1990 China too fanned Pakistan's ideal by pointing to the danger of Indian hegemony and the importance of seeking a settlement in Kashmir on the basis of self-determination. However it is unclear whether the expressed US and Chinese views rested on their convictions or whether they were opportunistic.

Distribution of military power

The distribution of military power in the subcontinent changed significantly between 1947 and 1971. There are four subperiods to consider: 1947–54 – from partition to the establishment of the US–Pakistan military alliance; 1955–60 – the period of induction of modern US arms into the subcontinent and its impact on India; 1961–65 – the period of India's military build-up, driven by the China and Pakistan threats; and the 1965–71 period, which was the aftermath of the 1965 war and the prelude to the 1971 war. For each period there are four questions to consider. First, was there a connection between arms build-up (military superiority) and war? Second, was there an arms race in either period in the form of continuous/frequent interactions among the major South Asian enemies, *viz.* India–Pakistan and India–China? Third, who was reacting to whom in each subperiod? Finally, what was the pattern, process and motive in the arms build-up of the smaller South Asian states other than Pakistan? We will address these questions for each subperiod.

In the first subperiod there was little by way of Indian military build-up. Military spending was less than 2 per cent of GNP. This was so even though the first Kashmir war had taken place in 1947–48 and Kashmir had been partitioned. In this subperiod the Indian military doctrine emphasised local military defence in Kashmir and marginal military modernisation with a focus on infrastructure development in the Himalayas. In the main, 'security' for India meant a search for stable political relations via diplomatic measures and modest military actions. Compared with India, Pakistan had a firm strategic idea and the military organisation to take Kashmir by force. This was behind Jinnah's orchestration of the tribal invasion in 1947–8. But the size of the Pakistani army was modest.

In the second subperiod there was no significant change in Indian military strength in relation to Pakistan or China. Pakistan showed a slight increase in military spending, but the standard sources of military data – the International Institute for Strategic Studies (IISS) and the Stockholm International Peace Research Institute (SIPRI) – do not provide data about US military aid to Pakistan. During this period Pakistan possessed a four-to-one ratio in its favour over India in tanks – a key indicator of military power in the region. So even though India was bigger, Pakistan was more powerful. There was a slight increase in Sri Lankan military spending during this period.

There was a rapid increase in military expenditure in the third subperiod as a result of the China–India war. Indian military expenditure increased from 1.8 per cent of GNP in 1960 to 3.6 per cent in 1965.

By 1965 Pakistan still had an edge in the crucial area of tanks but India had gained an advantage in the equally crucial area of military aircraft. Even though Pakistan's earlier military advantage was being eroded, when Pakistan went to war with India over Kashmir in 1965 it still had a clear edge over Indian military strength, and its arms were modern compared with India's. But to an extent Pakistan's qualitative advantage was cancelled out by India's quantitative edge in military manpower. During this period Sri Lankan military expenditure actually decreased, but that of Nepal showed a small increase.

In the fourth subperiod there was parallel growth in Indian and Pakistani military expenditure. Both grew on average by 6–7 per cent per year. This period is important because it also marked a serious effort by India to develop its indigenous defence industry. During this period both countries also achieved a modest naval build-up. Sri Lanka and Nepal too achieved a modest arms build-up.

What do all these numbers mean? Is there a relationship between arms acquisitions and war? The simple answer is yes. In each of the following cases, military superiority lay behind the decision to go to war. Pakistan had superior military organisation and overall strength in terms of usable military power (that is the government provided aid to armed tribals and 'on-leave' Pakistani army personnel were available to fight in Kashmir) compared with India's usable resources. This unequal military distribution led to the 1948 war. China had military superiority over India when it went to war. This was also the case with Pakistan in 1965 and India in 1971. So the connection between military superiority and war in self-evident.

This theory, however, breaks down in the post-1971 period. Here India has held military superiority over Pakistan but since 1971 the region has been free of war. It seems that the causal link between military superiority and war is explained by a crucial additional factor, that is, countries decide to fight if they possess military superiority and if, at the same time, the country's decision makers desire to change the status quo. In the 1948 war Pakistan wanted to make territorial gains in Kashmir. In 1962 China wished to bring India to heel in or-der to secure territorial gains and its other strategic objectives in the Himalayan region. In 1965 Pakistan fought an irredentist war in Kashmir. Finally, India had its own designs in the 1971 war: to help the Bangladeshis, to discipline Pakistan, to insulate the region from Chinese and US interventionist pressure, and to give a geopolitical focus to Indian coercive diplomacy.

Generally speaking, arms races are frequent but not an inevitable feature of international life. They are driven by two opposite motives

– to alter the status quo or to maintain it. There is no concrete evidence of a reciprocal interaction in arms acquisitions between India and Pakistan and China and India in the first subperiod. The pattern of reciprocal interaction first emerged in the 1955–60 subperiod and was active and intense during the 1960s, and particularly during the 1966–71 subperiod.

In the first subperiod there was no serious Indian reaction to Pakistani military activities, except to defend Kashmir. This was also the case between India and China. In the second subperiod India began to react to the massive (by subcontinental standards) influx of modern US arms into the area and its likely effect on internal and external relations in the region. In the second subperiod there was also a modest Indian reaction to China. In the third and fourth subperiods we see serious bilateral reactions in Indo–Pakistani and Sino–Indian attitudes and policies. In these subperiods the interactions were truly reciprocal and continuous.

Finally, the smaller South Asian states shared Pakistan's fear of Indian hegemony but their response in the military and diplomatic spheres differed from Pakistan's. The latter sought parity with India, war to regain Kashmir and sort out the Bangladeshis, an arms race to gain power, and alliance building with the United States, China and friendly Muslim states to put pressure on India and increase Pakistan's advantage. The other South Asian states chose not to adopt any of Pakistan's strategies or tactics. There were a number of reasons for this: there was no religious divide between these countries and India; there was no territorial dispute between these countries and India; often there were personal and ideological affinities among the leaders of the smaller South Asian states and Indian leaders; and finally there was a shared faith in the prospect of negotiating away differences by reaching a compromise between India – and its smaller neighbours. These reasons explain why these countries chose not to seek military solutions to problems between them and India; and why they insisted on political solutions to bilateral and regional issues that were based on the principles of compromise and compensation.

5 The Foreign Policies of India's Immediate Neighbours[1]

This chapter makes three points. First, Pakistan belongs to a separate category from the other South Asian states because it has historically been, and remains tied to the United States as a result of the military alliance between the two countries; it has been part, albeit not on a par with US allies in Europe and North Asia, of the US strategic framework during and since the Cold War. Pakistan is also tied up in a hostile relationship with India as a result of a long-standing territorial and ideological dispute over Kashmir, compounded by India's involvement in the freeing of Bangladesh from West Pakistani domination. The latter action enhanced Pakistan's sense of grievance about Indian policies.

The nuclear build-up in Pakistan, in response to its security and diplomatic needs in relation to India and the United States, distinguishes Pakistan from India's other immediate neighbours. Pakistan has also distinguished itself, in contrast with India's other immediate neighbours, by actively soliciting and gaining Chinese military, nuclear and diplomatic support. This increased the costs of India's defence programme and created an element of uncertainty and pressure on India by China that continues today, albeit in a lesser way.

These elements in Pakistani policies have created mutual suspicion and hostility, which leaves little room for peaceful coexistence as a long-term strategy or policy, although peaceful coexistence as a short-term tactic appeals to both countries. Following major political changes in Afghanistan since the mid-1980s and the changes in the former Soviet Union, could Pakistan advance its strategic and economic interests by building links with the emerging Islamic republics in the Central Asian sphere? Such a new channel could soften Indo–Pakistani rivalries.

Second, it appears that India has historically pursued a two-part policy towards its smaller immediate neighbours. With regard to Nepal, Bhutan and Sikkim up to 1975, and Sri Lanka and Bangladesh after 1971, Nehru's and Indira Gandhi's statements and policies, discussed in this chapter, explain one part of this policy. India's role with respect to the smaller and weaker states appears similar in a general way to the former USSR's relationship with Finland; that is, non-intervention in internal affairs unless they impinge on vital Indian security interests, and a pattern of intervention to preserve Indian security and regional order in neighbourly affairs but without a policy of territorial expansion. The other part of India's policy concerns Pakistan, where a posture of friendship and peaceful coexistence posture has been accompanied by a policy of maintaining and using coercive measures to keep Pakistan's territorial ambitions in check. The contrast between the two parts of India's policy are striking. On the one hand India has tried and succeeded thus far in keeping Nepal, Bhutan and Sri Lanka on a leash and preventing them from developing ties with China that could harm Indian vital interests. On the other hand no such attempt has been made with Pakistan. Rather the effort in the latter case has been to minimise the flow of US and Chinese arms into Pakistan. The contrasts are brought out by the pattern of Indian treaty relations with Nepal and Bhutan, by India's incorporation (following an internal referendum) of Sikkim into the Indian Union in 1975, by the Indo-Sri Lankan Accord of 1987 and by Indian economic pressures that led Nepal to accept the Indian rules of the game.

These two parts of Indian policy are clear from a study of its behaviour and, to a lesser extent, policies since the 1950s. Still, Indian objectives require clarification.

One explanation is that India is seeking to establish a cooperative and stable subsystem in the Indian subcontinent; this approach rests on peaceful coexistence as a long-term strategy or policy. This could work provided India avoids territorial aggrandisement of its immediate neighbours, advances the interests of these countries and their regimes, discreetly secures political pluralism in these societies and maintains regional order. Here India has been seen as acting in a manner consistent with a regional security regime that lay, minimum emphasis on coercion and recognises the value of the consent of weaker members of the region. Such consent should be gained not by coercion but by a commonality of political purpose and core values and development of an institutionalised process that enables the growth of internal democracy and continuous adjustment of the conflicting interests, perceptions and expectations of the decision makers. In this explanation India is seen as having been honest in its professed aims, and Indian involvement in the SAARC as a sign of a desire for friendship with neighbours based on economic and technical interests.

The second explanation rests on all of the above, but with one major difference. Here India's real motivation has been to secure regional dominance (as distinct from pre-eminence, which is based on consent and respect) and to use this as a step towards its long-standing dream of a seat at the table of the world powers. Thus India has disguised its real ambition by using the cover of its doctrine of a stable South Asian subsystem. In the first explanation India is assumed to be non-expansionist; in the second it is assumed to be expansionist in its policy aim, even if this is not hegemonic territoriality. In the second explanation the 'stable subsystem' is designed to pacify India's neighbours and prevent China and the United States from working against Indian interests.

The third explanation is that, since Nehru's time, India has learnt to draw blood as a result of its experiences with war and diplomacy in 1948, 1962, 1965, 1971 and the crises during the 1980s with Pakistan, Sri Lanka and Nepal; and having done so it has gained confidence in its ability to function as a regional policeman with US approval. Here changes in the regional and international environment during the 1980s and the 1990s have led to an incremental adjustment in the US perception of the value of benign Indian intervention in the affairs of its immediate neighbours other than Pakistan. The latter remains a special case in US policy for the reasons cited earlier.

The third and final point is that the number of domestic players involved in South Asian politics and foreign and military affairs has increased. A change in the size of decision-making structures in South Asian states, and variations in their sociology, attitudes and institutional interests, have complicated the making of foreign and military policy as well as the study of it. Usually the Foreign Office is seen as the central player in foreign affairs, but this is no longer true in South Asia. In the Nehru years, Indian foreign policy was the product of decisions by Nehru and a small circle of advisers. Other government departments and societal forces barely counted in issues concerning Kashmir, Pakistan, China, Tibet, the United States, the USSR and elsewhere. The grand design of foreign affairs and Indian interests and ambitions were articulated by Nehru and reflected the influence of a select few. Following the 1962 India–China war, the role of the armed services increased and the political weight of the Indian foreign office and the civilian Indian intelligence service declined as a result of the failure of its intelligence in 1962; the weight of Indian rightists (pro-US) and leftists (pro-USSR) increased and continued in a pattern of uneasy coexistence and polarisation within the Indian domestic structure. In the 1971 war, civilian Indian intelligence agencies and the military authorities worked well with Indira Gandhi and the prime minister's office. During the 1980s India's cabinet secretariat (which oversees the Indian intelligence agencies) and the Indian intelligence agency – the Research and Analysis Wing (RAW) – were active in the Sri Lankan and Indo–Pakistani campaigns. Often the channels of communication and decision making showed the weight of agencies other than the Indian Foreign Office.

Similarly, in Pakistan's case the decline of the authority of the Pakistani Foreign Office lies in the emergence of the military and intelligence agencies since the 1950s, and in the continuous decline of civilian control over these agencies during the past forty years. Following the downfall of Z. A. Bhutto in 1977, decision-making power shifted into the hands of those who controlled Pakistan's military, intelligence and scientific agencies. Here too the sociology, institutional interests and attitudes of the new decision makers showed a significant erosion in the central position and political authority of the Pakistani Foreign Office.

This chapter does not provide a detailed case study of the changing domestic structures and effects of increasing competition among domestic players, yet it suggests the need to recognise such changes in the foreign policy processes and policies of the states of subcontinent. Here inner tensions among competing domestic players affected policy results in interstate affairs.

NEIGHBOURS OTHER THAN PAKISTAN

The foreign policies of India's immediate neighbours, the Himalayan kingdoms – Nepal, Bhutan and Sikkim (which was absorbed in the Indian Union in 1975) – and Bangladesh and Sri Lanka are influenced by India, the dominant power in the region. The general rule was laid down by India's first prime minister, Jawaharlal Nehru, on 6 January 1950 in a statement on Nepal to the Indian Parliament (a policy pronouncement that has been applied to all the states in this group): '... much as we appreciate the independence of Nepal, we cannot allow anything to go wrong in Nepal or permit that barrier to be crossed or weakened, because that would be a risk to our own security'.[2] Nepal was in 'the throes of a revolution that threatened to result in political chaos'.[3] Indian policy towards Sikkim, Bhutan, East Pakistan (Bangladesh since 1971) and Sri Lanka (since the Indo–Sri Lanka Peace Accord of 29 July 1987) was based on the same consideration that Nehru applied to Nepal.

Pakistan, however, is in a category of its own. It resents India's intervention in Kashmir and East Pakistan, which resulted in the creation of the Republic of Bangladesh. Pakistan's foreign policies are therefore based on a fear of India on the one hand and a desire to challenge India's status as the major regional power on the other.

The concept of 'Finlandisation' could apply to the first group. By this we mean that the states in this group are obliged or compelled to adopt foreign policies that do not conflict with the security interests of India; just as Finland could not, in its external relations, threaten the national security of the USSR. Nehru's policy was restated by Indira Gandhi in more emphatic terms, because of greater challenges to India's geostrategy in the region. In July 1983 Bharat Wariaywalla wrote in *The Round Table* what he termed the 'national security state' of 'Indira's India'.[4] He meant that India under Indira Gandhi was characterised by high defence spending, mobilisation of the country's strengths against an external enemy ('often imaginary'), creation of a sense of beleagueredness and 'an expansionist foreign policy'. (The latter, in our view, was due to threats to India's security.) In fact Indira Gandhi was strengthening India's position in a more difficult context along the lines of her father's (Nehru) Nepal policy laid down in January 1950. Indira Gandhi's successor, Rajiv Gandhi, therefore acted no differently when political chaos and internal rebellion threatened the disintegration of Sri Lanka.

To take the first group of states. Their foreign policies have either been 'Finlandised' to various degrees, or they have been permitted some leeway as long as India's interests were not placed in jeopardy. Sikkim and Bhutan came into India's sphere of influence because of Indian uncertainties regarding the People's Republic of China (PRC). Nepal, Sri Lanka (until 1987) and Bangladesh were either manipulated or permitted freedom within a given safety net.

In the case of Sikkim, that country was faced with internal destabilisation and consequently became a problem to India's security. Indian intervention therefore followed the familiar lines. In June 1949 the Chogyal (king) of Sikkim requested India to help resolve his country's internal disturbances. On 5 December 1950 India signed a Treaty of Perpetuity with Sikkim, which made Sikkim an Indian protectorate. Later India made known its disapproval of the new chogyal, who ascended the throne in 1963.[5] But it was not until 1973, under Indira Gandhi, that India intervened. The immediate pretext was disaffection among Sikkim's Nepalese-speaking majority. The chogyal appealed to India for help. An agreement pledged that India would maintain law and order as well as Sikkim's internal administration. Internal reforms by way of an elected legislature with the chogyal as the formal head of state were instituted. In 1974 the elected legislature resolved that Sikkim should be annexed by India, and in February 1975 Sikkim became part of the Indian Union. These moves were to ensure India's security. India's moves in Sikkim in the period 1973–4 were guided by K. S. Bajpai, a top-ranking political officer. India has utilised the best possible skills in its diplomatic service in dealings with regional states.[6]

India was just as successful in securing dominance over Bhutan. Bhutan was as sensitive an area as Sikkim because of its proximity to the PRC. In August 1949 India signed a Treaty of Perpetual Peace and Friendship with Bhutan. India guaranteed non-interference in the internal affairs of Bhutan. In turn Bhutan agreed to be guided by India's advice in external relations. In 1959, with Sino–Indian relations at a low ebb, Nehru urged Bhutan to agree to establishing a road link with India. Indian troops, it was agreed, would go to Bhutan's assistance in the event of an emergency. On 28 August 1959 Nehru, in a statement to Lok Sabha, guaranteed the territorial integrity and borders of Bhutan and Sikkim. He added that aggression against either of these countries would be considered as aggression against India.[7] The obvious reference was to the PRC.

During the 1960s Bhutan had the twin problem of protesting about the PRC's incorporation of a neighbouring Llamaist region, Tibet (Bhutan had the same Llamaist Bhuddhist traditions), and of keeping India's presence in Bhutan at a low profile because of opposition from sections of the Bhutanese Buddhist elites to India's interference in their country and India's substantial presence there.

Again India's problem was to protect the high Himalayan Bhutanese border from incursions by the PRC. In this matter India received the cooperation of the royal government. However the king's prime minister, Jigme Dorji, who supported alignment with India rather than a Nepal-style non-alignment between India and the PRC, was assassinated in April 1964. Dorji's younger brother, Lhendup Dorji, succeeded him as acting prime minister but could not sustain his position because of the turmoil in the kingdom and the feelings among some of the elites against India. Lhendup Dorji, fearing for his life, fled to India shortly. Into all this was thrown Nari Rustomji, a friend of Jigme Dorji, as 'Indian adviser' in 1963. Due however to the confused situation in elite circles, Rustomji was recalled in 1966.

Bhutan, with India's cooperation, followed a gradual expansion of relations with states acceptable to India. It obtained membership of the United Nations in 1971 and joined the Non-Aligned Movement (NAM) in 1979. Despite occasional strains in their relationship, Bhutan continues to receive Indian economic aid and guidance on foreign policy. Bhutan can be described as an independent state enjoying Indian protection; it is not now truly an Indian protectorate.

In the case of Nepal, Nehru preferred to have the kingdom walk a tightrope in its relations with India and the PRC and to act as a buffer zone when it suited India's security interests. The Indo–Nepalese Treaty of 1950 provided for mutual consultation in the event of Nepal or Sikkim being threatened by an outside power. The treaty with Nepal was signed because of the PRC's claim to her 'traditional boundaries', which in unofficial chinese government statements included Bhutan, Sikkim, Nepal and Tibet.[8]

This 'special relationship' was maintained between India and Nepal until 1955, when the relationship suffered a strain. King Mahendra, who ascended the throne in 1955, had to cope with internal criticism that India was increasingly influencing Nepal's external relations and that Nepal's sovereign status was thereby being compromised. Mahendra decided to balance this opposition to India by entering into diplomatic relations with the PRC in August 1955. The PRC provided economic aid to Nepal. The prime minister of the PRC, Chou En-lai, visited Katmandu in January 1957 and April 1960. India too provided economic aid to Nepal. However India refrained from protesting against King Mahendra's affiliations with the PRC. There was a deterioration in Sino–Indian relations with regard to the border and it was not in India's interests to precipitate matters.

Between 1958 and 1959 the Indian National Congress's parallel organisation, the Nepalese National Congress, exerted pressure on King Mahendra and the king called for an election to be held in early 1959. B. P. Koirala, head of the winning Nepalese Congress, was appointed prime minister. Koirala's position towards India would have softened, but he held office only until 15 December 1960, when the king dismissed him and assumed all his powers. Mahendra reassured India and the PRC that he would maintain a neutral stance in Sino–Indian relations, which he did until his death in January 1972.

With the new king, Birendra, India utilised the distribution of river waters to keep Nepal in line. India entered into a bilateral agreement with Nepal in 1984 under which it would build 50 water schemes for that country. With the provision of water acting as a lever, Nepal has been prevented from pursuing policies not appropriate to India. The position now is that King Birendra has stated that his kingdom is not part of the subcontinent, rather it belongs to 'that part of Asia which touche[s] both China and India'.[9] King Birendra has thus successfully used the hostile relations between India and the PRC to secure for his country a position that has released him from excessive pressure from its two giant neighbours. However, in the final analysis Nepal has to follow New Delhi's dictates because of its economic dependence on India. Four to five million Nepalese are reported to work permanently in India, in addition to the 100 000 seasonal Nepalese migrant workers who cross the border into India each year.[10]

From its independence in 1948 to 1956, Sri Lanka (then Ceylon) adopted a foreign policy that showed a distinct fear of India. The island was internally stable and was not therefore a portentous threat to India. India intervened only when the Sinhalese–Tamil conflict reached the proportions of a major civil war after the anti-Tamil riots of July 1983.

Before the granting of independence by Britain, Ceylon's leader, Don Stephen Senanayake, negotiated a defence agreement with Britain in November 1947. The agreement permitted British military bases on the island in return for Britain agreeing to come to Ceylon's assistance in the event of attack. India did not consider these British bases a threat. Ceylon and India were both members of the Commonwealth and India enjoyed pride of place in the new Commonwealth. For Nehru, the Commonwealth provided a platform from which to communicate with the world.

Nonetheless Don Stephen Senanayake, now prime minister, stated in April 1949 that there was 'an undercurrent of apprehension regarding the long-term possibility of Indian expansion.[11] Senanayake's constitutional advisor, Sir Ivor Jennings, wrote in April 1956 that the prime minister was at the time of independence 'well aware' of the danger that 'India under the wrong leadership' could become 'aggressive'.[12] Sir John Kotelawala (prime minister 1953–56) caused some anxiety to Krishna Menon at the Bandung Conference of 1955 and shortly thereafter when the idea of Ceylon joining the South-East Asia Treaty Organisation (SEATO) was considered.[13]

An uncertain feeling towards India persisted, despite the change in government in 1956 and the formulation of a policy of 'dynamic neutralism' by the new prime minister, S. W. R. D. Bandaranaike.[14] This policy change implied Ceylon's involvement in the Non-Aligned Movement. The basic uncertainty among Ceylon's political elites was reflected in their expressed fear of India. In 1955 Bandaranaike, then leader of the opposition and founder leader of the Sri Lanka Freedom

Party (SLFP), had stated in a debate on making Sinhala the sole state language:

> I believe there are not inconsiderable numbers of Tamils in this country out of a population of eight million. Then there are forty to fifty million people just adjoining, and what about all this Tamil literature, Tamil teachers, even the films, papers, magazines, so that the Tamils in our country are not restricted to the Northern and Eastern provinces alone, there are a large number, I suppose over ten lakhs in Sinhalese provinces. And what about the Indian labourers whose return to India is now just fading into the dim and distant future? The fact that in the towns and villages, in business-houses and boutiques, most of the work is in the hands of Tamil-speaking people will inevitably result in a fear, and I do not think an unjustified fear, of the inexorable shrinking of the Sinhalese Language.[15]

In October 1956 J. R. Jayewardene, then a leading opposition spokesman of the defeated United National Party (UNP), censured the change to neutralism and alleged that 'leading Indians were saying that India should occupy Trincomalee when the British moved out.[16] All this despite Nehru's assurances in 1950 and 1959 that India had no intention of 'absorbing Ceylon'.[17]

The policy of dynamic neutralism was actively maintained by Bandaranaike's widow, Sirimavo, when she was prime minister (1960–65 and 1970–77). But even with the Bandaranaikes there was a fear of India. One reason was the developing ties between discontented Ceylon Tamils and Tamil political leaders in Tamil Nadu. Felix Dias Bandaranaike, who was Sirimavo Bandaranaike's principal cabinet advisor, remarked in private conversation that his government would call on the PRC for assistance if an Indian attack materialised.

These reservations notwithstanding, the Indian prime minister, Nehru, sent the foremost Catholic dignitary in India, Cardinal Valerian Gracias, to mediate in the dispute between the Catholic Church in Ceylon and Sirimavo Bandaranaike over her government's decision to nationalise all schools, the majority of which were owned by the Church. The deadlock created a major crisis for the SLFP government of the time. In 1971 Indira Gandhi assisted Sirimavo Bandaranaike in bringing under control the insurrection of the ultra-Marxist People's Liberation Front (the JVP), which at times seemed to overwhelm government forces. Thus India was ready to help Ceylon whenever domestic chaos threatened to upset the equilibrium.

Sirimavo Bandaranaike's occasionally independent foreign policy stances did not affect India's security interests. During her first term of office (1960-65) she functioned as an intermediary between India and the PRC on their border dispute. Her efforts brought no results but were appreciated by the governments of both states. The exercise gave the PRC an opportunity to improve relations with Ceylon. In 1971, during the Bangladesh crisis, Sirimavo Bandaranaike declared Ceylon's strict neutrality. Nevertheless Pakistani's aircraft were permitted stopover and refuelling rights at Ceylon's Bandaranaike airport en route from Pakistan to Dhaka (India had banned such flights over its territory). However the decision did not strain Indo-Ceylonese relations.

Even President Jayewardene's pro-West foreign policy and his government's progressive alienation from the NAM did not irritate India to the point of interference. However the growing conflict between Sinhalese and Tamils increasingly destabilised the island and caused concern in Tamil Nadu, an important political constituency for Rajiv Gandhi's government. The last straw was the intervention of hostile and unfriendly foreign powers (to India) and their agents in the island's affairs, especially from 1983-87. The granting of facilities to the Voice of America, which it was feared would broadcast low-frequency messages to US nuclear submarines deep in the North Indian Ocean, could have caused concern to the USSR and therefore to India. Article 8 of the Indo-Soviet Friendship Treaty of August 1972 required each side to prevent the use of its territory for military purposes that might be detrimental to the other side (to this end it is probable that the USSR regarded Ceylon as part of India's sphere of influence). Article 9 reinforced Article 8 by stipulating that neither side would assist a third party (probably the PRC or the United States) taking part in an armed conflict with the other side, thus ensuring the peace and security of their countries.[18]

The situation was made worse when President Jayewardene obtained the services of Pakistani, Israeli and British (unofficial) military advisors as well as arms from the Republic of South Africa. He claimed that he required foreign military assistance to quell the insurgency of the Tamil Freedom Fighters. Foreign involvement and the gradual engulfing of the island in a deleterious civil war compelled India to enter the scene, first as a mediator (1983-87) and later militarily (1987).[19] India's intervention was not part of a hegemonistic design nor an implementation of Indira Gandhi's alleged version of the Monroe Doctrine for South Asia, as various commentators have speculated. Rajiv Gandhi's action in 1987, on the contrary, was in total agreement with the policy on Nepal spelled out by his grandfather, Jawaharlal Nehru, in January 1950.[20]

In 1983–84 Indira Gandhi sent her minister for foreign affairs, Narasimha Rao, and the chairman of her Policy Planning Committee, G. Parthasarathy (who was also a member of the Indian cabinet), to investigate and try to resolve the Sinhalese–Tamil conflict. President Jayewardene's relationship with Parthasarathy was far from cordial, as the president indicated to A. J. Wilson in October 1983. Nor was the president willing to be persuaded by Indira Gandhi. Professor Wilson met with President Jayewardene in London in mid-1984, shortly after the latter's visit to President Ronald Reagan. The president did not seem hopeful of the results of his talks at the White House. But he was also hesitant when Professor Wilson urged him, before his visit to Indira Gandhi, to use her good offices to settle the increasingly rough civil war. According to reliable sources, Indira Gandhi did not trust President Jayewardene, and if he had accepted Parthasarathy's Annexure 'C' formula as a solution to the Sinhalese–Tamil problem, she would probably have insisted that her government monitor its implementation.

After Indira Gandhi's assassination, her successor, Rajiv Gandhi, tried unsuccessfully from 1984 to July 1987 to resolve the issue. Gandhi's foreign secretary, Romesh Bhandari, and his cabinet minister, P. Chidambaram, failed to persuade the two parties to agree to a mediated settlement. Failure resulted in Rajiv Gandhi himself negotiating the Indo–Sri Lankan Accord of 29 July 1987. The accord secured the Sri Lanka government's commitment to an India-devised peace plan that would end the civil war. More importantly President Jayewardene, in letters of exchange annexed to the accord, agreed to terminate the services of foreign military personnel and ensure Trincomalee as a harbour over which India would have prior participation involvement. India committed itself to guarantee 'the territorial integrity and unity' of Sri Lanka. Thus Indian intervention in the end provided for the safeguarding of India's vital interests; it was also an attempt at restoring equilibrium in the Sinhalese–Tamil conflict.

Following the resolution of the Sinhalese–Tamil problem, Rajiv Gandhi frequently consulted with Tamil Nadu's chief minister, M. G. Ramachandran. Tamil Nadu was an important constituency for Rajiv Gandhi's government. The accord did not bring the expected results. Sri Lanka's problems became aggravated by Sinhalese displeasure with the Indian military presence and opposition to the Indian Peace Keeping Force (IPKF) by the principal Tamil group of freedom fighters, the Liberation Tigers of Tamil Eelam (LTTE).

President Jayewardene himself aggravated the situation by his unwise pronouncements. He failed to placate moderate Tamil opinion, thereby polarising the Sinhalese and Tamils. He was most impolitic in his views on Indira Gandhi and on the Kashmir issue. In his state visit to New Delhi in 1978 as the guest of the government of Morarji Desai (1977–79), Jayewardene referred undiplomatically to Indira Gandhi's 'undemocratic' period of emergency rule. When told on his return that the statement would be taken amiss by Mrs Gandhi, President Jayewardene said he was confident that the Desai government was there to stay (which turned out to be an incorrect projection). On 27 August 1979, in a letter to the convenor of the Tamil Co-ordinating Committee in London (K. Vaikunthavasan), Indira Gandhi wrote: 'I... am horrified to see the enclosures. The Janata Party Government (of Morarji Desai) is going out of its way to be friendly with the present government of Sri Lanka. I doubt if they will wish to take up the issue of the sufferings of the Tamils in Sri Lanka. At the moment all attention is on our election but I shall see if it is possible to bring this issue to the notice of the public in some other way.'[21]

President Jayewardene was just as lacking in political sagacity in visiting General Zia Ul-Haq in Islamabad in April 1985. When asked on the phone from Canada why he had visited Pakistan when India was helping him to resolve his domestic crisis, his reply was 'Why shouldn't I?' The president acted even more unwisely in raising the issue of Jammu and Kashmir with General Zia. The Indian prime minister expressed concern, adding 'we were disturbed that he [Jayewardene] opened the Kashmir issue'. The president's statements on Indira Gandhi's emergency rule and Kashmir were a blunder, and an example of a powerless neighbour needlessly inviting the hostility of a powerful neighbour-state.

Sri Lanka's leaders, by and large, had no concept of foreign policy goals. The emphasis from independence centred on foreign aid. The Senanayakes (Don Stephen and Dudley) maintained the colonial attitude of reliance on Britain. Bandaranaike probably thought that involvement in the NAM would give him a place on the world stage. Beyond this goal, he did little to restructure foreign policy or formulate a strategy in terms of a world view. For example Sri Lankan academics – S. U. Kodikara and A. J. Wilson – helped set up a Ceylon Institute of World Affairs (CIWA),[22] and although the prime minister gave encouragement and participated in the inaugural meeting of the CIWA, he displayed no further interest in the progress and development of the institute, which to this day remains where it started in 1957.

Sirimavo Bandaranaike's involvement on the world stage was aimed more at domestic prestige. She lacked understanding of foreign policy orientations. At the meeting of Commonwealth leaders in 1961 she vigorously protested South Africa's application to remain in the Commonwealth after legislating for republican status. *The Times* (London) sardonically remarked that Mrs Bandaranaike had read from reams of typed sheets supplied to her by her cabinet confidant and advisor, Felix Dias Bandaranaike. Her role in 1962 as an intermediary in the aftermath of the 1962 Sino–Indian border war was of little significance. Her attempt to have the Indian Ocean declared a zone of peace at the UN General Assembly in 1971 gave her some exposure, but the Indian delegation had undertaken most of the groundwork. Though she received the plaudits of the more radical members of the NAM for her role in the movement's progress, her policy orientations were not part of a coherent pattern.

In the case of Bangladesh, Indira Gandhi did nothing more than follow Nehru's policy of safeguarding India's vital interests. S. M. Mujtaba Razvi described Indira Gandhi's policy as her version of the Monroe Doctrine in South Asia.[23] However our view is that she was following Nehru's policy on Nepal in 1950, though in a more difficult context. Razvi stated that Mrs Gandhi described South Asia as 'a troubled region' and he analysed her doctrine on 'Indian interests' thus: 'The idea behind this doctrine was that if law and order breaks down in any South Asian state, it should seek India's help to overcome destabilization, or solicit help from within the region but not to the exclusion of India.'[24] This view is not different from that of Nehru's case for intervening in Nepal should political chaos overtake that kingdom.

It was in these circumstances that Indira Gandhi intervened in East Pakistan. In order to ward off a possible threat from the PRC, she took the precaution of concluding a mutual assistance pact with the Soviet Union, known as the Indo–Soviet Friendship Treaty of August 1972. The decision to assist Mujibur Rahman in the creation of the state of Bangladesh probably had more to do with maintaining the stability of the South Asian system than with this pact.

India's relations with Bangladesh have been based on riparian rights, with Indira Gandhi's alleged Monroe Doctrine coming into play from time to time.[25] She had a satisfactory relationship with the first ruler, Mujibur Rahman, who was of course beholden to her. Mrs. Gandhi had assisted in the training and equipping of some 40 000 of Mujibur Rahman's own troops, the Mukti Bahini guerrillas, who played an important role in disrupting communications within Bangladesh, thereby making it easier for General Sam Manekshaw and his Indian forces to defeat the Pakistanis army.

Bangladesh started with good intentions, emulating the example of its secular neighbour and declaring itself the 'People's Republic of Bangladesh', but within four years Bangladesh developed troubles with India over the distribution of the waters of the two eastern rivers, the Ganges and the Brahmaputra. Then in November 1975 a coup finally brought General Ziaur Rahman into power, at least for a while.

General Rahman adopted a policy of distancing himself from New Delhi. One of his first acts was to abandon all cultural cooperation. In 1978 he renamed the republic 'the Islamic Republic of Bangladesh'. He emphasised Bangladeshi nationalism and he developed closer ties with Pakistan. Surjit Mansingh wrote in 1984 that from New Delhi's observations, 'Bangladeshi officials gained the reputation of being the toughest, most demanding and most sensitive of all national groups with whom the Indian government has regular dealings.'[26]

Internal destabilisation of Rahman's regime now began. Up to the general elections of 1977, when Indira Gandhi suffered defeat at the hands of the Janata Party led by Morarji Desai, guerilla raids on Bangladeshi territory were launched from Indian bases. Acts of internal sabotage were attributed to Indian *agents provocateur*. In the brief period when Desai was prime minister (1977–79) Indo–Bangladeshi relations improved. A five-year agreement was signed on 5 November 1977 under which Bangladesh was guaranteed a sufficiency of water during the dry months. But this was atypical of Indian external policy as moulded by the Nehru–Gandhi prime ministerships.

In June 1981 Lieutenant General H. M. Ershad took power after the assassination of General Ziaur Rahman, thus bringing about the failure of another regime before it had time to establish itself. General Ershad and India signed the Indo–Bangladeshi Accord of 31 May 1984, but the evidence suggests that relations between the two countries were not equal. There was a dispute over how the waters of the Ganges and the Brahmaputra should be distributed so that Bangladesh would not suffer. The Indian occupation of Purbasha Island in the Bay of Bengal was construed as an ill-considered act because of Bangladesh's claims over that island. India protested about the flow of Muslim migrants from Bangladesh to the Indian state of Assam. India's attempts to construct a barbed wire fence along the Bangladesh–Assam border as a way of controlling this migration added to General Ershad's displeasure. Bangladesh's problem was to emphasise its independence from India's beneficence. To accomplish this objective, Bangladesh sought to establish a separate Islamic identity. This left Bangladesh to look towards Pakistan for Islamic and emotional support. Ziaur Rahman's government obtained aid from the United States, the World Bank and Saudi Arabia and pro-Pakistani elements were, much to India's dismay, reinducted into the Bangladeshi government. Bangladesh will, in the final analysis, be obliged to refrain from actions that will affect Indian interests. The question of water and India's superior military strength leaves Bangladesh with little or no option.

PAKISTAN'S EXTERNAL RELATIONS

Resentment against India is rooted in Pakistan's foreign policy goals. The immediate post-partition problems, including Kashmir, are not the only causes. Pakistan has been a state in search of a national identity. It seeks reinforcement of its presence in the Indian subcontinent by challenging India's position as the dominant power. This seems irrational. India has a larger Muslim population than Pakistan. While Pakistan emphasises its Islamic identity, India maintains its secular character. India has 72 per cent of the land area of the subcontinent and 77 per cent of the population. Its sheer size and wealth in natural resources give India automatic pride of place. Nevertheless Pakistan's goal orientations have been directed at destabilising the Indian state system by, for example, encouraging the Khalistani Sikhs in their separatism, developing a nuclear profile and entering into strategic treaty arrangements that are at odds with India's policy of preventing South Asia from being drawn into the power politics of states outside the region.

Pakistan seeks to be taken note of in world affairs. Therefore Pakistan has close ties with the United States and seeks a position of vantage in the Middle East and Central Asian systems. Pakistan also maintains a relationship with the PRC as a counter to India. These policies have had no impact on the other states of South Asia discussed here. The latter have not sought to enter Pakistan's foreign policy network. This unwillingness is partly to avoid discomfiting India; in part it is self-preservation. At the same time, with the exception of Bangladesh, the other states do not envisage any advantage for themselves in Pakistan's external commitments.

As early as 1947 Pakistan's founder, Muhammad Ali Jinnah, decided that it was necessary to protect the newly independent state from Soviet aggression and 'Hindu imperialism'. Thus Pakistan looked for allies.

In September 1948 Liaquat Ali Khan sent a secret message to the British prime minister, Clement Attlee. He proposed a military alliance between his country and Britain against communism. Communism, he stated, posed a danger to Pakistan's stability. Nothing definite emerged from this overture.[27] Then on 24 June 1949 he told the British high commissioner in Pakistan, L. B. Grafftey-Smith: 'What I fear is that Great Britain and the world would look on with folded arms if India attacked us.'[28]

Britain did nothing to allay Pakistan's fears. Pakistan therefore, in its search for security, looked for allies in the Middle East and to the United States as an overall protector. The outcome was an agreement between Turkey and Pakistan on 19 February 1954. There was provision for both parties to strengthen 'peace and security in their own interest'. On 19 May 1954 Pakistan and the United States entered into a mutual defence assistance agreement. The United States agreed to provide military equipment and training to Pakistan's armed forces. Then followed the Manila Conference, which resulted on 8 September 1954 in the US-sponsored South-East Asia Collective Defence Treaty (SEATO). Pakistan was not satisfied with the provisions of the treaty. It did not arranged for a joint military command as in the case of NATO. The United States added further disillusionment by writing in a proviso to the treaty: US assistance would be provided only in the event of communist aggression. Pakistan ratified the treaty on 19 January 1955 but there was no guarantee that the United States, Britain or France would come to Pakistan's aid in the event of an Indian attack.

The Baghdad Pact, which Pakistan signed on 23 September 1955, proved no more useful. Other signatories to this pact were Britain, Iraq, Turkey and Iran. The United States, though a keen sponsor of the pact, remained a non-signatory because of Israel. The point in question was the attitude of Arab states to Israel. When the United States joined the military committee of the pact, the policy statement was again an assurance of protection against communism, not against India. The British position was similar. Thus Pakistan's diplomacy in this phase failed.

Pakistan's problem with India was the perceived aggression from that quarter, the troubles that followed partition and the dispute over Kashmir. At the start, Pakistan's Prime Minister Liaquat Ali Khan tried to sort out the post-partition problems with Nehru. On 8 April 1950 Liaquat Ali Khan signed an agreement with Nehru that ended the fleeing of Hindus from East Pakistan to West Bengal; it also introduced restrictions on Muslims leaving West Bengal for East Pakistan.

Earlier, contrary to his professed views on peaceful coexistence, Nehru had threatened in a speech in the Lok Sabha to use 'other methods' against Pakistan on the question of Hindu refugees flowing into India.[29] After the Liaquat Ali Khan–Nehru pact, Nehru stated: 'We have stopped ourselves at the edge of the precipice and turned our back to it.'[30]

In the following year there followed the crises over Kashmir. In April 1951 the Kashmiri head of state issued a proclamation for the purpose of convening a constituent assembly, which would decide 'the future shape and affiliations of the state'.[31] *The Economist* (25 August 1951) reported that the assembly would carry out 'its preordained part of formally voting for accession to India'. India amassed troops in East Punjab, Jammu and Kashmir.[32] Liaquat Ali Khan and his government prepared for the worst. The Pakistani army was far inferior to that of India in size and equipment. The crisis passed.

Pakistan's inability to establish its military capabilities in the Indo–Pakistani war of 1965, despite US military aid, marked a setback in Pakistan's bid to be a principal in the balance of power in South Asia. (A further setback followed with the break-up of the original state of Pakistan. As already discussed, in 1971 Bangladesh, with active Indian military assistance, seceded and became a state in its own right. Pakistan had hoped that the PRC and/or the United States would come to its assistance, but neither did.) Although United States provided military and economic aid to Pakistan, it was helpful to India, too. Pakistan laid much hope in the People's Republic of China, but beyond protestations of support, encouragement and some military aid, China did little. On 9 September 1965 the prime minister of China, Chou En-lai, denounced India as the aggressor in the Indo-Pakistani war of September 1965 and condemned the politics of 'US imperialism' and of 'the modern revisionists' of the USSR.

On 23 September 1965 both states agreed to end the war. Pressure had been brought to bear on them by Britain and the United States. The USSR called for a cessation of hostilities. On 10 January 1966, as a result of Soviet initiatives, Pakistan's President Ayub Khan, and the Indian prime minister, Lal Bahadur Shastri, signed the Tashkent Agreement. The agreement provided for a withdrawal by the two states to the borders they held prior to 5 August 1965. There was dissatisfaction in both Indian and Pakistani circles to the cencessions made by each party to the other. Shastri died of heart failure on 11 January 1966 at Tashkent. What was serious to India was that the USSR agreed to provide military aid to Pakistan. More ominous was the parity of treatment accorded to the two states by the USSR.

There was also the complicating factor of China's involvement with Pakistan. The Sino–Pakistani relationship was negotiated by President Ayub's foreign minister, Zulfikar Bhutto (1963). Bhutto concluded a Sino–Pakistani boundary agreement on 2 March 1963 under which large areas of northern Kashmir and Ladakh (a disputed territory held by India) were recognised by Pakistan as belonging to China. By August 1963 Bhutto's diplomacy had cemented the Sino–Pakistani relationship. Bhutto, however, failed to get the UN Security Council to discuss Kashmir, in part due to Nehru's death in 1964. In June 1966 Bhutto resigned from President Ayub's cabinet on medical grounds. He had however sensed the growing opposition to Ayub's regime. In particular, Pakistanis opposed the Tashkent Agreement as 'a sellout' to India. With Shastri's death in January 1966 Pakistan had to deal with a more formidable foe and a skilled diplomatist in Indira Gandhi.

Pakistan's policy towards India after the Bangladesh debacle was one to open rancour. President Zia Ul-Haq took steps to avoid Pakistan's encirclement, safeguard Pakistan from a 'menacing' India and strengthen the Islamic foundations of the state as a counter to what the Pakistanis thought of as an aggressive Hindu India.

President Zia sought assistance from China and the United States to break out of a possible Indo–Soviet encirclement. President Zia's policy was to improve US military ties with Pakistan, the excuse being that the United States needed bases in Pakistan to assist the Afghani resistance against the Soviets in Afghanistan. However US aid to Pakistan was balanced by Soviet assistance to India. The Pakistani government continues to maintain military links with China. To ensure easier border contact with China, Pakistan has disputed India's claim to the world's highest glacier, Siachin.[33] India claims that the glacier is part of Jammu and Kashmir. Siachin is a strategic link-up between Pakistan and China. New Delhi is concerned that this is one more instance of Sino–Pakistani military collaboration.

General Zia next tried, with a view to promoting Pakistan's image, to improve relations with the Arab states of the Middle East, but without success. Pakistan's support for Britain in the Suez War (1956) had alienated Arab nationalists. To a large extent this was repaired when an Islamic summit conference was held in Lahore in 1974 during the Bhutto years. But the conference, which might have provided positive support to Pakistan in its problems with India, failed to make headway because of Bhutto's personal ambitions to secure for himself the leadership of a Muslim bloc.

Pakistan also failed in its bid to establish closer relations with Iran:

in terms of sect, Pakistanis are Sunnis and Iranians Shiites. Pakistan has closer ties with Saudi Arabia and the relationship entails economic and military cooperation. Turkey and Iran had been lukewarm in their support of Pakistan under the CENTO agreement. Pakistan has thus had to depend almost wholly on US military aid and Chinese support.

The frustrated General Zia had a way out. This was to encourage Pakistan's scientific establishment's strenuous and persistent attempts to build a nuclear device. India exploded a nuclear device in 1974 and halted testing thereafter. The explosion was a warning to China not to Pakistan. During the 1980s Pakistan developed a nuclear weapons capability. But this was after the failure to attempts by Pakistan to persuade India to sign a treaty, the provisions of which included renouncing the manufacture or acquisition of nuclear weapons, and an offer to join with India in a system of mutual inspection of all nuclear facilities in the two countries on a bilateral basis.[34]

The Indian prime minister declined to sign a non-nuclear proliferation treaty with General Zia at their Delhi summit meeting on 17 November 1986. Both leaders, however, agreed not to attack each other's nuclear power installations. New Delhi did not accept General Zia's assurances to the UN General Assembly of 'Pakistan's irrevocable commitment not to acquire nuclear explosive devices'.[35] The Indian response was twofold:[36] (1) that Pakistan's proposals for joint inspections and safeguards were only made to enable Pakistan to gain time to develop nuclear devices, and (2) that Pakistan's suggestion for a nuclear weapons zone in South Asia did not take cognisance of China's nuclear capability. Indeed India had a valid point. As Pakistan's ally, and given the history of Sino–Indian conflict, mistrust and lack of transparency regarding China's strategic intention, China could always present a nuclear threat to India.

General Zia's third step was to strengthen the Islamic foundations of Pakistan. Ever since its creation, Pakistan had endeavoured to establish its identity by emphasising its Islamic character. Under General Zia, with Islamic fundamentalism rampant all over the Muslim world, it seemed politically rewarding to toe the line and establish a liaison with other Muslim states affected by Islamic fundamentalism. This could serve as a barrier to any attempt to bring Pakistan within India's orbit. Zia therefore declared that he would hold elections only after he was convinced that the future government would enforce the Islamic system. 'Sovereignty', he added, 'belonged to Allah...'[37] From Pakistan's point of view it was necessary for General Zia to enunciate this concept. With centrifugal forces encouraged by India and Soviet-backed Afghanistan there was a need to consolidate the internal unity of a disparate country.

Pakistan also faced a threat from the 1000 miles of border with Afghanistan – the Durand Line as it came to be called. Pakistan feared that the pro-Soviet government in Afghanistan could encourage the Baluchi and Pushtun secessionist movements. The Pro-Soviet president of Afghanistan promised support for the legitimate aspirations of the Baluchis and Pushtuns.

Since Zia-ul-Haq's death, Pakistan has seen several governments. National and provincial elections are now being accepted as the norm in Pakistan's internal political arrangements. Elections legitimise the political process in Pakistan, and they create opportunities for dialogue between Pakistan and India. However the military and intelligence services are still powerful in Pakistan's domestic and external affairs; the US–Pakistan strategic alignment is still powerful; and Pakistan and India are still diplomatic and military rivals. So the basic pattern of the relationship of conflict between India and Pakistan endures, albeit with a focus on confidence-building ventures to relieve stresses and strains that could lead to war. Here confidence building measures are tied to the value of a no-war Indo–Pakistan relationship of conflict.

THE SOUTH ASIA ASSOCIATION FOR REGIONAL COOPERATION (SAARC)

The group of seven (India, Pakistan, Bangladesh, Sri Lanka, Nepal, Bhutan and the Maldives) first met formally in 1981 and have had several meetings since. The SAARC is modelled on ASEAN. President J. R. Jayewardene of Sri Lanka and his prime minister, R. Premadasa, had made every effort to seek admission to ASEAN. But Lee Kuan Yew (the prime minister of Singapore) while sympathetic to Sri Lanka's aspirations, told the Sri Lankan government that the country's geographic location would prevent it from obtaining membership. The point of all this is that Sri Lanka was not happy about being involved in SAARC, where Indian dominance would prevail.

With a dominant power such as India and the ongoing conflict between the latter and Pakistan, there is more likely to be bilateral cooperation between states rather than the group converting itself into an economic community. Some members of the group have had their sovereignties curtailed by India (Sir Lanka and Bhutan). Others are economic vassals of India (the Maldives) or landlocked and depended on

India (Nepal). The SAARC is for trade, it is not a political forum. But extraneous issues such as terrorism have been raised at meetings even though the principal objective is to promote economic cooperation. Even in this field, cooperation is in selected areas of cultural and economic activities. Cooperation does not cover a wide range, the targeted areas being ones such as agricultural development, rural development, telecommunications, meteorology and health care. The SAARC may grow in time, but the main obstacles are the disputes between members.

CONCLUSIONS

One of the problems of South Asia is that for international purposes it has not been regarded as a subsystem. However, in the post-Cold-War context, with a new focus on the Asia–Pacific strategic and economic sphere, South Asia is being viewed as a subsystem in the Asia–Pacific sphere. As a subsystem, it would become the task of the international community to ensure its stability and equilibrium and give due weight to the opinions of its leaders. This does not happen at present. India is the only South Asian state where personalities such as Nehru and Indira Gandhi have been forced to reckon with. But a subsystem must also be a cohesive and internationally recognised grouping. South Asia does not function as one. This is because of India's desire to safeguard its vital interests and Pakistan's fear of Indian expansionism; also Pakistan wishes to challenge India's desire to be the stronger militarily. There is no documentation to prove the case, but South Asia, in our view, has become a troubled region where foreign powers cast their nets.

China does not wish India to emerge as the supreme power. Hence its support for Islamabad and its attempts to establish closer ties with Bangladesh and Nepal. China has also been interested in the events in Sri Lanka. In the late 1970s it took the position (according to information given to one of the authors) that it would prevent the emergence of two mini-states on the island. The reasons given was that the mini-states would become prey to Soviet machinations, and that Sri Lanka lay in the sea lanes from China to Africa. Thus China poses an obstacle to the emergence of a subsystem. US involvement in Pakistan, too, interferes with subsystemic development.

The fact of the Indo–Soviet alignment (1952–1990) did not alter the situation. There was no support for the view that India was 'a client state' of the USSR. The pact was one of mutual assistance and it was obviously intended to protect India against full-scale Chinese aggression.

Nevertheless the USSR connection created a problem for the formation of a subsystem.

Finally, there is the view that China looks on India as a rival in the world system. This rivalry, although limited now, also interferes in the formation of a subsystem in South Asia.

6 India and Pakistan in the 1980s and Early 1990s: Crises and Nuclear Activities

OVERVIEW

Following the 1971 war, the main thrust of Indo–Pakistani relations was to shift the controversies to the diplomatic level and to eschew the war option. The main diplomatic event was the Simla Accord, which was negotiated by Pakistan's President Z. A. Bhutto and Indian Prime Minister Indira Gandhi in July 1972. This accord spelled out several principles of interstate behaviour:

1. The principles included in the new charter were to govern bilateral relations.
2. Differences between the two were to be settled by peaceful means through bilateral negotiations.
3. Peaceful coexistence, respect for each other's territorial integrity and sovereignty and non-interference in internal affairs were prerequisites for good neighbourliness and durable peace.
4. The line of control in Jammu and Kashmir based on the 17 December 1971 ceasefire 'shall be respected by both sides without prejudice to the recognised position of either side'.[1]

Under Bhutto's leadership (1972–77) these principles governed Indo–Pakistani relations because Bhutto was preoccupied with domestic political and economic issues, and the distribution of power favoured India. A military coup in July 1977 brought Zia-ul-Haq to power, but, Pakistan remained internally preoccupied and Pakistan–US relations were mired in several controversies. The United States was concerned about Pakistan's nuclear programme as well as Zia-ul-Haq's position on democracy and human rights. The Soviet invasion of Afghanistan in December 1979 changed the regional context and the bilateral agenda of US–Pakistani relations. Pakistan became the frontline state through which the anti-Soviet coalition funnelled arms to the Afghan resistance. With a powerful international patron, the Zia-ul-Haq regime gained domestic and international legitimacy and a cover to develop new strategies to pursue its interests vis-à-vis India. During the 1980s these strategies triggered crises but not war between Pakistan and India, and they introduced the nuclear factor into the bilateral relationship. This chapter examines these issues.

Three processes dominated Indo–Pakistani affairs during the 1980s and early 1990s. The first process included arms-race strategies, war preparation, subversive action, hostile leadership rhetoric, hostile media campaigns and general mistrust of each other in elite perceptions. We call this the revisionist approach. This process has been at work in Indo–Pakistani affairs since the 1950s. It suggests that Indo–Pakistani relations are in a permanent crisis or a state of near crisis. Here Kashmir is the litmus test of a 'good' relationship. For Pakistan, securing Kashmir has remained the price – by war (1947–48, 1965), by subversive action (1947–8, 1965, 1980s to the present), by international pressure (1948–53, 1962 to the present) or by a combination of these strategies at different times. For India, cessation of hostile Pakistani support for armed insurgency in Kashmir and Punjab is the acid test of Pakistani good faith. This issue is more important than Pakistan's nuclear weapon development. The former is a sign of continuing Pakistani territorial irredentism and commitment to India's balkanisation. The latter is a sign that Pakistan seeks national security by nuclear means, which it sees as its right.

The second process was a strategy to develop confidence-building measures. Table 6.1 lists the main measures in this process.

The third process emerged in the late 1980s. It involved a strategy of incrementally developing Pakistan's and India's nuclear weapons capabilities to the extent that both are now seen as being nuclear capable but each country's capabilities have not been integrated into its military forces. For Pakistan, the strategy has been to gain weapons by clandestine means – by a large-scale, state-approved international smuggling operation (since the 1970s) and by risking a breach of understanding with its international patron, the United States (since the mid-1980s), on the nuclear issue.[2] India's strategy has been openly to develop dual-use technology (since the mid-1950s), to test a nuclear device (1974) and to develop a dual-use space and missiles capability (since the mid-1980s). Pakistan's strategy included using the Indo–Pakistani crises (1987 and 1989–90) to intensify its nuclear armament activity (more on this later). Table 6.2 chart's the progress of Indo–Pakistani nuclear developments. It reveals the absence, generally speaking,

Table 6.1 Indo–Pakistani confidence-building measures

Measure	Status in 1995
1. Sharing of information regarding military exercises	Agreed
2. Communications between military commanders	Agreed
3. Joint border patrols	Not Agreed
4. Prevention of violation of airspace by military aircraft	Agreed
5. Exchange of delegations of the armed forces	In progress
6. Prevention of acts detrimental to the maintenance of peaceful relations and non-interference in each other's internal affairs.	Not Agreed
7. Reiteration of resolve to abide by Simla agreement (that differences including Kashmir issue be settled by peaceful bilateral and other means).	Not Agreed
8. Agreement not to attack each other's nuclear facilities.	Agreed

of an Indian reaction in the nuclear sphere to Pakistan's nuclear activities, but on the other hand Pakistan has reacted to Indian nuclear activities since the mid-1970s.

Each process has a permanent place in both countries. The processes are interactive and dynamic, and no single process is dominant. The norms of these processes have generated tension in Indo–Pakistani relations and in the decision-making processes of the two countries because the norms are incompatible. As long as Kashmir remains a disputed area, the confidence-building process has limited use. Even an entrenched confidence-building process and a network of Indo–Pakistani agreements cannot change certain realities. The crux of the Indo–Pakistani problem is geopolitical and cultural, *viz*. India is big and Pakistan worries about asymmetry – India's economic and military strength is greater than Pakistan's, and there are more Indian Muslims than Pakistani ones. So equalisation requires India's balkanisation and nuclear development – the first to reduce India's power, and the second to increase Pakistan's power. Pakistan's Kashmir policy and its nuclear development is limiting the scope of the confidence-building process. At the same time the world community is supporting Indo–Pakistani confidence building, and significant sections of Indian and Pakistani public and elite opinion are interacting with world community elites. The Kashmiri and nuclear activities of India and Pakistan are being checked by the world community's demand to put all issues on the table and discuss them peacefully, and to move towards confidence-building activities.

The function of the nuclear factor has differed between India and Pakistan. Part of Pakistan's strategy has been the desire to equalise

Table 6.2 The 'escalatory potential' of Indo–Pakistani nuclear activities, 1947–89

Period	Technical activities	Diplomatic activities	Nuclear status
1940s–1960s	India begins to develop a nuclear programme: it acquires an unsafeguarded research reactor and seeks fuel recycling independence. 1964: India starts reprocessing. Mid-1960s: Pakistan rejects reprocessing and seeks a safeguarded research and power programme.	India rejects NPT and full safeguards. Pakistan rejects NPT, citing discrimination and 'geopolitical realities'.	Indian technical moves reveal a commitment to incrementally developing a nuclear wepons option. Pakistan's technical activities reveal a lack of commitment to the nuclear option.
1972–78	Pakistan moves towards plutonium bomb.	Pakistan claims that its nuclear programme has a peaceful intent.	Nil
1974	India explodes a nuclear device.	India denies intent to acquire nuclear arms.	Indian weapons potential exists.
1975–mid 1980s	Pakistan begins enrichment work, urarium bomb design and fabrication of components.	None	Pakistani weapons potential grows.
1987	Pakistan claims that it can make a bomb.	None	Pakistan's ability to make a nuclear weapon exists.
1989	India tests Agni, a ballistic missile.	None	Agni has ability to carry nuclear warhead.

Indo–Pakistani power. Here several strategies have been used: balkanisation of Indian border provinces, a conventional arms race and nuclear deterrence. The first and third are still in use. However the second failed because of India's determination to maintain asymmetry in conventional armament, because the influx of US arms into Pakistan is not guaranteed, and because Western sanctions have hindered Pakistan in its arms race with India. For Pakistan, given conventional arms asymmetry, nuclear power remains important to equalise India's advantage in conventional arms. Pakistan has also talked about an 'Islamic bomb', about Pakistan's bomb being a good thing for the Muslim world. Its words and actions indicate a willingness to share nuclear technology with friendly Muslim countries. Little, however, is known about nuclear relations between China, Pakistan, Iran and Iraq, and there is no clear evidence to indicate that Pakistan has given nuclear aid to friendly Muslim states. But combined with an overemphasis on Pakistan's leadership of the Muslim world (where Iran, Egypt and Saudi Arabia have a better claim), Pakistan's nuclear advertisement has sent the wrong signals to Pakistan's friends and enemies about its nuclear intentions.

For India, Pakistan's nuclear diplomacy vis-à-vis the Middle East is Pakistan's problem, but an indication that the nuclear leadership in South Asia has passed to Pakistan will create a problem for India that will have to be checked by technical and diplomatic countermeasures. Also for India, the assembly of Pakistani nuclear bombs and their integration into military machinery would require Indian nuclear retaliatory action in a military way if this is seen as adversely changing the security environment and India's security interests. Hence the need continually to upgrade the technical side of India's nuclear sphere, and to engage the Western world in a nuclear non-proliferation dialogue so that Pakistan does not gain an edge in its nuclear diplomacy and propaganda. But at the same time there is currently no need for Indian to possess nuclear bombs in order to equalise itself with Pakistan (or China) because the present level of Indian military strength and the pattern of Indian diplomacy is sufficient to manage contingencies in India's strategic environment in the 1990s.

In sum, the utility of the nuclear factor has differed between India and Pakistan because the asymmetrical distribution of power and threats has quite different implications for the two countries. The pattern of development of the three processes in the 1980s in both countries therefore reveal a fundamental shift from the requirement of a peaceful and bilateral resolution in the Simla Accord to a broadened set of competitive

Table 6.3 Processes in Indo–Pakistani affairs in the 1980s

Indicators of policy	Balkanise enemy-state[1]	CBM[2]	Nuclear and missile sphere
Activity	• *India*, moderate • *Pakistan*, high (mid-1980s to present)	Low in both countries	• *Pakistan*, moderate • *India*, moderate
Decision-making strength: motivation and organisational unity	• *Pakistan*, high (mid-1980s to present) • *India*, high	As above	• *Pakistan*, high • *India*, high
Posture	Semi-secretive	Public	Semi-secretive

Notes:
1. Hostile propaganda, arms race, subversive action and war preparation aimed at reducing the imbalance of power between India and Pakistan; for India the aim was to maintain the imbalance. This process relied on the use of diplomatic and conventional (non-nuclear) military measures.
2. Confidence-building measures.

and interactive processes that have become entrenched in the two countries. Table 6.3 explains the enlarged and complex scope of the new pattern of Indo-Pakistani strategic discourse.

This was the setting in which India and Pakistan engaged in crisis-making and crisis-management activities during the latter half of the 1980s. We now turn to a discussion of the two crises.

THE 1987 AND 1989–90 INDO–PAKISTANI CRISES: THE PATTERN OF BEHAVIOUR, THE PLAYERS AND THEIR CALCULATIONS

These crises revealed five aspects of Indo–Pakistani strategic behaviour:

1. Prime Minister Rajiv Gandhi's decision-making style was amateurish and it contributed to the origins of the 1987 crisis.
2. The pattern of India's military agenda and behaviour in the 1987 crisis differed from the agenda and behaviour of President Zia-ul-Haq and the Pakistani military in the 1987 crisis.
3. India's and Pakistani's agenda and behaviour in the 1989–90 crisis differed from the 1987 crisis.

4. Both crises revealed a highly volatile and complex Indo–Pakistani diplomatic and military discourse. The players, the issues, the calculations and the players' strategic concept varied. (There must be substantial adjustments in these areas if the two countries are to normalise their relationship.)
5. The nuclear factor played a role in each crisis, but it was not the driving element.

Rajiv Gandhi and the origins of the 1987 crisis

The 1987 Indo–Pakistani crisis refers to the 'Brass tacks' military exercise. This brought India and Pakistan close to war. During this crisis the nuclear factor played a role in President Zia-ul-Haq's/Dr A. Khan's behaviour.[3] This subsection describes the origins and the setting in which the Indian government embarked on 'Brass tacks' and the final subsection shows how Pakistan's nuclear posture changed under the cover of 'Brass tacks'.

The story begins in 1979, when the Indian government received information from a high-level Western scientific authority that Pakistan was going flat out to make a nuclear bomb. By 1981, Indian defence planners were arguing that if Pakistan had a bomb it was likely to use it. As a result of these inputs, by the early 1980s the Indian military's opinion was that India should go nuclear. In early 1985 Indian defence planners articulated the view that India must have a meaningful nuclear capability against China also.

The India military judged that the cost of a weapons programme was manageable. The Agni missile programme came out of this assessment, with a proposal to have a 5000 km range ballistic missile as a follow-up to Agni.[4]

This was the context in which 'Brass tacks' was conceived by the Indian government around October–November 1985. The decision to have a military exercise emerged at a regular meeting of the defence minister – Rajiv Gandhi was both prime minister and defence minister at the time. 'Brass tacks' was not on the agenda of this meeting, and there was no pressing crisis in Indo–Pakistani affairs that required political signalling via a military exercise. However Gandhi was keen to improve the training of the Indian air force and he wanted a large, integrated exercise. (The last major integrated exercise had taken place in 1952 and was called 'Vijay'.) Gandhi wanted the entire government of India to be involved in this exercise. At that time Gandhi was projecting the view that India was likely to become a militarily powerful country. Gandhi thirsted for a vast exercise and sought the involvement of all branches of the Indian government, including the Indian Railways, Air India and Indian Airlines for 7–10 days. Out of this the idea of 'Brass tacks' crystallised. 'Brass tacks' was not crisis driven. Rather it was driven by Gandhi's amateurish decision-making style, and his inability to think through an issue to its logical conclusion.

Indian and Pakistani military agenda and behaviour in the 1987 crisis

Apart from moving towards nuclear weapons and missile delivery systems so that India would have a meaningful nuclear capability to counter Pakistan's and China's challenge, the Indian military had two aims with respect to 'Brass tacks'. The main aim was to develop a mechanism to provide a rapid and integrated crisis response by all Indian government departments. Before 'Brass tacks' the Indian army had regularly conducted peacetime tactical exercises either without troops or with troops at the battalion level. These exercises were routinely held every four years. Fresh exercises were due in 1987, the last having been held in 1983. From a military point of view the 1987 'Brass tacks' exercise was important because a mechanised division had been formed, T-72 Russian tanks, helicopters and new air defence weapons had entered the picture and the question was how to integrate them into a fighting formation.[5] 'Brass tacks' involved 300 000 to 400 000 troops, that is, just under half the Indian army was moved from its peacetime stations during this exercise. Prior to 'Brass tacks', desert warfare training was a normal army activity but it took about three months to armour the training exercise and then another three months to decommission it; the training period itself lasted about three weeks. The new idea in 'Brass tacks' was to gain the ability to armour and de-armour rapidly. It was meant to improve India's rapid deployment capability and increase the morale of Indian troops who found themselves away from their families for a long period. The success of 'Brass tacks' caused fear in Pakistan and resulted in the subsequent crisis.

The second aim of 'Brass tacks' was represented by the 'Sunderji doctrine', named after General K. Sunderji, who was involved in planning 'Brass tacks'. This doctrine was based on the former idea of a standup fight in the Punjab. According to this doctrine it made no sense for India to fight Pakistan in the Punjab sector. Instead, the aim in Sunderji's thinking was to exploit the Pakistani Hyderabad–Sind–Indus River sector, which was 150 miles away. The second aim, therefore, was to test

India's desert operations capability in a military theatre that suited India geographically and was away from the Punjab military sector.

The chronology of events that led to the 1987 crisis was as follows.

1986: Political developments in India were complicated. Khalistan (Sikh independence) groups declared independence. India's Punjabis were nervous about Khalistan fearing that Pakistan might support Khalistani independence by mobilising troops on its side of the border. In addition the Babri Masjid/Ayodhya controversy flared up. In this controversy Hindus complained that Babur, a Mughal conqueror, had built a mosque at the birthplace of Lord Rama to celebrate muslim military victories. (Later the mosque was demolished by Hindu radicals.) All these developments agitated Indian public opinion and created domestic pressures on the political leadership to act resolutely.

September 1986: The first phase of 'Brass tacks' started. Indian railways officials were notified and they agreed to cancel trains at 24 hours notice to facilitate military movements for the exercise.

November–December 1986: Pakistan too was holding a routine military exercise at this time but the Pakistani units armour (whose peacetime location was Kherian, about 30–40 km from the Indian border) deployed for the exercise were not moved back.

December 1986: The second phase of 'Brass tacks' started. In this phase military briefings took place, small-scale military training without troop movement occurred and a military communications exercise was conducted.

16–20 January 1987: The third phase of the exercise started. Here troops began to move according to the exercise plan in areas east of the Rajasthan canal, south of Suratgarh and north of Bikaner. On 15–16 January 1987 Pakistan, under President Zia-ul-Haq's direction, moved its reserve strike force from Multan (its normal peacetime station) towards the Sulemain area. This move was intriguing. Normally reserves are not moved until there is a clear battle plan. The commitment of reserves is a real military and political signal in the subcontinent. For instance, in the 1971 war India and Pakistan did not use their reserve forces and Pakistan's reserve division stayed in Multan. In this context the forward commitment of Pakistani forces was seen as significant by India. If Pakistan felt threatened by 'Brass tacks' it could have used the hot line which had been in place since 1965, but this was not done.

Indian troop movement in 'Brass tacks' opened up an intriguing pattern of Pakistani military–political–nuclear behaviour. One conjecture is that Pakistan under President Zia-ul-Haq thought that Indian troop movement in the desert area of Rajasthan was a cover plant to go into Sind. Consequently, as noted earlier, Zia moved his entire reserve force towards the Indian border. This created a panic in Delhi because Indian troops had been moved away from the Punjab, normal train traffic had stopped and there was emergency movement of troops.

Zia's policies during 'Brass tacks' seemed to work at four different levels. First, *general policy*: Zia was quite clear that there should be no war with India. After the 1965 and 1971 wars a majority of Pakistani generals, including Zia, were cautious about the war option. Pakistan's political–military strategy rested on war avoidance (this was also the attitude of India's political and military leadership).

Second, *military tactics (escalation) and nuclear posturing*: in spite of the above by advancing his reserves Zia escalated the crisis. A. Q. Khan's interview with Indian journalist Kuldip Nayar occurred during the third phase of 'Brass tacks' (see note 3). Khan told Nayar about Pakistan's nuclear capability. The interview intensified Pakistan's nuclear posturing and revealed more details of its nuclear programme, even though Khan later denied discussing such issues with Nayar. If it is true that Pakistan crossed the nuclear weapons threshold in 1986,[6] the Khan interview was a nuclear warning signal – and it was viewed as such by the Indian government. Here a military crisis provided political justification for Pakistani's nuclear posturing, and the Zia/Khan interviews projected the Pakistani military's belief in nuclear weapons as the equaliser in the Indo–Pakistani conventional military asymmetry. 'Brass tacks' thus enabled Zia-ul-Haq to proclaim Pakistan's nuclear strength. The analytical link is between three elements of Zia's calculations: *war avoidance*; *tactical crisis making* by dramatically moving Pakistani reserves towards the Indian Punjab border; and *using a military crisis to publicise Pakistan's nuclear capability*.

Third, *testing India's choices*: by moving the reserves forward in an unprecedented manner, Zia created a dilemma for India that had the potential to disrupt its military exercise. India was faced with two options: to postpone 'Brass tacks' and redeploy its forces, or to carry on with 'Brass tacks', which would be risky if Pakistan's forward movement implied war. India chose the latter, but as a precaution on 16–17 January 1987 it airlifted infantry from Bangalore (south India) and moved it north-eastern reserves towards the Pakistan front. There were other options. One was to launch an air attack on the Pakistani forces in forward positions. This would only make sense if India planned a war with Pakistan, so it was not considered. Another was to use this crisis to reveal India's nuclear capability, but this was not done either. In any event 'Brass tacks' went on and to the outside world the exercise looked like a massive mobilisation now that Indian reserves from south and north-eastern India had entered the picture. On 21 January the Pakistani reserves (Multan division) started to withdraw and the threat was over. Given this pattern of Indo–Pakistani interactions, the assessment of the International Institute for Strategic Studies is wrong. The IISS made the following points:

1. First of all, in mid-summer India, in an attempt to block infiltration by Sikh terrorists for Pakistan, was reported to be amassing troops at the border. 2. Then Pakistan, in a departure from its usual training pattern, positioned some 14 of its 17 divisions at the frontier with India. 3. The crisis created by this military manoeuvring was eventually defused in February 1987 in a series of high-level talks at which a partial withdrawal of the troops massed on either side of the border was agreed, earlier pledges not to attack each other were repeated and both countries vowed to 'exercise maximum restraint and to avoid all provocative actions along the border'.[7]

By 21 January 1987 the crisis was over. Then the world media, the prime minister of India and the president of Pakistan entered the picture. The Indian media had maintained a silence during the crisis for reasons best known to it. Senior editors had received their first briefing on 18 or 19 January 1987 but nothing was reported. They received another briefing on 22 January for almost four hours by General Sunderji, and then the Indian papers started to publish articles on the crisis.

Fourth, *problems of inadequate communications and embroidered intelligence inputs*: 'Brass tacks' achieved its basic military aims, that is, the rapid deployment and withdrawal of forces in desert warfare conditions, and to achieve a close coordination between civilian and military agencies for this purpose. However the exercise produced a political crisis. 'Brass tacks' was not, in the opinion of the Indian authorities involved in the exercise, meant to signal a threat to Pakistan; yet it was seen as such by the Pakistani military and intelligence machinery. In hindsight the process of crisis escalation and deescalation between India and Pakistan looks like shadow boxing on both sides, however it must be recognised that the exercise revealed a lack of adequate communication arrangements, and this lack contributed to the escalation. The Indian government failed adequately to communicate the real purpose of 'Brass tacks' to Pakistan. Indian and Pakistani intelligence agencies have limited intelligence-gathering capabilities and yet they have a great responsibility to provide intelligence inputs in a timely fashion. Under these circumstances the intelligence services invent and interpret intelligence in a way that feeds the worst-case scenarios of the policy makers. This approach serves the institutional interests of the agencies and the career interests of members of the intelligence services. If a crisis is avoided, their intelligence warnings are projected as timely and effective. If a crises escalates, their worst-case projections are justified. The problem is that intelligence inputs have a limited factual basis and are heavily embroidered. In the case of 'Brass tacks', when the crisis was over Pakistani army officers, in private conversations with Indian officers, pointed to the alarming and distorted inputs by Pakistani intelligence as a factor that led to the crisis, the events of which are summarised in Figure 6.1.

A number of problems were thrown up by Indian and Pakistani decision making and behaviour in this crisis. There were three India-centred problems:

1. Lack of adequate Indian military communications with Pakistan regarding the nature and scope of 'Brass tacks'.
2. Lack of adequate communications between the Indian prime minister and defence minister, Rajiv Gandhi, and the Indian military staff.
3. Lack of adequate communications between the Indian government, the Indian press and the Indian people about the nature and scope of 'Brass tacks' and India's Pakistan policy.

There were two Pakistan-centred problems.

1. Lack of adequate Pakistani military communication with India regarding the reason(s) for the forward movement of Pakistani reserves.
2. Pakistani military intelligence was exaggerated.

Pakistan's and India's military and diplomatic agenda and behaviour in the 1989–90 crisis

When the 1987 crisis started India and Pakistan were already at odds. The 1989–90 crisis commenced with Pakistani provocation and threatened Indian retaliation. Deescalation and crisis management followed, but there was no settlement of the underlying conflict. The issues, the players and their calculations, and the regional and international environment differed between the two crises. The 1987 crisis occurred in the Cold War era, the Soviets were still in Afghanistan and Pakistan was important to the United States. The 1989–90 crisis occurred in the post-Cold-War era, the Soviets had left Afghanistan and US–Pakistan nuclear differences had begun to cloud the bilateral relationship. The

India and Pakistan in the 1980s and Early 1990s

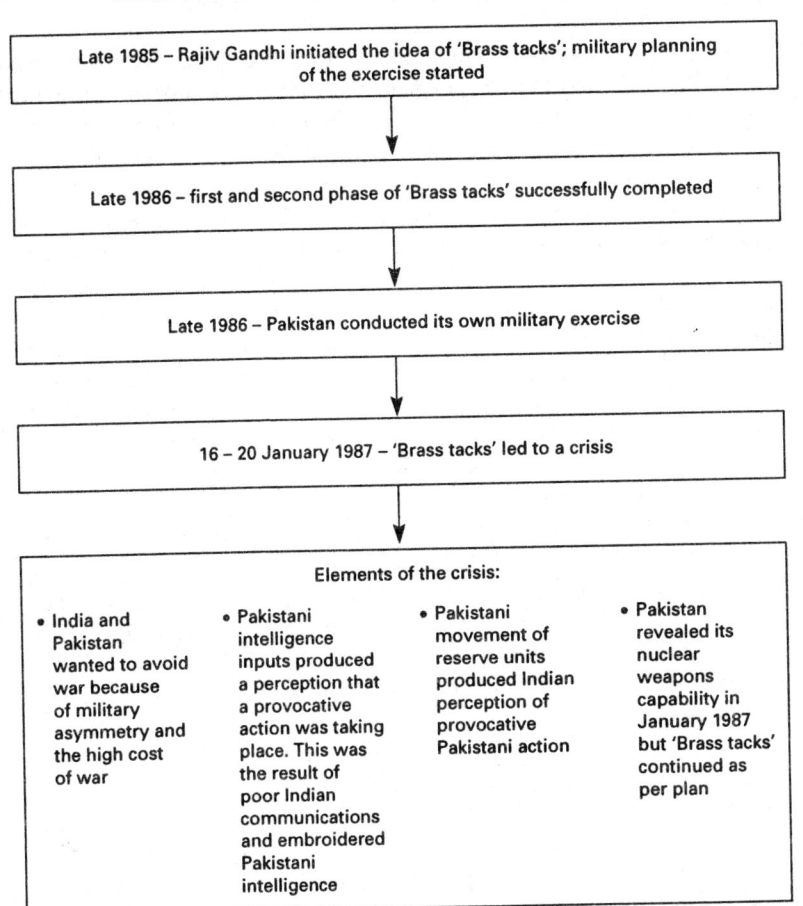

```
┌─────────────────────────────────────────────────────────────────────┐
│ Late 1985 – Rajiv Gandhi initiated the idea of 'Brass tacks';       │
│          military planning of the exercise started                  │
└─────────────────────────────────────────────────────────────────────┘
                                  │
                                  ▼
┌─────────────────────────────────────────────────────────────────────┐
│ Late 1986 – first and second phase of 'Brass tacks' successfully    │
│                            completed                                │
└─────────────────────────────────────────────────────────────────────┘
                                  │
                                  ▼
┌─────────────────────────────────────────────────────────────────────┐
│ Late 1986 – Pakistan conducted its own military exercise            │
└─────────────────────────────────────────────────────────────────────┘
                                  │
                                  ▼
┌─────────────────────────────────────────────────────────────────────┐
│ 16 – 20 January 1987 – 'Brass tacks' led to a crisis                │
└─────────────────────────────────────────────────────────────────────┘
                                  │
                                  ▼
```

Elements of the crisis:

- India and Pakistan wanted to avoid war because of military asymmetry and the high cost of war
- Pakistani intelligence inputs produced a perception that a provocative action was taking place. This was the result of poor Indian communications and embroidered Pakistani intelligence
- Pakistani movement of reserve units produced Indian perception of provocative Pakistani action
- Pakistan revealed its nuclear weapons capability in January 1987 but 'Brass tacks' continued as per plan

Figure 6.1 Summary of the 1987 Indo–Pakistani crisis

common denominator lay in the opportunity taken by Pakistan during both crises to advance its nuclear posturing and reveal its nuclear advances.

During the 1989–90 crisis Pakistan crossed the 'red line' in its nuclear work, which triggered the sanctions required in the Pressler Amendment. Our conjecture is that Pakistan clearly anticipated in 1989–90 that it would not get the 1990 certification by the Bush administration. Consequently the nature of Pakistan's nuclear strategy changed in this period. Several calculations dominated Pakistan's strategic behaviour at that time.

Pakistan saw two advantages in seeking a nuclear weapons capability. First, if Pakistan had nuclear arms and India did not, then war with Pakistan would no longer be an option for India. This could produced increased Indian political irresolution vis-à-vis Pakistan, and it could increase the margin of safety for Pakistan to conduct a proxy war in Punjab and Kashmir. Second, news of a Pakistani bomb could push or panic India into overt nuclearisation, which would reduce Western pressure on Pakistan. An overt Indian nuclear weapons programme was likely to legitimise Pakistan's clandestine nuclear activities, and Western attention would probably shift away from its focus on Pakistan, in the context of US legislation, towards India. The premise here is that the only thing that worried Pakistan was Western diplomatic pressure; if this could be diluted or diverted to India on the nuclear issue, then it would be a gain for Pakistani diplomacy on the nuclear and Kashmiri questions.

1989–90 also revealed a new Pakistani strategy on Kashmir and confidence that it was a winnable strategy. In essence Pakistani thinking at that time was based on several calculations. First, war was not really an option for India – Indian elites and public opinion did not want it. The break-up of Pakistan was likely to increase India's responsibilities. For example, who would run Sind if India won? In a war India would be bloodied even if Pakistan were defeated. Second, the Pakistani military could not survive an open-ended war with India and for this reason a majority of Pakistani generals did not want war. Third, given the above, it made sense to push India into a war situation by escalating Pakistani intervention in Indian Punjab and Kashmir. This would raise the costs of Indian defence. Hence a low-cost proxy war in Punjab and Kashmir made sense to the Pakistani military and intelligence community for several reasons. It would be sweet revenge for Pakistan's 1971 defeat in Bangladesh. It would lead to the recovery of Indian Kashmir, which should have gone to Pakistan in 1947–48. It would keep India on edge and it would foster Indian political and military irresolution in relation to Pakistan. Pakistan's aim was to develop a low-cost proxy war to force India to think about peace at any cost to India.

Pakistan's army chief, Aslam Beg, clearly spelled out his assessment and the Pakistani strategy. He emphasised that Pakistan had failed in earlier wars (1948, 1965 and 1971) because of a lack of strategic vision and because of inadequate political preparation of the people. In 1947–48, knowing that the Kashmiri people were not entirely on Pakistan's side, it led the attack with irregular forces to create chaos and make it difficult for India to defend Kashmir. Pakistan almost won,

India and Pakistan in the 1980s and Early 1990s

but the Pakistani irregulars failed to gain Srinagar. Nonetheless Pakistan gained a political advantage by making Kashmir a disputed issue, and it gained a military advantage by securing parts of the old Jammu and Kashmir kingdoms. The 1965 Pakistani campaign in Kashmir (carried out by Pakistani-backed guerillas) and the 1965 Indo–Pakistani war revealed that the Kashmiris were not at one with Pakistan. Pakistan gained no additional political or military advantage. Indeed the 1965 war gave Pakistan a bad name and it produced disadvantages for Ayub Khan, the army and Pakistanis in general. In sum, according to General Aslam Beg, Pakistan failed in 1948 and 1965 because the people were not ready for insurrection, they were politically ill-prepared and the irregular forces were undisciplined. The solution to this was to prepare the people for war by setting up two low-cost proxy war theatres – Indian Punjab and Indian Kashmir. This was a new element in Pakistani strategic planning after 1984; another was that Pakistan's nuclear activity and Indo-Pakistani normalisation talks provided a political cover for Pakistan's preparation for these low-cost proxy wars.

This is the background to the events that produced the December 1989–April 1990 crisis. Militancy in Indian Kashmir started on 31 July 1988. In 1989 a new Indian government was formed and it sought good relations with Pakistan. Indar Gujral, president of the Indo-Pakistani friendship society, became India's foreign minister, and he sought improved bilateral relations with Pakistan. For the first time a Kashmiri Muslim became the Indian home minister; he was in charge of internal and border security. In December 1989 Benazir Bhutto's Pakistan used an Inter-Services Intelligence (ISI) strategy, to which Aslam Beg lent his mind, to increase support for Kashmiri insurgency. The need for this came because of a change a government in Delhi. This confirms the theme in Pakistani strategic behaviour that was noted earlier; that is, it makes sense for Pakistan's military-dominated government to encourage militancy, activism and interventionism in Indian border provinces at times when the Indian government wants Indo–Pakistani normalisation (which is not always the case), and when India seems to be moving towards political normalisation in Indian Punjab and Kashmir. In Pakistan's strategy, Indian Punjab was linked to Indian Kashmir. Kashmir remained the prize but insurgency in Punjab increased Delhi's political and military costs and reduced India's confidence in holding Punjab and, consequently Kashmir.

How did the Indian government react to the crisis between December 1989 and April 1990? The crisis was played out at four levels.

First, at the Indo–Pakistani military level the military hot lines were active between the two countries. Hence there was no danger of war at any point in the crisis, unlike in the 1987 crisis.

Second, in the context of Indian politics the central government acted in a stern way against the Kashmiris. This was meant to identify the Kashmiri militants but it also had a negative effect. It humiliated the Kashmiris because large-scale counterinsurgency operations affected Kashmiri civilians as well.

Third, in Pakistani politics, between January and February 1990 Punjab premier Nawaz Sharif (Benazar Bhutto was the elected prime minister and Sharif and Bhutto were political enemies) hijacked the political process through an anti-India Kashmir campaign. The Sharif–Bhutto rivalry is a constant factor in contemporary Pakistani politics and Sharif's militancy on the Kashmir issue put pressure on Benazir Bhutto to do something. By early April 1990 she had started to talk like her late father, about a 1000-year war to liberate Kashmir.

Finally, on 9 April V. P. Singh, prime minister and defence minister of India, made a public statement that India must be prepared for war. This was merely a political signal to Pakistan. Nothing changed much on the ground but the Singh statement shifted the Indo–Pakistani relationship to the level of a political–psychological drama and a war of words. According to V. P. Singh's critics the political signal should have been given earlier to cool Pakistan's political rhetoric. In any event it cooled Pakistan's rhetorical enthusiasm for a 1000 year war but the ISI–army strategy to carry on with the proxy war in Punjab and Kashmir continued.

The matrix of players, concepts, calculations and issues

Thus far the discussion has outlined the patterns and processes of each crisis – who did what, when and why. The players were Indians and Pakistanis. (Americans were also players in both crises but lack of space has prevented us from studying the US role at this time.) The relationship between key players, their calculations, the issues and the underlying strategic concepts in each case is summarised below.

In the 1987 crisis the size of India's decision-making circle was small but the policy issues and debates showed a variety of cross-currents and fluidity. The key player in the decision to initiate the 'Brass tacks' exercise, which led to the 1987 crisis, was Rajiv Gandhi, and the issue was the need to improve Indian military training. To this end he wanted to organise a major military exercise, aimed at improving and testing Indian military logistics, although it was not believed that a war with Pakistan was necessary. In the second decision-making case, the key players were Rajiv Gandhi and Indian finance officials, and the issue concerned the future of Indian nuclear weapon development. Should India enter the nuclear sphere? How much would it cost? Should India sign the NPT? These questions indicated a softness in the nuclear stance of this body of decision-makers, and it showed a divergence from the officially declared policy of rejecting the NPT and maintaining the nuclear option.

In the third decision-making case the players consisted to Rajiv Gandhi and Indian military officials, and the issue was Indian missile development. The calculation was that Agni missile development must go forward to keep India abreast of modern technology and to develop a meaningful capability against China and Pakistan. This indicated a firmness in the pursuit of missile capability and contrasted with India's reluctance to undertake further nuclear tests after the 1974 explosion.

The players in fourth decision-making case were Rajiv Gandhi and Indian military and civilian officials, and the issue concerned India's South Asian policy. This case showed a broad consensus. The calculation was that India should be responsible for keeping regional order and it was in the interest of others to accept this approach. To maintain regional peace India needed military strength. Here the strategic concept stressed the value of a regional order under Indian leadership.

The fifth decision-making case involved Indian military officials and Rajiv Gandhi, and the issue concerned the quality and stability of Indian civil–military relations. The issue revealed a gap between the expectations of Indian military officials and the uneven quality of prime ministerial direction of defence affairs. Could India have an effective military posture and an effective policy if the prime ministerial direction was amateurish and the political will was ambivalent? The 1987 crisis highlighted this issue.

The sixth decision-making case was dominated by Indian military leaders, especially General K. Sunderji. The key issue concerned the value of war planning in peacetime that took into account changes in India's military capabilities and the value of adopting new military tactics to deal with possible contingencies in the Indo-Pakistani military theatre. Specifically, the intention was to develop methods for the rapid deployment and withdrawal of modern military formations and equipment for desert warfare, and to organise the 'Brass tacks' exercise on that basis. The context of this approach was a belief that war with Pakistan was not likely at that time, nor was it desirable.

In the seventh decision-making case, the key players were General

Sunderji and the Indian defence elite, and as in the second case the issue concerned nuclear weapon development. The professional view was that there must be a meaningful Indian nuclear weapon capability in relation to both China and Pakistan. The underlying strategic concept was that India needed to avoid the danger of nuclear blackmail by possessing a nuclear capability.

Finally, the eighth decision-making case involved the Indian military and the Indian space organisation, and the issue was space and missile development. The calculation was that Agni (an intermediate range missile) must be developed to give India a plausible nuclear defence against China should it become dangerous in the future. The strategic concept was to move towards a nuclear deterrence stance by possessing a missile delivery capability.

In the 1987 crisis the size of Pakistan's decision-making circle too was small, and the policy issues and debates showed a variety of crosscurrents and fluidity, as in the Indian case.

In the first decision-making case, President Zia-ul-Haq was the key player, along with the Pakistani military and intelligence agencies. The issue was to defend Pakistan against an Indian attack. Zia's plan was to engage in military brinkmanship by the forward movement of Pakistani forces, including its reserve formation, in response to India's 'Brass tacks' exercise. Zia's move was meant to induce Indian restraint, disorient India's war planning and test India's intentions. The strategic concept was to deter India by conventional means.

The key players in the second decision-making case were President Zia-ul-Haq, A. Q. Khan (the head of the nuclear enrichment project) and the military and intelligence agencies. The issue concerned Pakistan's nuclear activity and its stance. The intention was to convey to India and the United States that Pakistan possessed a nuclear weapon capability. The aims were to deter India by nuclear means and to induce the United States to attend to Pakistan's security needs. The strategic concept was that an increased Pakistani nuclear capability would act as an equaliser in a situation of Indo–Pakistani conventional weapon asymmetry.

The third decision-making case was dominated by Pakistan's intelligence apparatus. The issue concerned the role of intelligence in increasing a sense of danger rather than in setting problems. The theory was that military intelligence, which was based on few true facts and some wrong projections of enemy intentions and capability, was fostering a crisis atmosphere, and that it was serving the careers and institutional interests of intelligence officers rather than the national interest. In

1987 secret intelligence inputs into the political decision-making process manipulated the diplomatic and military behaviour of Pakistan.

In the 1989-90 crisis the size of the Indian and Pakistani decision-making units remained small and secretive; however the issues and calculations moved Indo-Pakistani relations from a state of ritualistic confrontation to a potentially deadly encounter. Because Pakistan instigated this crisis, we will first discuss its decision-making process. There were four strands to decision making in Pakistan at the time. The first concerned the belief of the Pakistani military and intelligence organisations that the Indian government was on the defensive in internal affairs, that Kashmir could be gained by force, and that the defeat of Pakistan in 1971 could be avenged. The aim was threefold: to encourage low-cost proxy warfare in Indian Punjab and Indian Kashmir, to avoid a general war with India, and to launch a public relations 'peace' initiative towards India that showed Pakistan's willingness to normalise relations and secure a bilateral non-proliferation deal.

The second strand involved the Pakistani military and nuclear establishments and it showed an appreciation of the value of an enhanced nuclear weapons capability and posture. The benefits would be threefold: it would deter India from war and neutralise India's advantage in conventional arms; it would enable Pakistan to intervene in Indian Punjabi and Kashmiri affairs without fear of a 1965-type retribution; and it would panic India into adopting an overt nuclear stance and this would result in US pressure on India. These calculations indicated connection between Pakistan's nuclear policy and its attitude towards Indian border provinces.

The third strand involved Pakistan's prime minister, the Foreign Office and the anti nuclear lobby. It stressed the value of regional non-proliferation and Indo-Pakistani nuclear disarmament brokered by the United States. Three purposes would be served: it would provide a cover for Pakistan's nuclear activities, in which case it was not intended as a disarmament measure; and at the same time it would further Pakistan's quest to be seen as a responsible regional and a global citizen in the important issue of non-proliferation; finally, if India agreed to nuclear disarmament, that would curb Indian strategic power. The fourth and final strand involved Benazir Bhutto, the prime minister, and the issue was her political struggle with Nawaz Sharif. In the 1989-90 crisis Benazir Bhutto used her father's rhetoric when calling for a 1000 year was to liberate Kashmir. Her political aim was twofold: to neutralise the opposition of Nawaz Sharif, who argued that Benazir Bhutto was soft on the Indians; and to downgrade Indo-Pakistani normalisation proceedings because historically Indo–Pakistani peace moves had provided Pakistani political leaders with no mileage in domestic politics.

In this crisis the Indian decision-making process had a single strand and was coherent in its approach to the issues of Kashmiri insurgency and border security with Pakistan. The aims of the Indian political and military leaders were as follows: stern measures were required to deny victory to Kashmiri insurgents and their Pakistani supporters; security of the Indian borders had to be maintained at all costs; a general war with Pakistan was unnecessary and avoidable; a public threat to fight another bloody war with Pakistan was necessary to calm the political temperature in Pakistani politics about Kashmiri and Indian affairs; and a strong public stance was needed to assure domestic public opinion about India's capacity to deter Pakistani adventurism. The 1989–90 crisis was resolved by political measures, and unlike the 1987 crisis it did not require Indian military manoeuvres or military signalling.

The role of the nuclear factor in the two crises

There were several instances of nuclear diplomacy in these Indo–Pakistani crises. In a loose way 'deterrence' defined Indo–Pakistani relations in the two crises. In 1987 and in 1989–90 the Pakistani government was deterred from going to war with India because of a fear of the consequences. This was a result of India's military superiority in conventional armament. However Pakistan was not deterred from its strategy of conducting a proxy war in Kashmir and Punjab. Despite massive arms aid from the United States in the 1980s, Pakistan failed to equal India's military strength. Furthermore, in the post-Afghanistan, post-Cold-War era, Pakistan's geostrategic value to the United States declined. These changes increased Pakistan's military and nuclear dilemma, and they cemented the antiwar attitude of the majority of Pakistani elites and opinion makers.

At the same time India was deterred from waging war against Pakistan. Even if it were to prevail militarily, the social costs of a military conflict were likely to be high given the religious dimension of the Indo–Pakistani conflict. Also, who would run key parts of a broken up Pakistan if India won the war? Did it make sense for India to go to war with Pakistan when it could be deterred by India's advantage in conventional arms?

Beyond this loose kind of deterrence lay a complex nuclear debate in Pakistan and India. Both countries had a choice between nuclear ambiguity, explicit nuclear deterrence and negotiated arms control.

India and Pakistan in the 1980s and Early 1990s

For Pakistan, nuclear ambiguity would have required a triad of non-renunciation of the nuclear option, a nuclear weapons capability and mixed nuclear signals. Explicit nuclear deterrence would have required the development of a stable regime, a well-defined intelligence, command, control and communications system, and a second-strike capability. Negotiated arms control would have required acceptance of the NPT or a regional deal. Each approach had its advantages and disadvantages, but nuclear ambiguity was safer than coming out in favour of nuclear arms.

Explicit nuclear deterrence has many advantagegs:

1. It removes dependence on allies and imported arms.
2. It strengthens a country's bargaining position.
3. It enhances national prestige as it signals technical competence and political will.
4. In the case of Pakistan, Pakistan can not achieve military parity with India, and if there is a high risk of Indo–Pakistani conflict, nuclear deterrence will offer the only hope of restraint, stability and peace. If India and Pakistan go nuclear simultaneously, deterrence and restraint will exist, as in East–West affairs in the past.
5. Overt Pakistani nuclearisation followed by a negotiated regional system of inspections and safeguards could lead to mutual restraint and trust.
6. Nuclear deterrence would give Pakistan a free hand to promote proxy wars in India.

Negotiated arms control too could offer Pakistan many advantages:

1. Pakistan's signature on the NPT could reduce regional tension.
2. Its adherence to the NPT would isolate India and increase world pressure on India to sign also.
3. Being a signatory could reduce the cost of participating in the Indo–Pakistani arms race.
4. Being a signatory could enable Pakistan to obtain substantial compensation from the United States.

Pakistan's current nuclear ambiguity has two disadvantages:

1. Nuclear ambiguity is creating uncertainty in Indo–Pakistani affairs and this is perpetuating the arms race. With uncertainty irrational decisions are possible.
2. Ambiguity is adversely affecting its aid relationship with the United States.

Explicit nuclear deterrence would have two disadvantages for Pakistan:

1. Evidence that Pakistan possesses a bomb would attract US sanctions.
2. Fear of the Pakistan bomb being an 'Islamic bomb' would arouse global concern because of the preoccupation with Islamic fundamentalism.

Negotiated arms control would have two disadvantages:

1. Pakistan could court Indian hegemony.
2. Pakistan's internal balance of power would be upset by internal opposition to the NPT.[8]

Between 1986 and 1990 Pakistan moved beyond the Reagan–Zia understanding not to cross the 5 per cent enrichment red line and the Zia–Khan posturing about Pakistan's nuclear capability emerged. These changes strengthened the triad in Pakistan's policy of nuclear ambiguity, but it did not take Pakistan into an overt nuclear stance. Before, during and after the 1987 and 1990 crises Pakistan's policy remained firmly anchored in this position. The weight of the deterrent aspect seemed to grow, but at the same time disadvantages surfaced.

The framework of India's nuclear calculations before, during and after the 1987 and 1990 crises differs from that of Pakistan. The picture is as follows.

For India, nuclear ambiguity required conventional deterrence based on military asymmetry, dual-use (civil–military) nuclear development and an ambiguous nuclear deterrence posture.[9] The requirement for explicit nuclear deterrence was the same as in Pakistan's case. A policy of negotiated arms control would have required adherence to the NPT or a regional deal. India saw two advantages in a policy of nuclear ambiguity:

1. This combination, rather than adopting a pronounced nuclear weapons posture, was diplomatically (externally) and politically (domestically) safe and it was adequate for national defence in foreseeable circumstance. It put pressure on China and Pakistan to exercise nuclear restraint vis-à-vis India.
2. It kept the United States attentive to India's security needs. India saw no advantage in an explicit nuclear policy or in negotiating over arms control.

Nuclear ambiguity no doubt had two disadvantages for India:

1. It perpetuated the nuclear controversy within India and between India and the United States.

2. If India's nuclear ambiguity had not been finely tuned, it could have negatively affected US–India relations.

Explicit nuclear deterrence would have been disadvantageous in that evidence of an assembled Indian bomb would have attracted US sanctions. Finally, negotiated arms control would have had several disadvantages:

1. China was a critical part of India's threat perception and therefore an Indo–Pakistani deal would have been inadequate by itself.[10]
2. Kashmir, not the nuclear issue, was the acid test in Indo–Pakistani relations, and a nuclear deal would not have addressed the fundamentals of the Indo–Pakistani conflict.
3. Arms control and arms reduction without threat reduction would have been a fraud. Threat reduction would have required mutual obligations between nuclear powers and threshold nations.[11]

SUMMARY

The nuclear issue has become a part of Indo–Pakistani crisis behaviour but it does not fit neatly into Western deterrence and arms control theory. There is an element of ambiguous nuclear deterrence at work in Indo–Pakistani strategic affairs, but care must be taken to study its parameters and role in a context-specific manner. Care must also be taken not to generalise and project the East–West nuclear deterrence concept onto South Asia. Several differences between superpower and South Asian circumstances justify such caution. First, the United States and the USSR were strategic adversaries but they did not hate each other culturally. In Pakistan's India policy, hatred of Hindus is a factor. Second, East–West arms control, especially after the Helsinki Agreement, was based on an acknowledgement of the utility of territorial status quo in arms control dialogues. This condition is absent in Pakistan's quest for a bilateral arms control deal with India. Nevertheless, as this chapter has shown, India and Pakistan have managed to develop a relationship of competitive coexistence.

7 Future Prospects

We have outlined the key elements that define the history, the process of development of South Asian international relations and the structure of the region's power relationships from 1947 to the mid-1990s. At the same time it must be recognised that the end of the Cold War has in part changed the international context in which South Asian international relations evolved in the past. A major consequence of the collapse of the USSR is that the overlay of superpower competition in regions of conflict (the Middle East, the Gulf, South Asia, South-East Asia, North Asia and southern Africa) is no longer a factor in regional diplomatic and military affairs. In the absence of the Soviet threat in these regions, US governmental interests and policies have changed to an extent: management of its rivalry with Moscow is no longer an element in US diplomacy and military policy. However the change in US policies may be studied more as an adjustment to current realities, including a preoccupation with the future of the US economy; and it may be studied as a continuation of an old US preoccupation, namely to prevent or at least slow the emergence of new independent centres of power and strategic thought that increase the uncertainties and costs of US diplomatic and military planning.

The Cold War has ended but in the Asia–Pacific sphere the secondary cold War Struggles of the past have emerged on to centre stage. The struggle between the United States and China remains sharp and it is occurring in an ideological sphere – for the United States the main issues are Chinese human rights abuses and lack of democracy, while for China, the main issue is US interference – and in a strategic sphere, where the issues concern the future of strategic relations and arms control in the region. Another struggle is between the United States and Japan. This pertains overtly to the economic sphere but there may also be a cultural undercurrent concerning the future destiny of Japan in Asian and world affairs. A third arena of struggle concerns the United States and regional powers – Iran, India and North Korea. Although the cases differ, a common theme runs through them all. It pertains to the US government's interest in disarming regional military powers, reducing the military and diplomatic independence of these countries and their ability to pursue their interests, and reducing if not eliminating the costs to the United States should these independent centres of power fully emerge to challenge US authority in regional and international affairs.

The end of the Cold War has created a belief in the United States that without the protection of the USSR these countries are now vulnerable to US pressure and blandishments. The model is the nuclear disarmament of post-apartheid South Africa. Just as US pressure led to destruction of South Africa's nuclear weapons the new struggle is aimed at achieving the same results – even though circumstances vary in Iran, India and North Korea. Here the US strategic concept had and still has a timeless value: it was not limited to the Cold War and the US–Soviet conflict; it has nothing much to do with the struggle between communism and capitalism or between democracy and dictatorship. The goal is to maintain US hegemony in the strategic and economic spheres in order to make the world safe for US interests, and to enhance the United States' freedom to advance its interests. This kind of freedom has nothing to do with liberty and democracy except in a superficial, cosmetic sense. In other words, the end of the Cold War has changed the cast by removing an old face from the stage, namely the USSR. But it has not changed the strategic orientation, the fundamental interests and the methods of the US government.

In the Asia–Pacific sphere this observation applies equally to other players, namely China, Japan, India and other lesser powers in the region. The United States and China have adjusted their military activities to the new realities. For China the process of military downsising and modernisation preceded the end of the Cold War and continued thereafter. For the United States the end of the Cold War also allowed a downsising of the US military presence in the Pacific region, but the adjustment was related to perceived threats. For the other players, military modernisation continues. There is renewed interest in the military development of the South-East Asian states, Japan and Australia. Recent studies point to a process of militarisation in the Asia–Pacific sphere when the end of the Cold War ought to have brought about the opposite. Obviously self-reliance remains the basis of each country's national security rather than dependence on international regimes in security planning. The United States is seeking the disarmament of others; not its own disarmament. It favours international regimes that reduce the military capability of its enemies or potential enemies; it does not promote or encourage international regimes that affect its freedom of action and its interests. Selective disarmament of enemies and selective development of friendly regimes to constrain enemies is the essence of the US approach to multilateral and bilateral diplomacy. This is also true of China and other Asian states.

These observations lead to the following conclusion. Even though the Cold War has ended and even though India is democratic, it is still attracting US pressure in the strategic sphere because it is independent minded and has a military capacity and an economic strength that add to US strategic planning costs. At present the pressure is limited to the nuclear sphere, but if the United States succeeds in this area then the pressure is likely to extend to the question of downsizing India's conventional military machinery to what the US government (with a Pakistani input) thinks is appropriate or legitimate for self-defence. Then will come the question of settling the Kashmir issue, which will diminish India's security and prestige. These pressures are placing India and the United States on a confrontational course in the 1990s.

We have studied the regional system of seven geographically contiguous and interactive states. Implicit here is the notion of boundaries between South Asia and the Gulf, between South Asia and Central Asia (including Tibet) and between South Asia and Southeastern Asia. The idea of systemic boundaries is well understood in the academic literature.[1] Boundaries mean that diplomatic, military, economic and cultural interactions between states and societies located across boundaries are less continuous, less intense and less significant compared with interactions among states and societies that are located within the geographical and systemic boundaries of a 'regional security complex', to use Buzan's term.

The boundaries that separate and distinguish the regions mentioned above defined regional international relations during the Cold War. A consequence of the end of the Cold War and of the break-up of the USSR is that the traditional or historical regional distinctions and boundaries that separate the regions are eroding. Although the process of erosion started during the Cold War it did not gain momentum until after the Cold War had ended. Consider the following changes in the strength of boundaries over the years.

First, the Soviet invasion of Afghanistan, and the flow of refugees and drugs from Afghanistan to Pakistan have significantly eroded the Pakistan–Afghanistan divide. Second, before and immediately after the communist revolution in China in 1949, the China–India boundary was porous: there was limited commercial, political and religious interaction between South Asia and Tibet. But when China and India went to war in 1962 the interactions ceased and a boundary was created.

Future Prospects

In 1993 China and India agreed to develop border trade and to withdraw their troops from the border areas. This agreement has made the border porous again to a limited extent in the context of an improved bilateral relationship. In this case there is a dynamic pattern of a boundary being porous, then solid, then porous again.

Third, following the detachment of Burma (now Myanmar) from India by the British imperial government in 1937, the Myanmar boundary remained porous; political, commercial, military and religious interactions were the main features of Indo-Myanmar relations. But with the emergence of Sino-Indian hostility in 1962 Myanmar distanced itself from India and a stronger boundary was instituted. With the exception of border smuggling and guerrilla activity in Indian and Burmese border provinces between the 1960s and the 1980s, the barrier between South Asia and Myanmar grew higher; that is, commercial and strategic interactions between South Asian states and Myanmar reduced while interactions increased between Myanmar and China from 1988 onwards.

Systematic and geographical boundaries of a region are not like frontiers; they are not buffers. They are not necessarily arenas where competing external forces interact. Boundaries are like fences that demarcate the limits of regional interactions. Boundaries differ from borders of countries within a region – boundaries may coincide with borders but they may also extend beyond them. Thus South Asia's regional boundaries extended to Tibet, Afghanistan and Myanmar and they included the economic zones of the South Asian states in relation to the Bay of Bengal, the Arabian sea and the Indian Ocean. However, the Gulf region did not fall within the region's systemic boundaries. An awareness of these boundaries has governed the conduct of official business of the South Asian states since 1947; they have also been recognised by the great powers and other members of the system of world states since 1947. No international law has defined South Asia's regional diplomatic and military boundaries. However the diplomatic and military practices of South Asian states between 1947 and the 1980s produced a pattern of regional and international diplomatic and military behaviour that is widely held to define the legitimacy of regional international relations. In this sense the boundaries reflect the empirical realities of South Asian international relations since 1947.

The Cold War has ended. The USSR has been eliminated as a factor in South Asian international relations following the collapse of Moscow as a centre of independent international thought, and following its inability to project Russian power into the Third World. There is an ongoing process of normalisation of relations between China and India.

From this one might surmise that the pattern of South Asian international relations is now firmly established. Such a conclusion is simplistic. There are new forces at work that are using the lull of the post-Cold-War world to put pressure on the Indocentric South Asian system of states and its regional boundaries. Apart from the pressure in the strategic sphere that is being placed on India by the Clinton administration, summarised below are other developments that must be included in any discussion of the future prospects of South Asian international relations.

First, *China's strategic orientation in relation to the peripheries of South Asia*. China and India have diffused the chill in their bilateral relations, a few trade routes have opened up in the border with Tibet, troop withdrawals are being phased in to correspond with confidence-building measures, and there is less tension on the border. Still there is much suspicion in Indian thinking about China and in Chinese thinking about India. There is a nagging worry about the new Chinese factor in Myanmar and the implications of Chinese actions in Pakistan and in the Gulf area. The worry relates to the fluidity in the regional environment from the Gulf to Myanmar and it concerns China's quest to be an economic and military superpower, a real Middle Kingdom in the twenty-first century. India does not figure in China's long-term calculations because India is not a major player in the global scene. Only the United States, former Soviet republics, Japan and Europe count in the Chinese view.

The end of the Cold War has changed the strategic environment and China is taking full advantage of the fluid situation. It seeks peace in the short term but its policy is simultaneously to make deals with the United States while blowing the whistle against it. It goes along with the United States on non-proliferation, trade and regional security issues in the Korean peninsula and South-East Asia, two spheres that are close to Chinese economic and strategic interests. Here China is getting close to Western mainstream concerns. But it is continuing to exert its power and authority by supplying missiles and arms to the Middle East and Pakistan, by developing a strategic foothold in Myanmar and the Bay of Bengal; and by using force to assert its territorial claims in the South China Sea.

China lacks the leverage to change European international relations. It cannot benefit by keeping South-East Asia in a melting pot because economic compulsions and proximity to China requires peaceful economic development of South-East Asia and of China's southern and coastal area. But it is not necessarily in China's interest to see the Gulf/Middle East settle down to a peaceful existence. With its missile diplomacy, China has been involved with Saudi Arabia, where the monarchical regime is despised by Iran and Iraq and where there is a potential power vacuum should the royal household fall to the demands of democratic or religious forces. China sells arms to Iran because it too blows the whistle against Western intervention in Gulf affairs and because China sees merit in the view that each nation has an inherent right to defend itself and to buy arms for this purpose. Chinese arms supplies to Pakistan are an expression of an old special relationship that was formed during the Cold War days: with the US embargo of military supplies to Pakistan, Pakistan is now even more in the Chinese sphere of influence.

In the context of US–China strategic competition and ideological struggle in the post-Cold-War era, instability in the area does not bode well for the United States, the lone superpower today, nor for India, the primary power in the subcontinent. In Pakistan the Shia–Sunni divide is now permanent. In recent years riots, curfews and the murder of Shia and Sunni clerics has become a regular feature in Pakistan. Afghanistan is a festering sore that cannot be healed because no one has a decisive advantage. If the Saudi Royal household falls, the United States will lose a lot, but if Pakistan and Afghanistan remain unstable, the United States will lose nothing. For the United States, the risks are high in the Gulf area, but for China, instability is fine in a faraway region if it reduces US authority. But stability is needed in areas close to the Chinese frontiers, such as South-East Asia, the Korean peninsula and Myanmar. The latter is a wedge between the Indian subcontinent and South-East Asia. It flanks the Bay of Bengal and the Malacca Straits. For China, Myanmar is an advanced strategic post where geography is on China's side, and its plains and economic resources are attractive for Chinese border trade and political and cultural influence. Myanmar has valuable natural resources. In contrast Nepal has no real geographical or natural advantage. Nepal has no strategic value for China; it has a nuisance value to keep India on edge, but now even this is limited. Through Myanmar, China could in the future put pressure on the north-east of India, on the Bay of Bengal and on the Malacca Straits in a worst-case scenario. But even if China does not act aggressively, without Myanmar on their side, India, Bangladesh and Thailand cannot come together. These are some of the obvious effects of China's pivotal position in the post-Cold-War era, although China's strategy took shape in 1988–89 before the Cold War ended.

What are the factors and the pattern of Chinese activities in Myanmar?

Up to 1988 China supported its ideological allies in Myanmar, the communists. Thereafter it switched its support to that state's military. After 1988 the focus was on giving China's backward Yunnan province, which faces Myanmar, a new hinterland. With about $ 1.2 billion of military aid and somewhat less than a billion in economic aid, China gained a strategic foothold for about 100 kilometres inside Myanmar's border with Yunnan province. Mandalay is now practically a Chinese town. Roads to Rangoon and Mandalay are being upgraded by Chinese experts and Chinese currency is in use in the new Chinese hinterland, where trade and tourism is growing. The Myanmar military has offered its ports to China. Some facilities are being used for Chinese radar activity. These could monitor Indian missile tests as well as its naval communications. Others, when developed, could service Chinese submarines. According to reliable naval information, in 1992 there was Chinese submarine surveillance activity in the Bay of Bengal. In peacetime, surface ships normally project goodwill, but submarine activity in peacetime implies reconnaissance and preparatory work for the future. The scale of Chinese aid and activity in this region is not the key element. Rather, it is the change in the strategic scenario as a result of a special relationship at a time when China is opening up to the outside world in Western and Indian thinking, and when economic reform rather than military strategy appears to be the new game being played. The pattern of Chinese activities indicates that it may be premature to write off the strategic side just because the Cold War has ended and China is seeking peace in its immediate neighbourhood.[2]

The special China–Myanmar relationship emerged in a particular context. Up to 1987–88 Myanmar was isolated and inward-looking. This was a domestic choice. After 1988 the world community isolated Myanmar because of its military crackdown against the democracy movement. China saw an opportunity, as did its neighbour's military, to overcome the situation. Ne Win, the behind-the-scenes controller of Myanmar, was always pro-Chinese, being three-fourths Chinese himself. His effort to bring about a working relationship bore fruit.

How did the country pay for the assistance of China? Four methods were used. First, money was diverted from the lucrative drug trade commissions that the authorities allegedly received. Although the Chinese have pressed the government to end the drug trade through China, the monetary incentive to continue the trade has prevailed. Second, timber and jade are used for bartering. Third, there are Chinese goodwill grants. Finally, there is speculation that the Myanmar embassy land sales in Tokyo may have been used as part payment or held in reserve to pay the Chinese. So, even though foreign exchange reserves are limited, the state has means of paying for Chinese exports.

Thus far press reports on Myanmar have dwelt on democracy and human rights. These are important issues, however the strategic side of the relationship also merits analysis in a volatile regional environment of changing geopolitics and geoeconomics.

Second, *Afghanistan's civil war and Pakistan*. The Soviet withdrawal from Afghanistan placed the issue of the country's future on the backburner. However Afghanistan is still unstable. There is an uneasy pattern of volatile alignments and animosities between the key Afghan players – Hekmetyar, Rabbani, Dosturm and Masood and others. The world community, including the United States, can live with an unstable Afghanistan but a key question needs to be addressed. If Hekmetyar (a fundamentalist, ambitious Pathan with a constituency in Afghanistan and Pakistan), or a similar figure fails to achieve a pre-eminent position in Afghan affairs, will he inevitably turn towards Pakistan with a view to securing a greater Pukhtoonistan, and seek the de facto partitioning of Afghanistan and Pakistan among the contending forces? Afghan politics reveal a mix of religion and ethnic politics mixed with arms and drug trading. This is a poisonous mixture. If it is applied to fragile Pakistani democratic politics, even with US aid Pakistan may not be able to contain the likes of Hekmetyar. Although the prospects of a change in Afghan–Pakistan geopolitics are not imminent, the undercurrents are entrenched, they are engaging Indian and Iranian attention and they may eventually attract US action.

Third, *arms control in South Asia*. Since the end of the Cold War the United States has increased its pressure on India to cap and eventually abandon its nuclear and missile programme. This plans is in the context of US pressure that led to the capping of Pakistan's nuclear-enrichment work but left intact its ability to make a few nuclear weapons. India has been reluctant to cap or roll back its nuclear programme in the absence of verificable international restraints on China and concrete moves towards real nuclear disarmament of the major powers. For India the issues are national security, its unwillingness to accept a lesser international status than China and its willingness to explore compensatory diplomatic and security measures that could give India a new deal with the United States. On the security issue there is evidence of a nuclearised Tibet.[3] This indicates an ongoing interaction, albeit in a secretive way, between Chinese nuclear activities and Indian missile and nuclear developments. This interaction is not provable; but nor is it disprovable. Our view is that India is not likely ever to accept a regional arms control arrangement that rests only on the principle of Indo–Pakistani parity, that it is not likely to accept an arrangement that does not simultaneously curb China in the strategic sphere, and that India is seeking a wider regional net beyond the framework of Indo–Pakistani arrangements. If India is uneasy about Chinese strategic intentions in Myanmar and the Bay of Bengal, then the question is whether regional arms control arrangements can be crafted that place verifiable limits on Chinese strategic activities in Tibet and the Bay of Bengal? Is there anything else that China can bring to the table?

Fourth, *The Kashmiri issue and normalisation in Indo–Pakistani and Indo–US affairs.* India is under intense pressure on the Kashmiri issue from four different directions. First, the insurgency in Kashmir shows the loss of faith among Kashmiris in the value of the political process and a new faith in the value of militancy in the Kashmir arena. Second, Pakistan's insistence that without Indian concessions on Kashmir, there cannot be meaningful Indo–Pakistan normalisation. Third, the Clinton administration is actively asserting the notion of Kashmir as a disputed territory, casting doubt on the validity of the Kashmir Maharaja's accession to India under Lord Mountbatten's advice, and downgrading the Reagan and Bush administration's emphasis on the Simla agreement as the way to settle Kashmir affairs.

Finally, there is internal pressure on the Indian government to act in two contradictory way. The first is to increase Kashmiri autonomy; the second is to fight insurgency by harsh measures. The first stance rests on the premise that after forty years of Indian rule, Kashmiris have nothing to show for their loyalty to India; that Delhi has failed to give legitimacy to its rule or build a pro-Indian Kashmiri middle class despite its lengthy opportunity to do so. The second stance rests on the premise that Pakistan and the United States want India to surrender on Kashmir; India should resist this, but the Indian government ought to be open to a dialogue on the issues so that future agreements may be crafted if and when the situation in Kashmir improves. If the second stance represents the dominant view of the Indian government, then the question is whether it is possible to shape a real dialogue on Kashmiri, Indo–Pakistani and Indo–US affairs other than to pursue confidence-building measures that alleviate stresses and strains in bilateral relations.

These observations are tentative and speculative as they concern a changing policy environment. They indicate a need to recognise that the regional agenda is complex and now includes issues and developments in geographical areas in the South Asian neighbourhood that impact on the South Asian regional security framework, even though they are not part of the region in the traditional sense of the word. Our study shows that bilateral initiatives involving India and Pakistan, India and China and India and its immediate neighbours have been important in alleviating stresses and strains in relationships. However, unless a broader security agenda is put in place, and an alleged 'outlaw' like Iran is given an incentive to play a constructive regional economic and strategic role, it is unlikely that academics and government officials will be able to forecast and control the developments and processes of South Asian international relations in the 1990s.

Notes and References

1 Introduction

1. The literature on Nehru's foreign policy is voluminous. The standard works the reader may find useful include the following: M. J. Akbar, *Nehru – the Making of India* (London: Viking, 1988); Michael Brecher, *Nehru: a political biography* (London, New York: Oxford University Press, 1959); J. S. Bright (ed.), *Important Speeches of Jawaharlal Nehru*, vol. II (New Delhi: Indian Printing Works, Didi); S. Gopal, *Jawaharlal Nehru*, 3 vols (Cambridge, Mass,: Harvard University Press, 1976–84); B. R. Nanda (ed.), *Indian Foreign Policy – The Nehru Years* (Delhi: Viking Publishing House 1976); Jawaharlal Nehru, *The Discovery of India* (Bombay: Asia Publishing House 1961).
2. This is from Karl von Clausewitz. According to him:

    As a total phenomenon its dominant tendencies always make war a remarkable *trinity* – composed of primordial violence, hatred and enmity, which are to be regarded as a blind natural force; of the play of chance and probability, within which the creative spirit is free to roam; and of its element of subordination, as an instrument of policy, which makes it subject to reason alone.
    The first of these aspects mainly concerns the people; the second, the commander and his army; the third, the government. . . . These three tendencies are like different codes of law, deep-rooted in their subject and yet variable in their relationship to one another. *A theory that ignores any one of them or seeks to fix an arbitrary relationship between them would conflict with reality to such an extent that for this reason alone it would be totally useless.*

    See Karl von Clausewitz, *On War* (Princeton University Press, 1976), p. 89, as quoted in Michael Howard, *The Causes of War and Other Essays* (Cambridge, Mass.: Harvard University Press, 1983), p. 4.
3. I am grateful to George Tanham of the Rand Corporation for this suggestion.
4. According to Barry Buzan, in B. Buzan and G. Rizvi (eds), *South Asian Insecurity and the Great Powers* (London: Macmillan 1986), pp. 21–22:

    The South Asian security complex, for example, has displayed a durable structure for nearly four decades. Its continuity resides in the primacy of India and Pakistan within the subcontinent, in the continuation of their treatment of each other as major rivals, and in the absence of any developments within, or external impositions upon, South Asia strong enough to break this pattern. Structure in this sense has endured despite the endless changes within and around the subcontinent. Internal changes, including the partition of Pakistan, have not altered the basic pattern of relations. Neither have external ones, which have so far tended more to reinforce, than to undermine, the existing bipolarity.

(See also Chapters 1 and 4 in the present volume.)

Furthermore, Professor T. P. Thornton, a former head of the South Asia Desk of the National Security Council staff of the White House, claims there is 'regional polarity' between India and Pakistan in South Asia. See S. P. Cohen (ed.), *The Security of South Asia* (New Delhi: Vistaar, 1988), p. 216.

Finally, Pakistan's Lieutenant General A. I. Akram, a former director of the Institute of Strategic Studies, notes that: 'When we study South Asia, we are really looking at India and Pakistan, for these are the protagonists of the subcontinent. When these two countries are at peace with each other, South Asia by and large is at peace. If the two countries have troubled relations, South Asia is uneasy. When the two fight, South Asia trembles. Lt. General Akram, 'Security and Stability in South Asia', in Cohen (ed.) *The Security of South Asia*, pp. 163.

5. For a discussion of this idea see Arthur Lall, *The Emergence of Modern India* (New York: Columbia University Press, 1981), ch. 1.
6. For Kautilya's political ideas see R. Choudhary, *Kautilya's Political Ideas and Institutions* (Varanasi: Chowkhamba Sanskrit Office, 1971); Adda B. Bozeman, *Politics and Culture in International History* (New Jersey: Princeton University Press, 1960), pp. 118–26; R. N. Dandekar, 'Artha, The second End of Man,' in W. M. Theodore de Bary (ed.), *Sources of Indian Tradition*, vol. I (New York: Columbia University Press, 1958; George Modelski, 'Kautilya: Foreign Policy and International System in the Ancient Hindu World', *American Political Science Review*, vol. 58, no. 3 (1964), pp. 549–60.
7. Lall, *The Emergence of Modern India*, op. cit., pp. 6–7.
8. Philip Mason, *The Men who Ruled India*, abridged edition (London: Jonathan Cape, 1985).
9. Leo E. Rose and Satish Kumar, 'South Asia', in W. J. Feld and G. Boyd (eds), *Comparative Regional Systems* (New York: Pergamon, 1980), pp. 268 and 264.
10. Clement R. Attlee, *As It Happened* (London: Heinemann, 1954); Michael Brecher, *Nehru: A Political Biography* (New York: Oxford University Press, 1959); Anthony Eden, *Full Circle: The Memoirs of Anthony Eden* (Boston: Houghton Mifflin, 1960); Harold Macmillan, *Tides of Fortune 1945–1955* (London: Macmillan, 1969); Escott Reid, *Envoy to Nehru* (Delhi and Toronto: Oxford University Press, 1981).
11. Louis J. Halle, *The Cold War as History* (New York: Harper & Row, 1975).
12. On this point, see Sisir Gupta, 'The Power Structure in South Asia: Problems of Stability', in M. S. Rajan and Shivaji Ganguly (eds), *India and the International System* (New Delhi: Vikas, 1981), p. 144.

> As China was getting united under a strong central authority, the Indian subcontinent was being divided into two independent and unfriendly states. These two developments together have radically altered the political map of Asia, and although the full impact of this change is perhaps yet to be felt, some of its effects on the politics of the Southern Asian region are already obvious. China has emerged as a powerful, active and revolutionary element in Asian politics; the question is how the authority that now

emanates from Peking will influence development in other parts of the continent. Although India under Nehru had for some time appeared on the world stage as one of its major actors, all the states of South Asia are relatively powerless and passive; the question is how to insulate them from interventionary pressure from outside and prevent violent internal changes in the countries of the region, in order to build a stable state system in the area.

13. The US assessment of the Soviet factor in Middle Eastern and South Asian international relations is revealed in the following words of Dean Acheson, a former US secretary of state:

> At the end of January 1951, in a letter to General Marshall, I asked the cooperation of the Defense Department in a review of American interests and policies in the whole area extending from the eastern Mediterranean to India. Over the past four years in an unplanned, undesired, and haphazard way American influence had largely succeeded French and British in that part of the world... and major conflicts were growing apace between the Arabs and the Israelis, between the nationalist movements in both Egypt and Iran and British interests and government, and between Pakistan and India. As the situation was developing, increasing opportunities were offered for the historic movement of Russia southward to warm water, to oil, and to mischief-making.

See Dean Acheson, *Present at the Creation* (New York: W. W. Norton 1969), p. 562.

Furthermore, according to a memorandum by the Joint Chiefs of Staff, issued on 24 March 1949, the South Asian countries, with the exception of Pakistan, had little strategic value for the United States. The main danger for the United States lay in the Soviet potential for dominating the area and the resulting problems this would represent in terms of hindering US access to raw materials and sea routes, and causing the US containment policy to fail. Otherwise, US strategic policy focused on Europe, the Middle East and the Far East, where it was believed more 'remunerative objectives' could be achieved. In short, US policy in this area was limited to preventing Soviet encroachment or alliances with the countries of this region, while at the same time cooperating with these countries (especially Pakistan) so as to use their facilities in military operations against the USSR in the event of war breaking out. See K. Arif (ed.), *American–Pakistan Relations I* (Lahore: Vanguard Books, 1984), pp. 15–17.

Extracts from informal US–UK discussions held in London in September 1950 cite Mr McGhee as emphasising the importance of Islam for the Muslim minorities in Central Asia (ibid.), p. 38.

Finally, according to a Department of State policy statement on Pakistan, dated 1 July 1951:

> Pakistan has the military manpower which could assist Near East countries in blocking Russian aggression especially through Iran. The Pakistani army, properly equipped would be in a position to send troops to Iran's assistance and so to fulfil one of the traditional functions of British–Indian troops in past wars. Furthermore, as Pakistan does not suffer from

the violent anti-Westernism and deep-rooted neutrality that prevent India from cooperating fully with the US and its allies, Pakistan might be persuaded to afford military bases to the US and the UK in the Indian Ocean area. Until Pakistan is relieved of threats to its territorial integrity, however, it cannot be persuaded to participate more actively with the US, UK and the UN in opposing aggression wherever it occurs (ibid., p. 57).

14. Gunnar Myrdal, *An Approach to the Asian Drama* (New York: Vintage Books, 1970), pp. 12–13.
15. Geoffrey Fairbairn, *Revolutionary Guerrilla Warfare: The Countryside Version* (Harmondsworth and Baltimore: Penguin, 1974), pp. 47–51.
16. *Financial Times of Canada*, 1 April 1991, p. 25.
17. Military theatres involving Indian troops in the First World War include the following: Malta, France, Belgium, Gallipoli, Salonika, Palestine, Egypt, Sudan, Mesopotamia, Aden, the Red Sea littoral, Somaliland, the Cameroons, East Africa, north-west Persia, Kurdistan South Persia, the Gulf of Oman, the length of East Persia from Mekran to Khorasan, Trans-Caspia, North China, and the north-west and north-east frontiers of India.

   The Second World War Indian contingent, on the other hand, fought in France, Karen, Iraq, Malaya, Burma, Hong Kong, Singapore, Italy, Sudan, Eritrea, Iran, Palestine, Syria and Greece.

   For details regarding the Indian contribution of military equipment and the number of combatants and casualties, see H. S. Bhatia (ed.), *Military History of British India* (New Delhi: Deep and Deep Publication, 1977), pp. 224–42.
18. See 'The Course of Asian Nationalism: Japan, China and the Indian Subcontinent', in J. Kennedy, *Asian Nationalism in the Twentieth Century* (New York: St. Martin's Press 1968), pp. 18–44.
19. Up to 1914, Britain did not think about Indian independence. See Hugh Tinker, *Men who Overturned Empires* (London: Macmillan, 1987), p. 5. In 1917 the secretary of state for India, Edwin Montagu, announced the aim of British policy, namely, 'the gradual development of self-governing institutions with a view to the progressive realisation of responsible government in India.... Substantial steps in this direction should be taken as soon as possible.... I would add that progress in this policy can only be achieved by successive stages', ibid., p. 6. From 1919 onwards, Indian nationalism gained ground under Gandhi's leadership. According to Tinker, the British left India because 'the short answer is that they went when they had to, when the advantages of empire expired', ibid., p. xii.
20. See ibid., p. 8. For more information on Ceylon, see ibid., p. 215, and J. E. Williams, 'The Joint Declaration on the Colonies: An issue in Anglo-American relations, 1942–1944', *British Journal of International Studies*, no. 2 (1976), pp. 267–92.
21. Tinker, *Men who Overturned Empires*, op. cit., p. 8.
22. Senator Larry Pressler, a ranking member of the Senate Foreign Relations Committee, emphasised the growth of a potential fundamentalist Islamic Confederation stretching in a continuous belt from Turkey down to Afghanistan, Pakistan and up to the former Soviet central republics ('India–

US Ties called "Best Ever"', *India Abroad*, 17 January 1992, p. 8.) According to the press, for some years the United States had been watching with growing concern the growth of Islamic fundamentalism in Lebanon, Iran and Pakistan and its potential for spreading in a crescent arching from Kashmir to Azerbaijan and even Xinjiang in northern China, where a Muslim revolt has been quelled by Chinese troops in 1990. It perceived India as the last secular barrier, or a 'frontline state' as one diplomat put it, against the 'fundamentalist threat'. (ibid., p. 8). Israeli analyses also stress a concern with Islamic fundamentalism.

23. Martin Wight, *Power Politics* (Markham, Ontario: Penguin, 1986), ch. 13.

2 The Structure of Power in South Asia

1. Barry Buzan and Gowher Rizvi, *South Asian Insecurity and the Great Powers* (London: Macmillan, 1986); Leo E. Rose and Satish Kumar, 'South Asia', in Werner G. Feld and Gavin Boyd (eds), *Comparative Regional Systems: West and East Europe, North America, the Middle East, and Developing Countries* (New York: Pergamon, 1980), pp. 237–73; Leo E. Rose, 'The Foreign Policy of India', in James N. Rosenau, Kenneth W. Thompson and Gavin Boyd (eds), *World Politics: An Introduction* (New York: Free Press, 1976), pp. 199–221; Leo E. Rose, 'India and Its Neighbours: Regional Foreign and Security Politics', in Lawrence Ziring (ed), *The Subcontinent in World Politics*, rev. ed (New York: Praeger, 1982), pp. 35–66; Stephen Philip Cohen (ed.), *The Security of South Asia* (New Delhi: Vistaar Publications, 1987).
2. Martin Wight *Systems of States*, (Leicester: Leicester University Press, 1977), provides the standard definition of systems of states.
3. Barry Buzan, *Regional Security – Working Papers 28/1989* (Copenhagen: Centre for Peace and Conflict Research, 1990), pp. 6, 10, 18–19.
4. Raimo Vayrynen, 'Regional Conflict Formations: An Intractable Problem of International Relations', *Journal of Peace Research*, vol. 21, no. 4 (1984), p. 340.
5. Buzan and Rizvi, *South Asian Insecurity*, op. cit., pp. 21–2.
6. Vayrynen, 'Regional Conflict Formations', op. cit., p. 352.
7. Ibid., p. 351.
8. Buzan and Rizvi, *South Asian Insecurity*, op. cit., p. 14.
9. Henry Kissinger, 'The New World Order: Made in the USA?', *Inside Guide*, June 1991, p. 17.
10. Sarvepalli Gopal, *Radhakrishnan: a Biography* (London: Unwin Hyman, 1989), p. 25.
11. S. M. Walt, 'Testing Theories of Alliance Formation: the Case of Southwest Asia', *International Organization*, vol. 42, no. 2 (Spring 1988).
12. Ibid., p. 277.
13. M. S. Rajan and Shivaji Gunguly (eds) *Sisir Gupta: India and the International System* (New Delhi: Vikas Publishing, 1981), pp. 154–5.
14. B. H. Farmer, *An Introduction to South Asia* (London and New York: Methuen, 1983), pp. 112–7.
15. Rajan and Ganguly, *Sisir Gupta*, op. cit., p. 144.

Notes and References

16. Ibid., pp. 150–7.
17. Ibid.
18. Ibid., p. 230.
19. Rose and Kumar, 'South Asia', op. cit., p. 244.
20. Ibid., p. 245.
21. Ibid., p. 263.
22. Ibid., p. 264.
23. Ibid.
24. Rajan and Ganguly, *Sisir Gupta*, op. cit., pp. 151, 224, 324, 330, 332–4.
25. Leo E. Rose, 'India and Its Neighbours', op. cit., pp. 36–8.

3 Polarity and Alliances in South Asia

1. A. Jalal, 'Inheriting the Raj: Jinnah and the Governor-Generalship Issue', *Modern Asian Studies*, vol. 19, no. 1 (February 1985), p. 50.
2. For details of military expenditure and force structures, see *Military Balance*, published annually by the International Institute for Strategic Studies, London.
3. S. P. Limaye, *US–Indian Relations: The Pursuit of Accommodation* (Boulder, Co: Westview Press, 1993).
4. 'India desperately needs a period of peace to build up its economy and stabilise its political structure'. See *India's Political and Economic Position in the East–West Conflict*, Office of Intelligence Research report no. 5526, Department of State, Washington DC, 15 May 1951, p. iv. 'The best deterrent to Communist aggression in the Far East is an economically sound India. If we succeed in the experiment in the Far East of combining democratic methods with the task of raising the living standards of the people we will have shown that the free world's way is better than the Communist way. Thus we will break down the Communist idea.' *Nehru's Attitudes Towards Communism, the Soviet Union and Communist China*, Intelligence Report no. 6269, Office of Intelligence Research, Department of State, Washington DC, 24 July 1953, p. 15. The authors thank Professor Arthur G. Rubinoff, University of Toronto, for providing copies of the 1951 and 1953 Intelligence Research reports.
5. Sisir Gupta points to the unity in civilisational terms of South Asian states and the conditions that could have helped create a cooperative system of states, but he then goes on to show the problems in Pakistani elite attitudes that inhibit Indo–Pakistani peace. See M. S. Rajan and S. Ganguly (eds), *Sisir Gupta: India and the International System* (New Delhi: Vikas Publishing, 1981), pp. 150–3.
6. S. Gopal, *Jawaharlal Nehru*, vol. 2 (Cambridge, Mass: Harvard University Press, 1979), ch. 3, especially p. 63.
7. Nehru thought the United States was naive and immature in foreign affairs. See ibid., especially p. 60.
8. Intelligence Report, *Nehru's Attitudes towards Communism, the Soviet Union and Communist China*, Office of Intelligence Research, Department of State, Washington, DC, 24 July 1953. Page 25 outlines Nehru's military preparations in north-eastern provinces and Nepal.
9. This was especially the case with regard to policy on Pakistan, Kashmir

and Tibet, as well as internal security issues. See Gopal, *Jawaharlal Nehru*, vol. 2, op. cit., pp. 38, 86–7; D. Das (ed.), *Sardar Patel's Correspondence*, vol. 10, *Relations with China*, 1945–50 (Ahmedabad: Navajivan Publishing House, 1974), pp. 328–47; G. S. Bajpai, 'India and the Balance of Power,' *The Indian Yearbook of International Affairs*, 1952, vol. 1 (University of Madras), pp. 1–8.
10. S. Gopal, *Radhakrishnan* (London: Unwin Hyman, 1989), ch. 10.
11. H. V. Hodson, *The Great Divide* (New York: 1985), Oxford University Press, pp. 441, 453–4, 466.
12. Ibid., p. 435.
13. Gopal, *Jawaharlal Nehru*, volume 2, op. cit., pp. 103, 106, 108, 195.
14. State Department Intelligence Report no. 6269, op. cit., pp. 23–6.
15. Das, *Sardar Patel's Correspondence*, op. cit., p. 338.
16. State Department Intelligence Report no. 6269, op. cit., p. 19.
17. Ibid., p. 23.
18. Ibid., p. 24.
19. Ibid., p. 25.
20. Ibid., pp. 24, 26.
21. This section draws on Gopal *Jawaharlal Nehru* and *Radhakrishnan*, op. cit.
22. Martin Wight, *Power Politics* (New York: Penguin, 1979), p. 18, distinguishes between 'politics of force' (*Machpolitik*) and politics of power.
23. Leo Rose, 'India and Its Neighbours', in L. Ziring, ed. *The Subcontinent in World Politics* (New York, Praeger, 1978), p. 38.
24. C. H. Heimsath and S. Mansingh, *A Diplomatic History of Modern India* (New Delhi: Allied Publishers, 1971), p. 204.
25. Ibid., ch. 8, especially p. 211.
26. A. Kapur, *Pakistan in Crisis* (London: Routledge, 1991).
27. Leo E. Rose and N. A. Husain (eds), *United States–Pakistan Relations*, Research Papers and Policy Studies no. 13 (Berkeley: Institute of East Asian Studies, University of California, 1985).
28. See Sino–Indian Aggreement on Tibet, 29 April 1954, and Chou–Nehru Joint Statement, 28 June 1954, in *Foreign Policy of India, Texts of Documents, 1947–59*, 2nd edn (New Delhi: Lok Sabha Secretariat, 1959). The first India–USSR Joint Declaration (the Bulganin–Nehru declaration) was signed on 23 June 1955, ibid.
29. These ideas are from E. Reid, *Envoy to Nehru* (Delhi: Oxford University Press, 1981), pp. 22, 56–7, 247–78.
30. To quote the State Department's policy on Pakistan (3 April 1950): 'the development of a Pakistan–India *entente cordiale* appears remote. Moreover, the vigor and methods which have characterised India's execution of its policy of consolidating the princely states, and its inflexible attitude with regard to Kashmir, may indicate national traits which in time, if not controlled, could make India Japan's successor in Asiatic imperialism. In such a circumstance a strong Muslim bloc under the leadership of Pakistan and friendly to the US, might afford a desirable balance of power in South Asia'. Cited in Kapur, *Pakistan in Crisis*, op. cit., p. 32.
31. This is based on Y. Vertzberger, *The Enduring Entente* (New York: Praeger, 1983), pp. 1–5.

32. Anthony Grey, *The Prime Minister Was a Spy* (London: Weidenfeld and Nicolson, 1983), p. 110.
33. Ibid., p. 140.
34. L. F. Rushbrook Williams, *The State of Pakistan* (London: Faber and Faber, 1962), p. 120; cited in Sisir Gupta, *Kashmir* (London: Asia Publishing House, 1966) p. 424.

4 Arms Race, War and Crisis in South Asia, 1955–71

1. I am grateful to Etel Solingen for this distinction.
2. M. Howard, *The Causes of War*, 2nd edn (Cambridge, Mass: Harvard University Press, 1984), p. 12.
3. E. Luard, 'Conciliation and Deterrence', *World Politics*, vol. 19, no. 2 (1971), pp. 167–89.
4. State intelligence report, July 1952, p. 24.
5. S. Gopal, *Jawaharlal Nehru*, vol. 2 (Cambridge, Mass: Harvard University Press), p. 43 and ch. 11.
6. C. H. Heimsath and S. Mansingh, *A Diplomatic History of Modern India* (New Delhi, Allied Publishers, 1971), p. 212.
7. Tariq Ali, *Can Pakistan Survive?* (New York: Penguin, 1983), pp. 76–80.
8. See note 19, Chapter 3.
9. The literature on the Sino–Indian war is voluminous but parochial. For two popular but one-sided accounts see N. Maxwell, *India's China War* (Bombay: Jaico Publishing House, 1971); and B. N. Mullick, *The Chinese Betrayal* (New Delhi: Allied Publishers, 1971).
10. See S. Ganguly, *The Origins of War in South Asia* (Boulder: Westview Press, 1986), pp. 83–4.
11. The literature on the 1965 war is one-sided. See Lars Blikenberg, *India–Pakistan: the History of Unsolved Conflicts* (Copenhagen: Dansk Udenrigsolitrsk Institut, 1972); M. Ashghar Khan, *The First Round Indo–Pakistan War 1965* (India: Vikas Publishing House, 1979); Kalim Siddiqui, *Conflict, Crisis and War in Pakistan* (Los Angeles: University of California Press, 1972).
12. See especially Tariq Ali, *Can Pakistan Survive?*, op. cit.; Sisir Gupta, *Bangladesh: A Struggle for Nationhood* (Delhi: Vikas, 1971); Robert Jackson, *South Asian Crisis* (London: Chatto and Windus, 1975); Leo Rose and R. Sisson, *War and Secession* (Los Angeles: University of California Press, 1990).
13. The standard sources are *The Military Balance* (London: International Institute for Strategic Studies, annual) and SIPRI (Stockholm, annual), but they provide little information for the 1947–68 period.
14. Cited in A. Kapur, *Pakistan in Crisis* (London: Routledge, 1991), pp. 27–8.
15. See S. P. Cohen, 'US–Pakistan Security Relations,' in Leo E. Rose and N. A. Husain (eds), *United States–Pakistan Relations*, (Barkeley: Institute of East Asian Studies, University of California, 1985), p. 16.
16. M. Ashghar Khan, op. cit., note 11.
17. Gopal, *Radhakrishnan* (London: Unwin Hyman, 1989), chapter 10.

5 The Foreign Policies of India's Immediate Neighbours

1. Originally published by A. Jeyaratnam Wilson in *Journal of Asian and African Studies*, vol. XXV, nos. 1–2 (1990). This chapter was revised by Ashok Kapur on the basis of suggestions by A. J. Wilson.
2. Quoted by Leo Rose in 'Bhutan's External Relations', *Pacific Affairs*, vol. 47, no. 2 (Summer 1974), p. 194. For an overall view see Ashok Kapur, 'Indian Foreign Policy: Perspectives and Present Predicament', *The Round Table*, no. 295 (July 1985), pp. 230–9.
3. Rose, 'Bhutan's External Relations', op. cit.
4. Bharat Wariavwalla, 'Indira's India: A National Security State?', *The Round Table*, no. 287 (1983), p. 282.
5. Leo E. Rose and Margaret Fisher, *The Politics of Nepal: Persistence and Change in an Asian Monarchy* (Ithaca, NY: 1970), pp. 122–3.
6. For these and other details, see Surjit Mansingh, *India's Search for Power: Indira Gandhi's Foreign Policy 1966–1982* (New Delhi: Sage, 1984), pp. 282–3, and 'Asianism' in Sudershan Chawla, *The Foreign Relations of India* (California and Belmont, 1976) pp. 52–5, 121.
7. Rose and Fisher, *The Politics of Nepal*, op. cit., p. 150.
8. For further information, see Rose, 'Bhutan's External Relations', op. cit. The information that follows on Rustomji, the Dorjis and developments in Bhutan is from Rose, ibid.
9. See Leo Rose, *Nepal: Strategy for Survival* (Berkeley: University of California, 1971), p. 280; S. M. Mujtaba Razvi, 'Conflict and Cooperation in South Asia', *The Round Table*, no. 299 (July 1986), p. 276.
10. Surjit Mansingh, *India's Search for Power: Indira Gandhi's Foreign Policy 1966–1982*, op. cit., p. 287.
11. Quoted in T. A. Keenleyside, 'Nationalist Indian Attitudes Towards Asia: A Troublesome Legacy for Post-Independence Indian Foreign Policy', *Pacific Affairs*, vol. 55, no. 2 (Summer 1982), pp. 228–9.
12. In 'Crown and Commonwealth in Asia', *International Affairs* (London), vol. 32, no. 138 (April 1956).
13. See Sir John Kotelawala, *An Asian Prime Minister's Story* (London: G. Harrap, 1956).
14. For an exposition of 'Dynamic neutralism' under the title 'Neutralism and Cowardice', see *The Foreign Policy of Ceylon: Extracts from Statements by the Late Prime Minister, Mr. S.W.R.D. Bandaranaike and Texts of Joint Statements issued by him and Visiting Heads of States* (Colombo: Ceylon Government Press, 1961, revised and enlarged), pp. 10–11.
15. *Parliamentary Debates* (House of Representatives), vol. 23, column 684.14.
16. *The Times* (Ceylon), 2 October 1956.
17. At the Commonwealth Foreign Ministers' Conference in Colombo in January 1950, *Ceylon Daily News*, 16 January 1950 and again in 1959, see S.U. Kodikara, *Indo–Ceylon Relations Since Independence* (Colombo: Lakehouse, 1965), p. 21.
18. The full text of the treaty is in Appendix C of Mansingh, *India's Search for Power*, op. cit. pp. 387–9.
19. For the stages of India's involvement before the Indo–Sri Lankan Accord, see A. J. Wilson, *The Break-up of Sri Lanka: The Sinhalese-Tamil*

Conflict (London: Hurst, 1988).
20. For the full text of the Indo–Sri Lankan Accord, see *Tamil Times*, vol. VI, no. 10 (August 1977).
21. This letter was given to Professor A. J. Wilson by K. Vaikunthavasan for perusal.
22. At that time, Professor A. J. Wilson was a political science faculty member of the Department of Economics, University of Ceylon. S. U. Kodikara was in the Department of History of the same university and specialised in Indo–Ceylonese relations, including the decitisenisation of Indian plantation workers.
23. Razvi, 'Conflict and Cooperation', op. cit.
24. Ibid.
25. The information that follows on Bangladesh is derived from Razvi, ibid., and Mansingh, *India's Search for Power*, op. cit.
26. Mansingh, ibid., p. 269.
27. Anita Inder Singh, 'Post-Imperial British Attitudes to India: The Military Aspect, 1947–51', *The Round Table*, no. 296 (October 1985), p. 365.
28. Ibid.
29. S. M. Burke, *Pakistan's Foreign Policy: An Historical Analysis* (London: Oxford University Press, 1973), p. 57.
30. Ibid., p. 58.
31. Ibid., p. 59.
32. Nehru's position on Kashmir was that: 'as far as we are concerned, it is desirable for us from a strategic point of view that Kashmir should be with us'; quoted in A. P. Rana, *The Imperatives of Non-Alignment: A Conceptual Study of India's Foreign Policy Strategy in the Nehru Period* (Delhi: Macmillan, 1976), p. 34.
33. Razvi, 'Conflict and Cooperation', op. cit., p. 271.
34. Ibid., p. 270.
35. General Zia is quoted in Ravzi, ibid., p. 271.
36. Ibid.; see also Ashok Kapur, 'Nuclear Proliferation: South Asian Perspectives' (review article), *Pacific Affairs*, vol. 57, no. 2 (Summer 1984), pp. 304–10.
37. See Ataur Rahman, 'Pakistan: Unity or Further Divisions', in A. Jeyaratnam Wilson and Dennis Dalton (eds), *The States of South Asia* (London: Hurst, 1982), p. 205.

6 India and Pakistan in the 1980s and Early 1990s

1. The text is in Mansingh, *India's Search for Power*, (New Delhi: Sage, 1984) pp. 390–1.
2. A. Kapur, *Pakistan's Nuclear Development* (London: Croom Helm, 1987).
3. On the 'Brass tacks' military exercise, see S. R. Weisman, 'On India's Border, a Huge Mock War', *New York Times*, 6 March 1987, p. 1; *IISS Strategic Survey 1986/87* (Oxford: Oxford University Press, 1987), p. 142. According to the report of the Carnegie Task Force on Non-Proliferation and South Asian Security, Dr A. Q. Khan, the head of Pakistan's nuclear enrichment programme, was quoted as saying in January 1987 that, 'what the CIA has been saying about our possessing the bomb is correct. . . .

They told us that Pakistan could never produce the bomb... but they know we have done it': *Nuclear Weapons* and *South Asian Security*, Carnegie Endowment for International Peace, Washington D.C. 1988, p. 18. In a highly publicised interview, President Zia ul-Haq said, 'Pakistan has the capability of building the bomb. You can write today that Pakistan can build a bomb whenever it wishes. Once you have acquired the technology, which Pakistan has, you can do whatever you like'. Zia added, however, that Pakistan still has no actual plan to make nuclear weapons, 'Knocking at the Nuclear Door': *Time,* 30 March 1987, p. 42.

4. Interview, New Delhi, 1991.
5. Pakistan's military expenditure also grew rapidly during this period due in large part to military aid from the United States, China and Arab countries. In 1980 Pakistan turned down an offer of US aid because the amount was too small. In 1981, an aid package valued at $3.2 billion over five years (half of which was to be for military purchases) was negotiated (SIPRI, *World Armaments and Disarmament Yearbook,* London: Taylor and Francis, 1982, p. 123). In 1986 a new US–Pakistan military and economic aid package worth $4.02 billion between 1987 and 1993 was announced (SIPRI, *World Armaments and Disarmament Yearbook*, Oxford University Press, 1987, p. 141).

In India's 'ambitious' 1985–90 defence plan the emphasis was on 'the modernisation and replacement of equipment to secure greater firepower, mobility and more modern means of communication, and on self-reliance in the production of weapons and import substitution' (SIPRI, *World Armaments and Disarmament Yearbook*, Oxford University Press, 1987, p. 139). For further details, see IISS, *The Military Balance*, Annual, (Oxford: Oxford University Press), and 'The Indian Sub-Continent', *Military Powers*, vol. 5 (Paris, Société 13c, 1990).

6. See Kapur, *Pakistan's Nuclear Development*, op. cit., chapter 7.
7. *IISS Strategic Survey*, op. cit., p. 142.
8. Air Commodore Aliuddin, 'Pakistan's Nuclear Dilemma', *Seaford House Papers* (London: Royal College of Defence Studies, 1990).
9. According to the Indian defence minister, 'The nations, which are also militarily significant powers have adopted nuclear deterrence as their basic security doctrine. India does not subscribe to the doctrine of nuclear deterrence. However, India just cannot afford to overlook the fact that three major nuclear powers operate in its neighbourhood and Pakistan is engaged in a nuclear weapons programme. If we are to influence these major powers and attempt to ensure that they do no indulge in nuclear threats, then it becomes inescapably necessary for us to reckon with their nuclear deterrence belief concepts. As our Prime Minister said in the third UN special session on disarmament, "Left to ourselves, we would not want to touch nuclear weapons but when tactical considerations, in the passing play of great power rivalries, are allowed to take precedence over the imperatives of nuclear nonproliferation, with what leeway are we left?"' Speech by the Indian defence minister, K.C. Pant, at MIT, 1 July 1989, 'Philosophy of Indian Defence', reprinted in *Strategic Digest* (New Delhi: Institute of Defence Studies, 1989), pp. 481–2.
10. Ibid., p. 481.

11. '... that there must be reciprocity of obligations between nuclear weapon powers and the threshold nations. If the former would agree to a phased programme of elimination of nuclear weapons, the latter should not cross the nuclear threshold': ibid., p. 482.

7 Future Prospects

1. B. Buzan and G. Rizvi (eds), *South Asian Insecurity and the Great Powers* (London: Macmillan, 1986), chapter 1.
2. Interviews, New Delhi, 1992; interviews, Washington DC, 1993; B. Lintner, 'Arms for Eyes: Military Sales Raise China's Profile in Bay of Bengal', *Far Eastern Economic Review*, 16 December 1993, p. 26.
3. *Nuclear Tibet: Nuclear Weapons and Nuclear Waste on the Tibetan Plateau*, report by the International Campaign for Tibet, Washington DC, 1993.

Index

academic and policy setting 1947 8–15
   orientation of literature 10–13
Acheson, D. 72
Afghanistan
   academic and policy setting 13
   and China's strategic orientation 161
   civil war 163
   foreign policies 111
   future prospects 158, 159
   India and Pakistan 1980s–1990s 133, 144
   and Pakistan 83, 128, 130
   patterns and trends 17
   polarity and alliances 54
   structure of power 39, 44, 45, 47
Africa 131
Agni missile programme 139, 150
Akbar 6–7
Aksai Chin 88
alignment patterns 1947–mid-1990s 19
alliances 92–3, 102–3
   see also under polarity
Annexure 'C' formula 121
Arab–Israeli war 98
Arif, K. 34
arms control 163–4
arms race as policy tool 79–80
Aryans 5
Asianism 84
Assam 18, 63, 124
Association of South East Asian Nations 35, 130
Attlee, C. 126
Aurangzeb 7
Australia 157
Ayoob, M. 11, 28
Ayub Khan, M. 128

Babri Masjid/Ayodha controversy 141
Babur 141

Baghdad Pact 73, 126
Bajpai, K.S. 65, 66, 116
Baldwin, H. 59
Baluchis 105, 130
Bandaranaike, F.D. 119, 123
Bandaranaike, S.W.R.D. 118–20, 122–3
Bandung conference (1955) 74, 118
Bangladesh 2, 4, 131
   academic and policy setting 8, 10
   and China 85, 161
   foreign policies 111, 114, 115, 120, 123–5
   and India and Pakistan 99, 102, 106, 109, 146
   and Pakistan 83, 127, 128
   patterns and trends 16, 18
   polarity and alliances 51
   and South Asia Association for Regional Cooperation 130
   structure of power 22, 41, 44, 45, 47
   war and war avoidance 80, 89–91
Beg, A. 146, 147
Bengal 18, 126
Bengal, Bay of 124, 164
Bengalis 105
Bhandari, R. 121
Bhuddism 116
Bhutan 47
   academic and policy setting 8, 10
   foreign policies 111, 112, 114, 115, 116–17
   and India–China war 94
   patterns and trends 19
   polarity and alliances 54, 66, 68, 71
   and South Asia Association for Regional Cooperation 130
   structure of power 22, 31, 44, 45
Bhutto, B. 147–8, 151

Index

Bhutto, Z.A. 82, 88, 89, 103–4, 114, 128, 133
Birendra, King 70, 117–18
Bowles, C. 56, 62
Boyd, G. 10
Bradnock, R.W. 13
'Brass tacks' exercise 139–40, 141–5, 148, 150
Brecher, M. 24–5
British India 6
British merchants 7
British power 5
British–Indian treaty relations 4
Bryroade, H. 58
Burki, S.J. 57
Burma 1
  academic and policy setting 15
  arms control 164
  and China's strategic orientation 160, 161, 162, 163
  future prospects 159
Bush, G. 164
Buzan, B. 10, 23, 24, 27, 28–30, 35, 36, 38, 41–2

Callard, K.B. 57
Canada 8
Cantori, L.J. 25, 30
Caroe, Sir O. 56, 58, 59, 76
Catholic Church 119
CENTO agreement (Central Treaty Organisation) 12, 73
Ceylon *see* Sri Lanka
Chakma tribals 18
Chidambaram, P. 121
China 77, 78, 131, 132, 165
  academic and policy setting 11, 12, 14, 15
  arms control 163–4
  arms race 80
  and Bangladesh war 90
  failure to contain India or stimulate revolution 84–6
  foreign policies 111–13, 115–20, 123
  future prospects 156, 157, 158, 159
  and India and Pakistan 1980s–1990s 137, 139, 140, 149–50, 154, 155
  and India–Pakistan Kashmir war 89
  and Indo–Pakistani wars 99, 101–3, 105–10
  and Pakistan 83, 125, 127, 128, 129
  patterns and trends 16, 17, 18, 19, 20
  polarity and alliances 53–5, 60–6, 69–73, 75
  strategic orientation 160–3
  structure of power 30, 32, 35, 37–41, 43, 46, 48–50
  variables in South Asian wars 1960s–1971 87
  see also under India; United States
Chogyal, King of Sikkim 115
Chou En-lai 73, 74, 94, 117, 127
Christianity 6
Chumbi valley 68
Clinton, B. 160, 164
Cohen, S.P. 24, 27, 36
Cold War 5, 58, 111, 144, 161
  arms race, war and crisis 77–8, 81–2, 86, 93
  ending of 54, 65, 156–60
  power structure 44, 49
Commonwealth 118, 123
communism 75, 76
competing paradigms of regional security 24–6
cooperation formation *see under* stability
Curzon, Lord 44

Dalai Lama 88
Desai, M. 1, 15, 122, 124
diplomatic conflict *see under* stability
Dorji, J. 116
Dorji, L. 116
Dostum, A.R. 163
Dulles, J.F. 72
Durand Line 130

East India Company 7
Egypt 137
elite/national interests 93–5, 103–6

Index

Ershad, H.M. 124
Europe 9, 81, 92, 111, 160

Feld, W.J. 10
fifth alignment 72-5
Finland 112
Finlandisation 115
first alignment 56, 57
Foreign Office 113, 114
foreign policies 111-32
  Bangladesh 114, 115, 120, 123-5
  Bhutan 114, 115, 116-17
  China 115, 116, 117, 118, 119-20, 123
  Kashmir 115, 122
  Nepal 114, 115, 117-18, 121, 123
  Pakistan 115, 120, 122, 123, 124-30
  Sikkim 114, 115-16, 117
  South Asia Association for Regional Cooperation 130-1
  Sri Lanka 114, 115, 118-19, 118-23
  Tibet 116, 117
  United Kingdom 118, 120, 122
  United States 120, 125
  USSR 115, 120, 123
fourth alignment 66-72
  Himalayan kingdoms 68-70
France 126
future prospects 156-65
  Afghanistan's civil war and Pakistan 163
  arms control 163-4
  China's strategic orientation 160-3

Gandhi, I. 1, 15, 105, 111, 113-15, 119-24, 128, 131, 133
Gandhi, M. 75, 81
Gandhi, R. 1, 15, 115, 120-1, 138-40, 144-5, 148-9
Ganguly, S. 11
Germany 14
Goa 4
Gopal, S. 34, 64, 65
Gracias, Cardinal V. 119

Grafftey-Smith, L.B. 126
Greece 5
Gulf 1, 43, 75, 156, 158, 159, 160, 161
Gujral, I. 147
Gupta, S. 11, 44-6, 47-9

Hare, R.A. 100
Harrison, S.S. 34, 59
Heimsath, C.H. 69
Hekmetyar, G. 163
Helsinki Agreement 155
Himalayan kingdoms 2
  and British-Indian treaty relations 4
  and China 84, 85
  cooperative and hostile relations 69-70
  and India-China war 88, 91, 92, 95, 96
  Indian policy and attitudes 80
  and Indo-Pakistani wars 102-3, 107, 108, 109
  patterns and trends 15
  polarity and alliances 51, 55-6, 60, 63, 67, 70-3
  structure of power 35, 49
  treaty relations 68-9
  variables in South Asian wars 1960s-1971 87
  see also Bhutan; Nepal; Sikkim
Hindus/Hinduism 42, 107, 126, 141
  Muslim divisions 3, 79, 80
  imperialism 32, 125
  India 6, 18, 100, 127, 128
  Pakistan 31, 89, 98, 103
historical legacy 5-7
Hitler, A. 14
Holt, H. 74

India-China war 1962 88, 91-7
  alliance relationships pre-1962 92-3
  distribution of military power pre-1962 96-7
  elite and national interests pre-1962 93-5
  strategic concepts 95-6
  threat perceptions 91-2

Index

Indian Foreign Office 114
Indian Mutiny 1857 7
Indian National Congress 7, 117
Indian Peace Keeping Force 121
Indo–Bangladeshi Accord 1984 124
Indo–Nepalese Treaty (1950) 117
Indo–Pakistani affairs 3–4
Indo–Pakistani wars 97–110
  distribution of military power 108–10
  elite/national interests 103–6
  peacetime external alignments 102–3
  peacetime threat perceptions 99–101
  strategic concepts 106–7
Indo–Soviet alignment 1952–90 131
Indo–Soviet Friendship Treaty 120, 123
Indo–Sri Lankan Accord 1987 112, 114, 121
Indonesia 27, 102
Indus River agreement 47
Inter-Services Intelligence strategy 147–8
International Institute for Strategic Studies 108, 143
interstate relations 29
Iran 5, 161, 165
  Baghdad Pact 126
  military aid for Pakistan 102, 128–9
  nuclear power 43, 137, 157
  power structure 47
  regional power 156
  regional subsystem 27
Iraq 126, 137, 161
Israel 35, 70, 98, 120, 126

Jammu 31, 122, 127, 128, 133, 147
Janata Party Government 122, 124
Japan 9, 86, 156, 157, 160, 162
Jayewardene, J.R. 119, 120, 121, 122, 130
Jehangir 7
Jennings, Sir I. 118

Jinnah, M.A. 52, 53, 57, 73, 97, 100, 108, 125
Junagarh 34
JVP *see* People's Liberation Front

Kapur, A. 57
Kashmir 2
  academic and policy setting 12
  arms race 79
  and China 84
  foreign policies 111, 113, 115, 122
  future prospects 158
  India and Pakistan 1980s–1990s 133–5, 146–8, 151–2, 155
  and India–China war 93, 94, 96
  Indian policy and attitudes 80
  and Indo–Pakistani wars 97–8, 100–10 *passim*
  and Pakistan's external relations 125, 126, 127, 128
  patterns and trends 18
  polarity and alliances 52–3, 57, 60, 61, 64, 73, 75
  and Rann of Kutch war 88
  structure of power 31, 32, 33, 34, 39, 40, 46, 49
  and United States 86–7
  see also under Pakistan; wars
Kashmir, Maharaja of 97, 164
Kautilyan tradition (*realpolitik*) 6, 7
Kazakstan 43
Kennedy, J.F. 81
Khalistan Sikh independence groups 125, 141
Khan, A.Q. 81, 103–4, 127, 139, 142, 147, 150
Khan, G.I. 154
Khan, L.A. 57, 60, 126, 127
Khan, Y. 99, 104
Kissinger, H. 30, 48, 81, 85, 87, 99, 103, 106
Kodikara, S.U. 122
Koirala, B.P. 117
Korea 39, 60, 65–6, 156, 157, 160, 161
Korean War 9, 32, 73
Kotelawala, Sir J. 118
Kumar, S. 10, 44–5

Ladakh 128
Liberation Tigers of Tamil
    Eelam 121
Lin Piao 74

McGhee, G. 62
McMahon Line 63, 73, 84, 94
Mahabharata 5
Mahendra, King 70, 117
Maldives 2, 4
    academic and policy setting 8
    patterns and trends 16
    polarity and alliances 54
    and South Asia Association for
        Regional Cooperation 130
    structure of power 22
Manekshaw, S. 124
Manila Conference 126
Mansingh, S. 69, 124
Mao Tse-tung 74, 84, 85, 94
Mason, P. 7
Masood, A.S. 163
Mediterranean 9
Menon, K. 60, 61, 65, 66, 118
Middle East 9, 12, 14, 81
    and China's strategic
        orientation 160, 161
    future prospects 156
    and India and Pakistan
        1980s–1990s 137
    and Indo–China war 91, 92, 94
    and Indo–Pakistani wars 100
    and Pakistan's external relations
        125, 126, 128
    polarity and alliances 75, 76
    structure of power 31, 43, 48
military conflict *see under* stability
military crisis 18
military power, distribution of 96–7,
    108–10
Moghuls 2–3, 5, 6, 7
Mohamed, G. 56, 57
Monroe Doctrine for South
    Asia 120, 123
Mountbatten, Earl 3, 61, 64, 164
Muhajirs 105
Mujtaba Razvi, S.M. 123
Mukti Bahini guerrillas 123–4
Muslim League 100

Muslims/Islam 2, 3, 73, 79, 135,
    137, 147, 161
    academic and policy setting 12,
        13
    foreign policies 111, 125, 129
    historical legacy 5, 6
    Islamic summit conference 128
    leaving West Bengal for East
        Pakistan 126
    migrants from Bangladesh 124
    patterns and trends 16, 17, 18
    separateness 106–7
    structure of power 21, 31, 42–3,
        44, 46
    variables in South Asian wars
        1960s to 1971 89, 95, 97,
        102, 103, 110
Myanmar *see* Burma
Myrdal, G. 9

Nayar, K. 142
Ne Win 162
Nehru, J. 1, 3, 4, 7, 43, 55, 67, 76
    academic and policy setting
        1947 8–9
    China's failure to contain India
        or stimulate an Indian
        revolution 84, 86
    fifth alignment 72, 73, 74
    foreign policies 111, 113–19,
        121, 123–4, 126–8, 131
    fourth alignment 67, 71
    patterns and trends 15
    second alignment 56, 59
    stability via regional military and
        diplomatic conflict and
        cooperation formation 32, 33,
        35
    third alignment 60–4, 65, 66
    transformation of Indian policy
        and attitudes 81
    United States's failure to contain
        India 86
    variables in South Asian wars
        1960s–1971 88, 89, 93–4, 96,
        97, 98, 102, 105
Nepal 4, 131
    academic and policy setting
        8, 10

and China's strategic orientation 161
foreign policies 111, 112, 113, 114, 115, 117–18, 121, 123
and India–China war 94
and Indo-Pakistani wars 109
Nepalese National Congress 117
patterns and trends 16, 17, 19
polarity and alliances 54, 63, 66, 68, 69, 70, 71
and South Asia Association for Regional Cooperation 130
structure of power 22, 29, 31, 35, 44, 45, 46
Nigeria 27
Nixon, R. 59, 75, 81, 85, 87, 99, 103
Non-Aligned Movement 117, 118, 120, 122, 123
non-Aryans 5
North America *see* Canada; United States
North Atlantic Treaty Organisation 126
nuclear factor 136, 152–5
Nuclear Non-Proliferation Treaty 81, 87, 129, 136, 149, 153–4

overview 1–5

Pacific 14, 156, 157
Pakistan 2, 77, 78, 131, 165
academic and policy setting 8, 9, 10–11, 12, 13, 15
and Afghanistan's civil war 163
arms race 79, 80
and Bangladesh war 89, 90
and China 84–5, 160, 161
external relations 125–30
failure to balkanize or balance India and liberate Kashmir 82–3
Foreign Office 114
foreign policies 111, 112, 113, 114, 115, 120, 122, 123, 124–5
future prospects 158
and India–China war 91–7 *passim*
and Indian policy and attitudes 81
patterns and trends 16, 17, 18, 19

People's Party of 104
polarity and alliances 51–6, 75, 76; first alignment 56, 57; second alignment 56, 58–9; third alignment 60, 61; fourth alignment 70, 71; fifth alignment 72, 73, 75
and Rann of Kutch war 88
and South Asia Association for Regional Cooperation 130
structure of power 21, 22, 23, 27–34 *passim*; enmities and friendships 37, 38, 39, 40, 41; history of development 42–50
and United States 86–7
United States–Soviet and United States–China detentes 82
see also Indo-Pakistani; Pakistan and India; wars
Pakistan and India 1980s–1990s 133–55
confidence-building measures 135
1987 crisis 139–40, 145; and military agenda and behaviour 140–4
1989–90 crisis and military and diplomatic agenda and behaviour 144, 146–8
nuclear activities 136, 152–5
players, concepts, calculations and issues 148–52
processes in affairs 138
Pandit, Madame 62, 65, 66
Panikkar, K.M. 61
Parthasarathy, G. 121
Patel, S. 3, 60, 61
Pathans 105, 163
patterns and trends 15–20
alignment patterns 1947–mid-1990s 19
incidence of war, military crisis and terrorism 18
People's Liberation Front (JVP) 119
insurgency 4, 41
polarity and alliances 51–76
first alignment 56, 57
second alignment 56, 58–9

third alignment 60–6
fourth alignment 66–72
fifth alignment 72–5
policy and attitudes, transformation of 80–1
Policy Planning Committee 121
power structure 21–50
  competing paradigms of regional security 24–6
  development 42–50
  interstate relations 29
  regional security issues 27
  regional subsystem formation 23, 27–8
  security interdependencies 28–9
  stability via regional military and diplomatic conflict and cooperation formation 30–42
  western paradigms 22–3
Premadasa, R. 130
Pressler Amendment 145
Punjab 18, 83, 105, 127, 134, 140–2, 146, 147, 151, 152
Purbash Island 124
Pushtun secessionist movement 130

Rabbani, B. 163
Radhakrishnan, S. 32, 60, 64, 65, 66
Rahman, Sheikh M. 104, 123, 124
Rahman, Z. 125
Rajan, M.S. 11
Rama, Lord 141
Ramachandran, M.G. 121
Rann of Kutch 18, 87
  war 1965 88
Rao, N. 1–2, 121
Ray, A.K. 57
Reagan, R. 121, 154, 164
realpolitik 6
regional conflict *see under* stability
regional security issues 27
regional subsystem formation 23, 27–8
Reid, E. 34
Research and Analysis Wing 114
Rivzi, G. 10, 28, 36

Rose, L. 8, 10, 36, 44–5, 46, 47–8
Rustomji, N. 116

SAARC *see* South Asia Association for Regional Cooperation
Sabha, L. 116, 127
Sati 6
Saudi Arabia 125, 129, 137, 161
SEATO *see* South-East Asia Treaty Organisation
second alignment 56, 58–9
security interdependencies 28–9
Senanayake, D.S. 118, 122
Shahjehan 7
Sharif, N. 148, 151
Shastri, L.B. 1, 98, 105, 127
Shia-Sunni divide 161
Shiites 12
Sikhs 18, 125, 141, 143
Sikkim 4
  and China 85
  foreign policies 111, 112, 114, 115–16, 117
  and India–China war 94
  patterns and trends 19
  polarity and alliances 54, 63, 66, 68, 70, 71
  structure of power 31, 44
Simla Accord 133, 164
Sindhis 105
Singapore 70, 96, 130
Singh, V.P. 148
Singh, W. 89
Sinhalese 18, 119, 120, 122
Sinhalese–Tamil conflict 118, 121
Sinkiang 84, 88
Sino–Soviet Friendship Treaty 92
South Africa 14, 120, 123, 157
South Asia Association for Regional Cooperation 112, 130–1
South-East Asia Collective Defence Treaty 126
South-East Asia Treaty Organisation 73, 118
Spiegel, S.L. 25, 30
Sri Lanka 2, 4, 131
  academic and policy setting 8, 10, 13, 15

Index

Ceylon Institute of World Affairs 122
foreign policies 111–15, 118–23
Freedom Party 118–19
and India–China war 94, 95, 96
and Indo-Pakistani wars 108, 109
patterns and trends 16, 17, 18
polarity and alliances 51, 54, 55, 70
and South Asia Association for Regional Cooperation 130
structure of power 22, 29, 31, 35, 44, 45, 47
stability via regional military and diplomatic conflict and cooperation formation 30–42
alignments 36–7, 42
balance of interests 35–6, 41
balance of power theory 31, 35, 41, 42
balance of threat theory 31, 32–3, 35, 41, 42
balancing and bandwaggoning 31, 32–3, 34–5, 42
conflict formation 34–5, 36, 42
cooperation formation 34–5, 36
enmities and friendships 37–8, 39–41
external alliance activity 33–4
regional security structures 30
Stalin, J. 35, 62, 64, 65, 75, 94, 101, 102
Stockholm International Peace Research Institute 108
strategic concepts 95–6, 106–7
Sunderji doctrine 140
Sunderji, K. 140, 143, 149–50
Sunnis 129, 161

Taiwan 96
Tamil 18, 119, 120, 122
Co-ordinating Committee 122
Freedom Fighters 120
Nadu 119, 120, 121
separatism 13, 41
see also Sinhalese–Tamil conflict
Tashkent 82, 89, 90, 98
Agreement 127, 128
terrorism 18

Thailand 161
third alignment 60–6
threat perceptions 91–2, 99–101
Tibet 1
arms control 163–4
and China 84
foreign policies 113, 116, 117
future prospects 158, 159
and India–China war 1962 88
and Indo-Pakistani wars 107
polarity and alliances 60, 61, 63, 66, 68, 69, 71
structure of power 44
Treaty of Perpetual Peace and Friendship 116
Treaty of Perpetuity 115
Tribhuvan, King 4
Truman, H. 9
Turkey 5, 102, 126, 129

United Kingdom 3
academic and policy setting 8, 9, 14, 15
foreign policies 118, 120, 122
future prospects 159
and Indo-Pakistani wars 98, 106
and Pakistan's external relations 126, 127
polarity and alliances 51, 54, 55, 56, 61, 64, 66, 67, 68, 71, 75
structure of power 31, 35, 44
see also British
United National Party 119
United Nations 3, 93, 94, 102, 106, 117
General Assembly 123, 129
polarity and alliances 60, 65, 75
Security Council 64, 73, 82, 98, 128
structure of power 31, 32, 33
United States 77, 78, 131
academic and policy setting 8, 9, 11, 12, 14
and Afghanistan civil war 163
and Bangladesh war 90
and China 81–2, 84, 85, 160, 161
failure to contain India 86–7
foreign policies 111, 112, 113, 120, 125

future prospects 156, 157, 158
and India and Pakistan
  1980s–1990s 133–4, 144, 146,
  148, 150–5
and India–China war 88, 91–7
and India–Pakistan Kashmir
  war 89
and Indian policy and
  attitudes 80
and Indo–Pakistani wars 98–103,
  106–8, 110
and Pakistan 83, 126–30
patterns and trends 16, 17, 19
polarity and alliances 52–60, 65,
  70–6
–Soviet detente 81–2
structure of power 30–5, 37–9,
  41, 43, 46–50
USSR 1, 77, 78, 131, 132
  academic and policy setting 9,
    12, 14
  and Afghanistan civil war 163
  and India and Pakistan
    1980s–1990s 133, 144, 155
  and Bangladesh war 90
  and China 84, 85, 160
  foreign policies 111, 112, 113,
    115, 120, 123
  future prospects 156, 157, 158,
    159
  and India–China war 88, 91, 92,
    93, 94, 95, 96
  and India–Pakistan Kashmir
    war 89
  and Indian policy and
    attitudes 80
  and Indo–Pakistani wars 98, 99,
  100, 101, 102, 103, 106
  and Pakistan 83, 125, 127, 128,
    129–30
  patterns and trends 16, 17, 19
  polarity and alliances 53–4, 56,
    58–64, 66, 72–6
  structure of power 30–5, 37–41,
    43, 46–9
  see also under United States

Vaikunthavasan, K. 122
Vandenbert, General H. 58
Vayrynen, R. 25–6, 27–8, 30, 34,
  42
Venkataramani, M.S. 34
'Vijay' integrated exercise 139

Walt, S.M. 26, 30–1, 32–5, 41–2
Wariaywalla, B. 115
wars 87–110
  Bangladesh war 1971 89–91
  incidence of 18
  India–China war 1962 88, 91–7
  India–Pakistan–Kashmir war
    1965 88–9
  Indo–Pakistani wars 97–110
  Rann of Kutch war 1965 88
  value of and avoidance 80
Weil, T.E. 100
Williams, R. 74
Wilson, A.J. 121, 122
World Bank 47, 125

Yew, L.K. 130

Zia Ul-Haq 83, 122, 128–30,
  133–4, 138–9, 141–2, 150, 154